D1360493

ML
2831
.S68
1974b

CHOICE, Mar. 1969) and *English song-books, 1651–1702* by C. L. Day and E. B. Murrie (1940). In addition, a list of the principal manuscript song-books from 1600 to 1660 is given. For the undergraduate and graduate reader.

LIBRARY
Lander College
Greenwood, S. C. 29646

English Song
Dowland to Purcell

English Song
Dowland to Purcell

Ian Spink

99084

Charles Scribner's Sons, New York

First published 1974
© Ian Spink 1974

Copyright under the Berne Convention. All rights
reserved. No part of this book may be reproduced in any
form without the permission of Charles Scribner's Sons

Printed in Great Britain
Library of Congress Catalog Card Number 73-9488

SBN 684-13621-X (Cloth)

Contents

List of Illustrations

Preface

This is a critical and stylistic study of English Song in the seventeenth century. For the most part, detailed matters of bibliography and biography are excluded, not because they are unimportant, but because they have already been covered to a considerable extent elsewhere, whereas the musical development from Dowland to Purcell has not been traced before, other than briefly.

My work is founded on two bibliographical tools: first and foremost C. L. Day and E. B. Murrie's *English Song-Books, 1651–1702* (London, 1940); secondly, a thematic index of manuscript songs of the period 1620–60 which I began as long ago as 1956. In this connection the published work of Vincent Duckles and John P. Cutts has been a great help. Both started earlier in the field and consequently I was able to benefit considerably from their researches. This sort of thing—discovery, indexing, examination and evaluation of sources—is the spade-work of textual criticism, and its fruits were born in what may, in some degree, be regarded as a complementary volume to this book, my edition of 'English Songs, 1620–1660' published in *Musica Britannica*, Vol. 33 (Stainer & Bell, 1971). So far as biography is concerned, my original plan was to provide information about the lives of the composers dealt with, but it soon became clear that this would inflate the size of the book without bringing proportional advantages. The imminence of *Grove 6* was the final argument that persuaded me to abandon the biographical aspects of this study.

Although I have described the treatment as critical, this is not the primary intention, which is really more modest—to provide a survey of the song literature of the period. To do this it was necessary to examine as wide a selection of material as possible, and in the process I have looked at almost 5000 songs. Of course, many of them never got a second glance, but they all helped to build up a general picture, for it is the general picture which establishes critical norms. It is true that Dowland and the lutesong composers have received attention from musical scholars before, and I was at first unwilling to add to the literature on this topic but for the fact that it seemed essential to the unity and whole perspective of my subject to do so. On the other hand, there is nothing published which treats Purcell's songs with anything like the attention they deserve. Arguably, they are his finest works. Indeed, the fact that the musical genius of both Dowland and Purcell manifested itself in song would be reason enough for such a book as this, I believe, quite apart from the rewards which have come from exploring the period between. The history of song is central to the English tradition, and in tracing its development through the seventeenth century we are dealing with one of its richest periods. This being so, it would be a nice (if increasingly improbable) irony that Dowland and Purcell should turn out to be Irish after all!

It is a pleasure to acknowledge help from many quarters: firstly, from friends and colleagues who have encouraged me, answered queries, lent material and assisted unselfishly in other ways; secondly, from the Universities of Birmingham, Sydney and London which have subsidized my work in one way or another during the past seventeen years; thirdly, from the librarians and staff of the following libraries, to whose governing bodies thanks are also due for permission to use and publish material in their possession—the British Museum, London; the Bibliothèque Nationale, Paris; the National Library of Scotland, Edinburgh; the Bodleian and Christ Church Libraries, Oxford; the Fitzwilliam and Magdalene College Libraries, Cambridge; the University Libraries of Edinburgh and Glasgow; the Library of Trinity College, Dublin; the Library of Lambeth Palace, London; the Library of St. Michael's College, Tenbury; and the New York Public Library, New York. For permission to reproduce various portraits grateful acknowledgement is due to the Dean and Chapter of Salisbury Cathedral, and to the Faculty of Music at Oxford University, as well as to the governing bodies of the National Portrait Gallery, London, and the Kunsthistorisches Museum, Vienna.

Ian Spink

Royal Holloway College,
University of London
1974

Part one

Lutesong
and
continuo song

1 John Dowland
and the lutesong

When, in 1597, John Dowland published his *First Booke of Songes or Ayres* with alternative versions to be performed either as solo songs with lute accompaniment, or as four-part ayres, he was following a practice well established on the Continent. The first printed collection of songs catering for this mode of performance consisted of arrangements of *frottole* published by Petrucci in 1509. Thereafter numerous collections of *frottole*, *chansons*, *villancicos*, *lieder*, madrigals, psalms and religious songs were printed in Italy, France, Spain and Germany. In England, nothing of this sort came out until near the end of the century, though a few manuscripts furnish evidence that lute-accompanied song was practised, for which, in any case, there is considerable literary evidence.[1]

The contents of these manuscripts hardly prepare us for the wealth and comparative sophistication of lutesong publications beginning in 1597.[2] It was probably the undoubted success of Dowland's first book that encouraged the others thereafter: that and the probability that Peter Short, the music printer, had recently acquired a font of lute tablature to facilitate such publications. (William Barley's *New Booke of Tabliture*, published the year before and containing songs with bandora accompaniment, used wood blocks.[3]) Short printed Morley's *Canzonets Or Little Short Aers* the same year as Dowland's book, and, in the remaining period of his activity, lutesong books by Cavendish (1598), Jones (1600 and 1601), Rosseter and Campion (1601) and Dowland (1603).

Unlike the madrigal, which was an exotic import, the lutesong belongs to the main development of indigenous English song, which in the sixteenth century had passed from the 'freemen's song' of Henry VIII's time, through the simple part-songs of the middle of the century, to the Elizabethan consort song brought to its perfection in William Byrd's *Psalmes, Sonets, & songs* (1588) and surviving in Orlando Gibbons' so-called *Madrigals* (1612).[4] It is from the consort song with its 'first singing part' that the contrapuntal element in the serious lutesong derives, rather than the madrigal. Instrumental preludes and interludes between the lines are, of course, transferred to the lute, but the same relationship between voice and accompaniment persists. The influence is clear in the ayres of Michael Cavendish (*C1598*) where an initial point is frequently worked out on the lute before the voice enters, and continues dove-tailing cadences with anticipatory imitations of subsequent lines. This was a fairly common procedure for dealing with an unfrivolous text among the more conservative and contrapuntally inclined lutesong writers—Thomas Morley, for example, though his opening preludes are usually free.[5]

Ex. 1a 'Who is it that this dark night' (Sidney)   Thomas Morley *(M1600)*

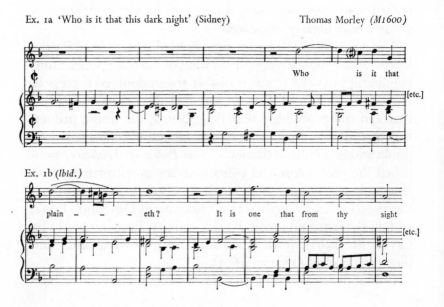

Ex. 1b *(Ibid.)*

16

Lighter songs draw on the tradition of the ballad and the dance; their characteristics are therefore melodic and rhythmic. It has been suggested that the important dance element in the songs of Dowland represents a French influence, but though he was in France for a time (1580–84) direct indebtedness is difficult to pin-point.[6] In any case, songs were made to dances in England as well as France. As the grammarian Webbe said:

> . . . neither is there anie tune or stroke which may be sung or plaide on instruments, which hath not some poetical ditties framed according to the numbers thereof: some to Rogero . . . to Galliardes, to Pavines, to Iygges, to Brawles, to all manner of tunes which everie Fidler knowes better then myself.[7]

To some extent it may have been the presence of a number of already popular instrumental pieces with 'ditties framed' that helped to make Dowland's *First Booke of Songes or Ayres* such a success—enough to warrant further editions in 1600, 1603, 1606 and 1613. It includes Sir John Souch's Galliard ('My thoughts are winged with hopes'), Captain Piper's Galliard ('If my complaints could passions move'), the Earl of Essex's Galliard ('Can she excuse my wrongs'), the Frog Galliard ('Now, O now, I needs must part'), and 'Awake sweet love' which is also known as an instrumental piece. But significantly, pride of place is given to the song 'Unquiet thoughts'. Dowland's obsessive melancholy thus appears from the outset and is never far away in any of the song books. Sleep and death are sought to provide a longed-for release from earthly cares, and al-

Ex. 2 'Come again, sweet love doth now invite'   John Dowland (*1597*)

To see,   to hear,   to touch,   to kiss,   to die

though this was very much an affectation of the time it was one which clearly excited an acutely personal response in him. Death, of course, has a sexual connotation too—but even when this is absent or heavily overlaid, his treatment of the idea frequently has an erotic intensity (Ex. 2). In 'Come heavy sleep' we are wrenched from the key of G major by an impassioned plea which breaks through all restraints of counterpoint.

Ex. 3 'Come, heavy sleep'   John Dowland (*1597*)

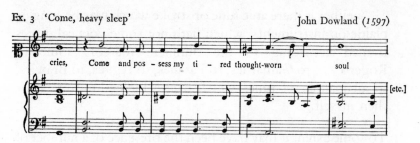

Although Dowland provided an alternative partsong version of this song (as he did for all the others in his first book) such highly personalized sentiments presuppose a solo singer, and there is evidence that some of his partsong arrangements are adaptations of instrumental accompaniments (just as Campion admitted his own were). For not only are they aesthetically inappropriate in many cases, technically they are often unsatisfactory.[8] The technical deficiencies mostly relate to the awkward verbal underlay of the lower parts, and though an accompaniment of viols would mitigate these defects, it is clear that frequently we are dealing with lute texture rather than true polyphony. The individual lines are, in themselves, neither vocal nor instrumental in character, and it is significant that Dowland gives himself away in small details such as in 'Burst

Ex. 4 from 'Burst forth, my tears'   John Dowland (*D1597*)

forth my tears', where the lute's idiomatic treatment of a suspended fourth at 'love provokes' is literally transcribed into
the alto in a way quite foreign to vocal or instrumental polyphony (Ex. 4).

Increasingly the soloistic nature of the lutesong is asserted.
Beginning with his *Second Booke of Songs or Ayres* (1600) Dowland left certain songs as solos—the first eight—though the
bass part remains texted and the table of contents describes
them as 'Songs to two voices'. But the underlay suggests that
this part is instrumental rather than vocal in conception. The
title page does indeed stipulate that these songs are to be performed 'with the Violl *de Gamba*' supporting the lute; more-

Ex. 5   'I saw my lady weep'   John Dowland (D1600)

over, the repetition of the words of the opening line of 'I saw my lady weep' three times in the bass can only be regarded as foreign to the essential nature of the song, forced on the music as some sort of compromise (Ex. 5).

In this book the *'semper dolens'* side of Dowland—passionate, melancholy, resigned—appears still more clearly. The prevailing mood is established at the outset. Following 'I saw my lady weep' comes the famous *Lachrimae Pavane* 'Flow my tears', then 'Sorrow, sorrow stay', No other song book can ever have begun with three such songs. In 'Sorrow, sorrow stay' counterpoint and the sustained vocal line give way to declamation and chords at the words 'pity, pity, pity' and 'no hope, no help', a throwback to the idiom of the Elizabethan choirboy playsongs in moments of anguish (and to Dowland's own 'Come, heavy sleep') and a foretaste of the electrifying outburst towards the end of 'In darkness let me dwell' (R *1610*). But generally the lute accompaniment of these expressive songs is a continuous web of polyphony, sometimes participating thematically with the voice but more often content to unwind in long lines drawn out by suspensions and prolonged by avoidance of direct cadences, superbly subtle in harmonic and rhythmic nuance.

In the latter part of the book the mood lightens a little in such songs as the exquisite 'Shall I sue, shall I seek for grace', but the only one that is completely carefree is 'Fine knacks for ladies'. The more extrovert side of Dowland is revealed in his *Third and Last Booke of Songs or Aires* (1603). Here and there gay chanson rhythms and a general lack of complication bring other composers to mind; Rosseter, for example in 'What if I never speed', Jones in 'Fie on this feigning'. And while only Dowland could have written 'Weep you no more sad fountains', the collection as a whole is less emotionally indulgent than the earlier books. Yet restraint, far from inhibiting force of expression is able to sublimate it, raising it to a higher level where it can outlast the heat of the moment. One song in particular has this sublime quality—'Time stands still', a rapt contemplation of feminine beauty seen in eternity. Nothing is allowed to disturb the mood of breathless wonder. The harmonic materials are of the simplest, the melody itself does not exceed a fifth in range, yet the song is as affecting as anything Dowland wrote.

Despite the title of the third book, Dowland's last lutesong publication was *A Pilgrimes Solace* (1612). The tone of its preface suggests a disappointed man resentful of intrigues—real or imagined—against him, and envious of the recognition given to younger men while he still lacked a court appointment. He wrote:

> I againe found strange entertainment since my returne [from Denmark]; especially by the opposition of two sorts of people that shroude themselves under the title of Musitians. The first are some simple Cantors, or vocall singers, who though they seeme excellent in their blinde Division-making, are meerely ignorant, even in the first elements of Musicke . . . yet doe these fellowes give their verdict of me behinde my backe, and say, what I doe is after the old manner . . . The second are young-men, professors of the Lute, who vaunt themselves, to the disparagement of such as have beene before their time, (wherein I my self am a party) that there never was the like of them . . .

As if to defy those who criticized him for being old fashioned, many of the songs in this book are retrospective in style. The links with the consort song are unmistakable, especially in the sequence of religious pieces (nos. 12–17), and there are three songs (nos. 9–11) which actually have an obbligato treble-viol part in consort with the voice (lying beneath the viol), lute and bass viol. Needless to say the expressive idiom of these songs, 'Go nightly cares', 'From silent night' and '*Lasso! vita mia*' differ from the consort song of his youth, but the basic constituents—'first singing part' and polyphonic accompaniment—remain the same. Nor is the technique of contrapuntal continuity vastly different. However, there are distinctly modern features in some of the songs in this book too. The declamatory element is more pronounced, not so much in the 'mille, mille' repetitions of 'Lasso! vita mia', which are illustrative rather than expressive (and anyway the presence of consort parts precludes free declamatory treatment) but in 'Welcome black night' and 'Cease these false sports' where we may perceive a new orientation. The fact that these were probably written for a masque celebrating the wedding of Theophilus, Lord Walden (Dowland's patron) to Lady Elizabeth Home in March 1612 is, as we shall see, significant. Here declamation begins to oust melody, and continuo homophony all but replaces polyphony in the accompaniment.

The finest example of Dowland's 'old manner' is not to be found in any of his own publications, but among the three songs he contributed to his son's *Musicall Banquet* (1610). 'In darkness let me dwell', though probably written in 1606 or soon after, recalls the style of 'I saw my lady weep' (*D1600*) in the restless counterpoint of its accompaniment and the long sustained vocal phrases. But the emotional intensity is even greater, and at the climax it bursts out uncontrollably.

Ex. 6a 'In darkness let me dwell'   John Dowland *(D1610)*

Ex. 6b (*Ibid.*)

Dowland has discovered the limitation of the polyphonic style. The pathetic repetition of the first line at the end of the song, and the final cadence, which, being phrygian, gives no promise of rest or ease, confirm this as one of the most profoundly moving songs ever written. It typifies Dowland at his best; the brooding melancholy and the conservative technique pushed as far as it will go to achieve an intensity of expression unequalled in England until Purcell.

*

But Dowland speaks only for Dowland. There is another view of the lutesong which Campion propounded (in R*1601*).

What Epigrams are in Poetrie, the same are Ayres in musicke, then in their chiefe perfection when they are short and well seasoned. But to clogg a light song with a long Praeludium, is to corrupt the nature of it. Manie rests in Musicke were invented either for necessitie of the fuge, or granted as a harmonicall licence in songs of many parts: but in Ayres I find no use they have, unlesse it be to make a vulgar, and triviall modulation seeme to the ignorant strange, and to the judiciall tedious . . . But there are some, who to appeare the more deepe, and singular in their judgement, will admit no Musicke but that which is long, intricate, bated with fuge, chaind with sincopation, and where the nature of everie word is precisely exprest in the Note, like the old exploided action in Comedies, when if they did pronounce *Memeni*, they would point to the hinder part of their heads, if *Video*, put their finger in their eye. But such childish observing of words is altogether ridiculous, and we ought to maintaine as well in Notes, as in action a manly cariage, gracing no word, but that which is eminent, and emphaticall . . .

Such were Campion's views on the elaborate and artificial style of the consort song, and lute ayres derived from that style. The *Booke Of Ayres* which he and Philip Rosseter published in 1601 provides persuasive justification of this view. The collection contains 21 songs by each composer; Campion's, on the whole, being a shade dull and four-square compared with his friend's. Rosseter's songs compel enthusiastic admiration despite the narrow range in which he worked.[9] 'Ayres have both their Art and pleasure' Campion said (R*1601*), but whereas the pleasure is easily grasped, the art is elusive. Rosseter has an exquisite melodic sense which we recognise in terms of the contour of line, rhythmic structure and tonal organization. A seemingly infallible gift enables him to vary phrase-lengths while still holding them in balance, an attractive feature exemplified in such songs as 'If I hope, I pine'. This natural feeling for balance functions at a higher level too. Almost all his songs are in two sections; the first opening out freely, usually without recourse to direct repetition; the second, closing in again and focusing the material through sequential repetition towards the 'point' of the song. It is a truly organic process of expansion followed by contraction—like breathing—and somehow, with Rosseter, as natural. 'What then is love but mourning' provides a short but perfect example.

Although Campion's songs are slightly disappointing after Rosseter's there are some good ones among them.[10] In their joint collection (*R 1601*) he does, in fact, cover a wider range of style than Rosseter, but without quite discovering where his true talents lie. He is most agreeable in triple-time songs like 'Follow your saint', 'Thou art not fair' and 'The cypress curtain of the night', of which there are quite a number—considerably more than in Rosseter's half of the book. His success is less marked in common time. Nevertheless, there are some charming ones, among which 'Hark all you ladies that do sleep' is perhaps the most delicate. Mention should also be made of 'Come let us sound with melody'—*musique mesurée à l'antique* according to the principles of Baïf's *Académie*. Though Campion was an opponent of rhyme and a firm advocate of quantitative metres in his *Observations in the Art of English Poesie* (1602), this is the only setting in which he applies these principles. The result was hardly promising.[11]

Campion was to die before Rosseter, to whom he left his whole estate wishing 'that it had bin farr more'. Rosseter published no songs after 1601; Campion another 95 in four books, besides a few in his masque publications. In this respect it is Rosseter's legacy one wishes had been the greater. Although the title-pages of Campion's songbooks give no dates, it seems probable that the *Two Bookes of Ayres* came out in 1613 or soon after, the first 'Contayning Divine and Morall Songs', the second 'Containing Light Conceits of Lovers'. Unlike the 1601 collection, and unlike the later pair of song books (*C 1618*), these songs are also furnished with partsong arrangements. As Campion says:

These Ayres were for the most part framed at first for one voyce with the Lute, or Violl, but upon occasion, they have since been filled with more parts, which who so please may use, who like not may leave . . .

It is interesting to note that only two of the 42 songs in these books are in triple time, compared with the generous sprinkling of such songs in half the number in *R1601*. This fact is hard to account for—it is perhaps a sign of increasing literary self-consciousness, and a move from the dance—but it very much limits the variety and overall attractiveness of the collection. Indeed, there is really very little of musical interest in the first book. Most of them are in simple hymn-tune style, 'Never weather-beaten sail' being a quite well-known and above average example. The first song in the collection, 'Author of light' is probably the best and at the same time the least typical. The flexibility of the vocal line even suggests Dowland, while chromaticism at the end gives force to the concluding line of the poem:

And their sharp pains and grief in time assuage.

Campion is more at ease when it comes to the 'Light Conceits of Lovers'. Most of them are in the same AA:B: form as the 'moral' songs, but in general they show more variety and rhythmic interest. There is even one song in the book which begins in five time (Ex. 7).

Again, one of the best is one of the least typical. 'Give beauty all her right' has a lovely supple line, extremely free (for Cam-

Ex. 7 'Sweet exclude me not'   Thomas Campion *(C1613)*

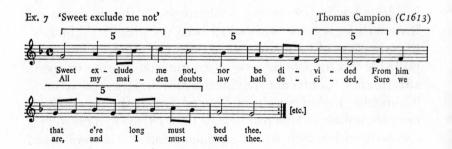

pion) considering the regularity of the 66 66:88 stanza, with pairs of triplas expanding and contracting the natural phrase lengths (Ex. 8).

Ex. 8 'Give beauty all her right'   Thomas Campion *(C1613)*

The Third and Fourth Booke Of Ayres were dedicated to Sir Thomas Monson and his son respectively. Thus publication dates from about the time of Sir Thomas's release from prison early in 1617, cleared of suspected complicity in the murder of Sir Thomas Overbury. The dedication seems to imply that some of the songs had been written in earlier years:

These youth-borne Ayres *then, prison'd in this Booke,*
Which in your Bowres much of their beeing tooke . . .

and the preface to the fourth book mentions 'three or foure Songs that have beene published before, but . . . you shall finde all of them reformed eyther in Words or Notes'. However, taking the two books together some general advance in style is discernible. The rhythmic element has become noticeably more subtle and Campion less open to the charge of being four-square. Implied triplas, even changes into and out of triple time as in 'Break now my heart', are absorbed naturally into the melodic flow, which is now more graceful. But this increased freedom brings in its train the danger of diffuseness, something he does not altogether avoid even in a song like 'O never to be moved' which begins so promisingly. One or two songs show incipient declamatory traits, the opening of 'Kind were her answers' for example; still more 'O sweet delight'. But it is as a simple melodist that Campion appears at his best in these books, in such songs as 'Shall I come sweet love to thee' where words and music, meaning and mood, come together as perfectly as can be expected when composer and poet are one, or in the rapt beauty of 'Could my heart more tongues employ.'

Ex. 9 'Could my heart more tongues employ'   Thomas Campion (*C1618*)

Campion's reputation as a song writer has probably been exaggerated in the past. The fact that he was a notable poet probably helped to bring his songs into greater prominence than they would have achieved otherwise, while songs like 'Never weather-beaten sail' and 'There is a garden in her face' may have recommended him to a taste raised on hymns and sentimental ballads. A composer like Robert Jones was at a disadvantage in both respects and (predictably enough) it was Peter Warlock who readjusted the critical balance between the two.[12] The trouble with them both is that they wrote too much. The best songs of each would fill a delightful book and make one thirst for more; as it is, there is a surfeit.

In fact, Jones as a melodist pure and simple is arguably superior to Campion, though the contrapuntal element is present in his songs to a much greater extent, and rarely to advantage. Of his five books of ayres, the second and last contain exclusively solo songs. His output as a whole shows him to have been an uneven composer, becoming increasingly careless and unselfcritical, prone to tediousness in serious mood yet with a lively rustic vein. Between these two extremes he offers a number of songs rivalling the best of Campion and Rosseter; among them 'What if I seek for love of thee', (*J1600*) and 'Go to bed, sweet muse' (*J1605*). 'Lie down, poor heart' (*J1600*) is a successful example of a polyphonically conceived lutesong, but several of the more solemn ayres in the second and fourth books are merely dull, spun out with interludes between lines dutifully anticipating thematic material to follow. Nor are his lighter songs free from this reproach. Some of the duets in the last part of *Ultimum Vale* (1605) and the first part of *A Musicall Dreame* (1609) handle the imitative style deftly—notably, of course, 'Sweet Kate'—but in the more melodic ayres, redundant chords or routine imitations often disrupt the flow and balance of phrases thus accentuating the tendency to ramble, while odd turns of harmony (even when not mistakes in the tablature) disturb rather than beguile.

Even so, there is no denying Jones a prominent place among the lutesong writers, despite obvious deficiencies. It would be invidious (and impossible) to rank the others, for each can show a song or two which wins our admiration. After all, it is the definition of a minor composer, perhaps, that he is capable of producing a small-scale masterpiece at least once in his life. And though for convenience, we may make comparison with Dowland on one hand and Campion on the other, it is rarely a clear case of imitating one or the other. Minor composers they may be, but each establishes his own identity.

Michael Cavendish and Thomas Greaves are, in some ways, old fashioned, though fortunately they do not inherit the legacy of 'woeful wights' and 'doleful dumps'. Both are Arcadians: Cavendish a country gentleman; Greaves lutenist to one. The former's *Ayres in Tabletorie* (1598) adapt the consort song to voice and lute. But he is able to avoid that cumbrous heaviness which is all too frequently a feature of the style. He manages equally well whether the mood is serious, as in 'Fair are those eyes' or light-hearted, as in 'Love, the delight of all well-thinking minds'. He can slip in and out of three time easily and occasionally throw counterpoint to the winds and produce as good a tune as anybody—'Love is not blind' for example. The first 14 songs in the collection are printed with lute accompaniment and without partsong versions (though the bass is texted). Two appear later in the book as five-part madrigals. A further six are provided with alternate four-part settings, and the book ends with eight madrigals.

Greaves' *Songes of sundrie kindes* (1604) include solo songs, consort songs ('for the Viols and Voyce') and five-part madrigals. There are distinct echoes of Cavendish's book here, even direct quotation, as we find comparing' Ye bubbling springs' with Cavendish's 'Cursed be the time' (Ex. 10). On the whole Greaves is less dependent on polyphonic texture and has a stronger melodic sense although his lute parts often bandy motifs with the voice. His metrical structure is varied, but at

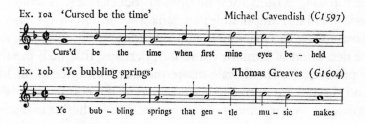

Ex. 10a 'Cursed be the time'   Michael Cavendish (*C1597*)

Curs'd   be   the   time   when   first   mine   eyes   be - held

Ex. 10b 'Ye bubbling springs'   Thomas Greaves (*G1604*)

Ye   bub - bling   springs   that   gen - tle   mu - sic   makes

30

the same time easy and natural. 'Shaded with olive trees' shows all these qualities at their best.

For all that it survives incomplete, Morley's *First Booke of Ayres* (1600) comes as close as any single volume to encompassing the complete range of expression found in the lutesong repertoire.[13] Hardly surprisingly, his technique is superb, yet nothing could be more artless than 'With my love my life was nestled'. 'Mistress mine, well may you fare' is equally entrancing, while 'It was a lover and his lass' (sung in *As You Like It*) epitomises Morley's unique ability to combine musical sophistication with popular appeal. Yet there is a side to Morley at variance with the common notion of him, one which emerges in such songs as 'Come, sorrow, come' and 'I saw my lady weeping', and even challenges comparison with Dowland in his *'semper dolens'* mood. Indeed both composers published settings of 'I saw my lady weep[ing]' in 1600 which show striking similarities not only of mood but also of material. Both are in A minor and maintain a rhapsodic, non-imitative, yet contrapuntal continuity in the accompaniment. The songs begin similarly, and there are even closer resemblences later: compare especially the passages marked x and y in Ex. 11 with those in Ex. 5 (p. 19).

Whether this may be taken as indicating the influence of one composer on the other (and if so, which on which) is doubtful, but it certainly underlines the similarity of their idiom, and shows that Morley was a match for Dowland on his home ground.

Tobias Hume's *Musicall Humors* (1605) consist primarily of instrumental pieces but should be noticed if only on account of 'Fain would I change that note', and absolute *non pareil* among the works of the worthy but woeful Captain, and as graceful a song as any of the period.[14] 'Tobacco, tobacco' is something of a curiosity; so too is 'The Souldier's Song' ('I sing the praise of honour'd wars'), a programmatic battle piece in which the accompaniment imitates 'The great Ordenance', 'Kettle Drumme' and 'Trumpets'. Hume advocated the bass viol

Ex. 11a 'I saw my lady weeping'   Thomas Morley (*M1600*)

rather than the lute as the ideal instrument for song accompaniments, and believed that 'from henceforth, the statefull
instrument *Gambo Violl*, shall with ease yeelde full various and
as devicefull Musicke as the Lute'. His *Poeticall Musicke* (1607)
is unremarkable for any reason connected with the few songs
it contains.

Francis Pilkington shares something of Dowland's approach to the lutesong. But many of the contents of his *First Booke Of Songs* (1605) are rather turgid, the melodic line conceived as an element of polyphonic texture rather than as a focus in itself and rarely shaped with anything like Dowland's expressive elegance. Within the galliard form he can forget counterpoint for a while and allow his gift of melody free rein, but even at its best it is somewhat stiff. There is little that is easy and natural; the simple, unaffected line of 'Rest sweet nymphs' is unfortunately not typical. For the rest there is some evidence of technical competence (he was, after all, an Oxford B.Mus.) but little of the true spark of genius. His literary taste was refined but conventional, and he did better when he turned to the madrigal.

John Bartlet reminds one of Jones. Two-thirds of the contents of his *Booke of Ayres* (1606) were furnished with alternative four-part arrangements and these are often the more successful versions. There are some engaging pieces. The duet 'Whither runneth my sweet heart?' is well known, as is 'Of all the birds that I do know'—somewhat indelicate beneath its symbols yet as delicate musically as one could wish. The serious songs are afflicted by dullness and the old fashioned consort style, though 'Go wailing verse' approaches Dowland's technique and mood quite successfully. With Bartlett one imagines that the partsong versions came first; the imitations are, generally speaking, so integral to the texture and superior in this respect to Jones's. Yet he can also think melodically and 'I would thou wert not fair' has the elegant simplicity of Rosseter or Campion at his best.

This is not the place to consider Giovanni Coprario's two songbooks published in 1606 and 1613 to mark the death of the Earl of Devonshire and Prince Henry respectively; nor Alfonso Ferrabosco's *Ayres* (1609) which bear more directly on the development of the declamatory style—they will be dealt with later. But John Danyel's *Songs* (1606) mark one of the peaks of the lutesong school.[15] Undoubtedly there are a number of attractive light ayres in the book, but it is not on them that Danyel's claim to fame rests. It is the serious songs which mark him out as second only to Dowland in expressive power. If anything, his writing is even more intense than Dowland's; the emotions seem more tortured, whereas Dowland's convey a resigned, world-weary quality. This aspect of Danyel's expressive language is most convincingly demonstrated in the second song of the 'Chromatic Tunes' cycle (nos. 13–15) where the music provides a harrowing, almost frightening, commentary on the text.

> *No, let chromatic tunes, harsh without ground,*
> *Be sullen music for a tuneless heart;*
> *Chromatic tunes most like my passions sound,*
> *As if combined to bear their falling part.*

A milder example of the same sort of thing is to be found in the setting of his brother Samuel's 'Like as the lute delights', where once again musical terminology is matched by appropriate devices—which, perhaps, is mere punning, but to what effect!

> *Else harsh my style, untuneable my Muse:*
> *Hoarse sounds the voice that praiseth not her name . . .*

Here phrases such as 'heart strings, *high tuned*', 'the *warble* of the sound', 'a wailing *descant*', 'whose due *reports*', 'pleasing *relish*', 'no *ground* else' are all depicted in the music; 'warble' and 'relish' by ornamental passages, 'descant' and 'ground' against a hexachord *cantus firmus* in the accompaniment, 'report' by close imitations between voice and lute, 'high tuned' by a high cantus part. Such traits are characteristic of a madrigalian mentality, and though Danyel was not a madrigalist his style is highly artificial nevertheless.

As with Dowland the basic structure of the dance is frequently discernable. 'Eyes look no more' is obviously a pavan and even quotes Dowland's *Lacrimae.* (Danyel's song also occurs as a lute piece with the title 'Rosamunde' in certain manuscripts.) 'Let not Chloris think because' is equally obviously a galliard, as is 'He whose desires', though of quite a different kind. The same tripartite structure is to be found in more developed form elsewhere, notably in the cycle 'Mrs. M. E. her Funeral tears for the death of her husband' (nos. 9–11) where each of the three songs becomes a strain of the pavan. The 'Chromatic Tunes' cycle takes the process a stage further. Here each strain assumes the dimensions of a fantasia, yet the unified mood and the characteristic tonal layout (I–V:V–V: I–I) imply the pavan.

Beside Danyel, Thomas Ford seems facile, yet this is a view not altogether fair. Charm such as his is always welcome. His *Musick Of Sundrie Kindes* (1607) contains only ten songs and a dialogue, but among them are not only such justly admired pieces as 'Since first I saw your face' and 'There is a lady sweet and kind', but the deliciously swooning 'Fair, sweet, cruel', the wistful 'What then is love', or the more forthright 'Now I see thy looks were feigned'. The taste is exquisite, the technique that of the harmonised tune with here and there some motivic interplay between tune and accompaniment.

Although George Handford's book of *Ayres* in manuscript bears a dedication to Prince Henry dated 1609, it was never published. It was not a great loss. Nor, had the same fate befallen John Maynard's *XII Wonders Of the World* (1611) would we have been much the poorer. Maynard's 'wonders' are, in fact, 'characters'—*The Courtier, The Divine,* etc.,—but the music is feeble and adds nothing at all to the subjects represented.

Robert Dowland's miscellaneous collection entitled *A Musicall Banquet* (1610) is an important publication deserving attention on account of a number of Italian songs in it, and three by his father. It is also interesting because it supplies us with songs by several composers not otherwise known as songwriters: Anthony Holborne, Richard Martin, Robert

Hales and Daniel Batchelar among them. Two of the poems set are by Robert Devereux, Earl of Essex: Richard Martin's attractive 'Change thy mind since she doth change' and Batchelar's 'To Plead my faith' the beginning of which is virtually the same as that of his best-known galliard.

William Corkine's first book of *Ayres* (1610) contains a number of charming songs. One or two would have done more than justice to Campion. Some are simple and tuneful like 'Think you to seduce me so', others are more elaborate in style, such as the delightfully teasing 'Sweet, let me go'. His setting of Anthony Munday's 'Beauty sat bathing' is superior to both Jones's and Pilkington's. It is more than usually complicated for Corkine, with an imitative introduction for the lute and some charming details, notably the word-painting on 'cool streams ran beside her' and some high spirited 'Fie, fies' towards the end. His *Second Booke of Ayres* (1612) is less rewarding, though 'Shall a smile or guileful glance' is as pleasing as anything in the earlier collection. It is worth noting that 13 of the songs in this book are without tablature accompaniment or alternative partsong versions. Instead, they are to be sung 'to the Base-Violl alone'. This, of course, was how nearly all the songs of the next generation were written, though Corkine makes no reference to realising the bass as a continuo—indeed, the title seems to preclude it.

Though the title-page of Martin Peerson's *Private Musicke* (1620) refers to the possibility of a kind of continuo accompaniment ('. . . for want of Viols, they may be performed to either the Virginall or Lute, where the Proficient can play upon the Ground . . .') the music, like the words, is really quite old fashioned. The songs are, in fact, consort songs with verse and full sections, though melodic in their appeal. Among the best in the book are 'At her fair hands', and the gently complaining 'Ah, were she pitiful as she is fair'.

There is little in John Attey's *First Booke Of Ayres* (1622) to give cause for regret that he failed to produce a second, or, for that matter that it brings the English school of lutesong publications to an end. (No more solo songs came out in print for the next 30 years.) 'On a time the amorous Silvy' is poor Jones; 'Vain hope, adieu!' is poor Dowland. Only 'Sweet was the song the Virgin sung' invites a second look, though hardly meriting Warlock's description of it as a 'flawless work of serene beauty which forms a fitting conclusion to this golden period of English song'.[16]

And so the English lutesongs come to an end, not with a bang but a whimper. It need hardly be said that Dowland's genius overshadows the whole school. In style, too, he covers the complete range, for though Danyel challenges strongly as a composer of undoubted power in his serious songs, and Rosseter is matchless in lighter ayres, no one comes as close to spanning these extremes as Dowland. Morley alone suggests that he might have done so had he lived long enough to follow up his *First Booke of Ayres* with a second or third. The others— Bartlett, Cavendish, Corkine, Ford, Greaves and Pilkington —were minor composers each of whom came close to perfection once or twice. Yet Dowland alone has real stature, and as a composer of songs dominates the beginning of the century just as surely as Purcell does the end. It is hard to follow such geniuses; inevitably some sort of fresh start needs to be made.

2 The new men and the new music

The accession of King James VI of Scotland to the English throne in 1603 was an event which promised great things; certainly, for better or worse, it was to usher in a new era. New men looked to the Court to advance themselves and their causes, and while the King turned to matters of state and religion, his Queen, Anne of Denmark, took up the arts—in particular the arts of poetry, design and decoration, music and dancing, lavishly combined in the Masque. Inordinate sums were spent on these entertainments, and the talents of Ben Johnson and Inigo Jones were employed in their production. Not only the King, but the Queen and Prince Henry each had their own households, including sizable musical establishments. Indeed, Whitehall in its Jacobean heyday stood out in contrast to the pinch-penny conservatism of Elizabeth's court which as an artistic centre had lacked distinction. In her reign it had been to the country house and the great families that musicians and poets looked for patronage. The dedications alone of many madrigal and lutesong publications bear testimony of this, and the role of household or personal musician was one which many respectable composers enjoyed; that, or the service of the Church. Elizabeth's court musicians on the other hand included few composers of repute, apart from those in the Chapel Royal.

It is true that country house patronage did not disappear during the seventeenth century, but undoubtedly it diminished. Increasingly the court became the artistic focal point of the nation, and its glamour and prestige drew the best mu-

sicians in a way which Elizabeth's had not done. The move
from the country house to the court was, of course, a reflection
of a larger social and political phenomenon. No doubt the
process had already begun in the latter years of Elizabeth's
reign, but it accelerated in the early Stuart period. Economically it was a time of increasing difficulty for the gentry, and
while many sought an easy way out of their troubles by in-
stalling themselves in town in the hope of pickings at court,
others who stayed at home in the country failed to live up to
their responsibilities as landowners. Both James I and Charles
I had occasion to order those gentlemen without a London
house of their own to return to the country and perform their
traditional duties. The feudal concept of the landowner was
declining, and with it the obligation of patronage.

For those young gentlemen who desired a place at court, the
way in (appropriately enough!) was through one of the Inns of
Court. Young blades down from Oxford or Cambridge sharp-
ened their wits there. Free from the discipline of the University
and diverted with all London had to offer, it was natural that
an atmosphere of youthful high spirits and intellectual vigour
should give rise to new ideas—in the arts, science, religion and
politics. A new wave was about to break and (as always) it is
not difficult to sense that an older generation disapproved of
the way things were going:

'More geese than swans now live, more fools than wise',[1]
puts the sober Elizabethan view nicely.

So too in music. As we have seen, John Dowland felt it per-
sonally, and set himself against the *avant garde*. Admittedly he
was given to peevishness when he felt that his reputation had
been insufficiently recognized. He had long coveted a place
among the royal musicians. As early as 1594 he had hoped for
preferment, but his Catholicism (he said) was against him, and
it was not until 1612 that he was appointed to the King's
Musick as composer and lutenist. Approaching 50 and famous
throughout Northern Europe, he probably resented the up-
starts whom he found there already, among them Alfonso

Ferrabosco who had come strongly into the limelight by providing songs for court masques since 1605 and whose praises were sung in verse by Ben Jonson. Similarly, the still younger Robert Johnson (whose father's place as a lutenist Dowland had sought in vain in 1594) could have come in for some obloquy.[2]

These two composers were certainly in the vanguard, and Nicholas Lanier—who may already have appeared on the scene under the powerful patronage of the Earl of Salisbury—even more so, whereas Dowland could not, or would not, refute the imputation that 'what I doe is after the old manner'. It was not entirely true, however. One or two of his songs do foreshadow the new declamatory style, notably 'Far from triumphing court,' (*D1610*).

Ex. 12 'Far from triumphing court' (Lee)   John Dowland (*D1610*)

It seems to have been written for an occasion associated with the declining years of Sir Henry Lee, Ranger of Woodstock and erstwhile Champion of Queen Elizabeth, at whose retirement from office in 1590 an earlier song by Dowland, 'His golden locks' (*D1597*) had been sung. 'Far from triumphing court' dates from after the Queen's death and probably marks the occasion when Queen Anne visited him at Woodstock in 1608.[3] Its style is symptomatic of trends observable not only in a few of Dowland's songs, but particularly in some of Ferrabosco's *Ayres* (1609). A more declamatory treatment of the voice is immediately noticeable, together with a chordal type of lute accompaniment characterized by a harmonically static bass. It is significant that these traits are to be found mainly in ceremonial or masque songs such as 'Far from triumphing court' and those written by Dowland for Lord Walden's wedding celebrations, and Ferrabosco's songs for Jonson's court masques.[4]

Ferrabosco's songs for the *Masque of Beauty* (1608)—nos. 18–22 in the *Ayres*—demonstrate this new 'heroic' style as does 'If all the ages of the earth' (*F1609*) from the *Masque of Queens* (1609) sung 'by that most excellent *tenor* voyce, and exact singer (her Mᵗⁱᵉˢ servant, mʳ Io Allin)'. In particular, the opening illustrates the declamatory nature of the voice part and the continuo type of accompaniment (Ex. 13). The effect is immediately arresting, and matches the high-flown verse admirably. Its ceremonial character is obvious, and as far removed from the delicious trifling of Rosseter as from the fervour of Danyel. Above all the aim seems to have been to make the words audible in a large hall (a new Banqueting Hall had been opened in Whitehall in 1608), clearly declaimed above an accompaniment sometimes of several lutes. Subtleties of harmonic nuance or polyphonic elaboration were unnecessary.

Ex. 13 'If all the ages of the earth' (Jonson: *Masque of Queens*, 1609)

Alfonso Ferrabosco (*F1609*)

Now and again there is word repetition, sequence or imitation towards the end of a song, but only rarely. The general harmonic treatment is simple, with the same chord frequently held or repeated over several bars and stereotyped use of ♯ 4 ♯ cadences. The style is thoroughly diatonic, though as a personal idiosyncrasy Ferrabosco often equivocates between tonic major and minor.

A possible parallel with developments in Italy comes to mind immediately, and the question arises as to how far Italian influences, direct or indirect, are involved. It has to be admitted that the vogue for things Italian was at its height at the end of the sixteenth century and that it persisted into the seventeenth. The taste for Italian madrigals, and the Italian influence on the English madrigal, is the most persuasive evidence of this ultramontanism, and we can be sure that printed books from Italy, madrigals and (after 1602) monodies, were sought after and studied with interest. Yet their availability in the early years of the seventeenth century does not seem to have extended much beyond the madrigalian repertory, and indicative of this is the fact that Francis Tregian did not include any monodic pieces in his vast anthology of mainly Italian vocal and instrumental music compiled while in the Fleet Gaol as a recusant from 1609 to 1619.[5]

However, there is little doubt that certain composers affected the Italian style (either as they knew or imagined it) and even set Italian words. But Dowland's '*Lasso! vita mia*' (*D1612*) is not a monody. Nor are Jones' Petrarch settings, '*Ite, caldi sospiri*' (*J1609*) and '*S'amor non è*' (*Ibid.*) for they are tied down by written-out lute parts. The freedom of declamation which comes with the *basso continuo* and an improvised accompaniment is denied this music, whereas it is the essence of *le nuove musiche*. Indeed, the fact that figured basses are virtually nonexistant in England before the 1630's itself suggests that Italian monody was not well known.

The presence of Italian musicians in England could have facilitated the dissemination of the new music. Someone who may have played a part in introducing it was Giovanni Maria Lugario, Queen Anne's Italian musician, who entered her service in 1607 after employment at the court of Mantua where he was a colleague of Monteverdi. Apparently he was in correspondance with Ottavio Rinnuccini in 1606 and he may be assumed to have been familiar with the Italian musical scene.[6] Likewise Angelo Notari of Padua, one of Prince Henry's lutenists, who arrived from Venice about 1610, and whose *Prime Musiche Nuove* containing a few solo items was published in London in 1613.[7] It has been shown that he was the compiler of a manuscript (BM Add. MS 31440) containing—among other things—Italian monodies and continuo madrigals, some of which are found in printed books dating, preponderantly, from around 1620. The presence of a string of 11 items from Monteverdi's seventh book of madrigals (1619) suggests that the contents were assembled after Notari's arrival in England, probably after 1620. Apparently Caccini is unrepresented in the manuscript, and so far the only traceable monodies are from Raffaello Rontani's fifth and sixth books of *Varie Musiche* (1620–22).

No doubt there was more coming and going between England and Italy than we have record of now, and more Italian music available (apart from madrigals, etc.) than the few samples that survive. Even so, it is surprising that there is not more evidence of Italian traits in English songs of the period. By and large the lutesong writers were untouched, and one gets the impression that Italianate composers such as Ferrabosco and Lanier had not so much heard the 'new music' as heard *about* it.

But from about 1610 onwards examples of Italian monody began to be accessible to English musicians through publications such as Robert Dowland's *Musicall Banquet* (1610) and Notari's collection. Caccini's '*Amarilli, mia bella*' seems to have enjoyed wide popularity, and was even adapted to English words ('Miserere my maker' in Add. MS 15117).[8] It is among the Italian songs printed in the *Musicall Banquet*, and occurs in three other manuscripts, including Tenbury MS 1018–9 which contains numerous songs by Caccini and seems to derive from Italian sources prior to the appearance of *Le Nuove Musiche* in 1602.[9] The same manuscript contains five Italian settings by Alfonso Ferrabosco; one, a setting of Guarini's *'Occhi stelle mortale'* (probably earlier than the others since an English version was published in the *Ayres* as 'O eyes, O mortal stars') and three of passages from the same poet's *Pastor Fido*.[10] Clearly these songs are conscious attempts at imitating Italian monody. In them Ferrabosco manages to achieve a degree of expressive force and declamatory power surpassing his English masque songs.

Similar traits have been noticed by some in Coprario's *Songs of Mourning* (1613) bewailing the untimely death of Henry, Prince of Wales. Coprario had travelled on the Continent and probably visited Italy, adopting the Italian form of his name (Cooper) which he retained on his return. Dowland may have come into contact with the *Camerata* in 1595 while in Florence, early enough to have heard Caccini's songs; and Coprario, too, may have had first-hand experience of the new music, though the report that he had taken part in 'the production of the first opera' has not been substantiated.[11] Whatever (if any) his experiences in Italy may have been, he does not show much trace of them in his *Funeral Tears* (1606) on the death of Charles Blount, Earl of Devonshire. Nor do the *Songs of Mourning* argue convincingly in favour of first-hand Italian influence, for though the solo voice is more declamatory, the accompaniment is a long way from being conceived as a continuo. His three songs in Campion's Masque for the Earl of Somerset's wedding (1613) are even less remarkable—from any point of view.

Quite the opposite applies to Nicholas Lanier's single contribution to the same masque, 'Bring away this sacred tree' (*C1614*), which he himself sang in the role of Eternity.[12] This song represents a concentration of most of the tendencies we have been considering. The vocal line is suitably heroic in its declamation and has much in common with the style of Ferra-

bosco's masque songs, though the wide leaps which characterize the latter's line have been restricted. But it develops the
older musician's methods a stage further, by reducing the
accompaniment to mere chords, and stabilizing the harmonic
range. This song is really the earliest ayre that is clearly of the
same type as that which was to flourish over the next 30 years.
Without being more than a thoroughly effective piece it marks
the point to which Ferrabosco had been leading.

The new style, then, was born and grew up in the masquing

Ex. 14 'Bring away, this sacred tree' (Campion: *Somerset Masque*, 1613)

Nicholas Lanier (*C1614*)

hall. Actually, fewer masque songs survive from the period
immediately after 1613 than before; however, the *Ayres that
were Sung and Played at Brougham Castle . . . in the Kings Entertainment* (1618) by George Mason and John Earsden put the
declamatory techniques already observed in the masque songs
of Ferrabosco and Lanier to good effect, notably in 'The Farewell Song' ('O Stay, sweet is the least delay') and the gipsy's
atmospheric incantation 'The shadows dark'ning our intents'.[13]

Following the break-up of the Jonson-Ferrabosco partnership sometime after 1612, Nicholas Lanier became the principal

composer for the court masques. He had already made a name for himself in these entertainments (was he perhaps one of Dowland's despised 'simple Cantors, or vocall singers')? and, indeed, the impression one receives from letters and other records of this time is of a courtier, first and foremost, making his way. His subsequent career—not only his appointment as Master of the King's Musick—certainly suggests that he put his talents to advantageous use. North's description of him as 'a very ingenious *vertuoso*' was apt.[14] According to Jonson, Lanier 'ordered and made both the Scene, and the Musicke' for the masque *Lovers Made Men* (1617); moreover '*the whole Maske was sung (after the Italian manner)* Stylo recitativo'. In *Vision of Delight* (1617)—another masque for which Lanier wrote the music—Jonson notes that '*Delight* spake in song (*stylo recitativo*)'.[15] We cannot assume, however, that recitative was thus an accomplished fact, for these observations are only found in the 1637-40 edition of Jonson's works, and virtually none of the music survives—only a roughly notated, highly embellished treble part of a setting of the words 'I was not wearier' (N) from the *Vision of Delight*.[16] In so far as it tells us anything, it bears an affinity with the type of declamatory ayre already established in England rather than with true recitative (Ex. 15).

In this form it is certainly nothing out of the ordinary run of English masque songs of the time, and it conforms, too, with the only other masque song by Lanier we have from this period, the song 'Do not expect to hear' (P) from the *Masque of Augurs* (1622).[17] Although '*that excellent paire of kinsemen, Mr. Alphonso Ferrabosco, and Mr. Nicholas Lanier*' collaborated over the music for this masque, this particular song is ascribed to Lanier and still gives no suggestion of familiarity with Italian recitative. This was to come later with his *Hero and Leander*.

The earliest and closest approach to recitative is found in the Dialogue—usually a musical setting of a short dramatized incident between a nymph and a shepherd, or of some biblical or mythological anecdote.[18] Already in the dialogues of Ferra-

Ex. 15 'I was not wearier' (Jonson: *Vision of Delight*, 1617)

Nicholas Lanier (N - ornamented treble only)

I was not wea – ri- er where I lay

[reconstruction of 'original']

By frozen Ti - tan's side to - - - - night

Than I am wil - ling now to stay, And be a part of

7   #6

your de-light; But I am ar - gued by the day

A - - gainst my will to bid you come

bosco we are on the brink of true recitative, particularly in the last of the three in his *Ayres*, 'Tell me, O love'. As yet the style is insufficiently flexible to serve as a vehicle for naturalistic musical conversation, but the continuo tendencies in the accompaniment are clear, and this was a necessary preliminary before the vocal parts could loosen up and develop declamatory suppleness.

As in his masque songs, Lanier's dialogues take Ferrabosco's style a stage further. The continuo role of the accompaniment is no longer tentative, the declamation is freer and the stiff alternation that we find in Ferrabosco is now more fluid, partly because of the irregular breaking of lines between the singers and the use of enjambements. But the nature of the form offers Lanier little opportunity to display such dramatic and expressive ability as he may possess, and a few moments of touching pathos are the only rewards.[19]

Although overrunning the chronological limits of the present chapter by a few years, a further look at the dialogue will not be out of place here. Its continued vogue in the 1630's reflects the platonic pastoralism of the court under the influence of Queen Henrietta-Maria, and, significantly, all the court composers contribute to it.[20] But outside court circles another species of dialogue was being cultivated, one far less effete though also less sophisticated. These were the mythological and biblical dialogues of Robert Ramsey and John Hilton.[21] In place of coy question and answer there is a more powerful dramatic confrontation in such subjects as *Dives and*

[1] Nicholas Lanier, *c.* 1625 (?). (Sir Anthony Van Dyck. Kunsthistorisches Museum, Vienna)

Abraham, Saul and the Witch of Endor, Paris and Oenone, Vulcan and Venus, Orpheus and Pluto (among Ramsey's dialogues in *L*), and *The Judgement of Paris, The Judgement of Solomon, The Temptation of Job* (among Hilton's in *P*). Secular and sacred, they bear a direct relationship to opera and oratorio, which is really what they are on a small scale.

It is difficult to say exactly when these dialogues were written, though the fact that Ramsey and Hilton were both Cambridge men and acquainted with each other offers some clues. Any investigation needs to take into account the likely date of the earliest of two important manuscripts containing these dialogues: Bodleian MS Don.c.57 (*L*). At first sight, the clear association of Ramsey and the poet Robert Herrick in this manuscript suggests that a piece such as the dialogue between Orpheus and Pluto could have been written while they were both at Cambridge—Herrick graduated in 1617, the year after Ramsey. But other evidence argues more strongly for a later date. In fact, the early part of the manuscript cannot be earlier than 1631 since no. 4 is Hilton's 'Charon, come hither Charon', a dialogue between Charon and Hobson, the Cambridge carrier (celebrated in verse by Milton) who died on New Year's Day, 1631.[22] Bearing in mind, too, that Ramsey was organist of Trinity College from 1628, the presence of several items by Hilton (who graduated from Trinity in 1626), of the only known song by Stephen Mace (father of Thomas Mace and 'Singing Man' at Trinity from 1627 to 1635), of a dialogue by Ramsey (Woe's me, alas') set to a poem by 'Mr. Riley' (possibly the Thomas Rylye at Trinity from 1626 to 1630, and a Fellow later)—all these point to the years about 1630 as the period of origin of the Cambridge repertoire in the manuscript. There is even a song deploring the death of Charles I's first-born son two hours after his birth on 13 May 1629:

> *How short a time of breath was lent*
> *Unto our prince . . .*
> *Born to three crowns, dead in two hours,*

The peaceful child desired a truce
Betwixt the Rose and Flower de Luce.

Certainly there are songs earlier than 1630 in this manuscript, but most of them belong to a fairly widely circulating general repertoire, whereas the Cambridge items seem to concentrate about 1630. Nor is the Ramsey-Herrick partnership incompatible with this date, since Herrick, though no longer a Fellow, seems to have been in residence at Trinity Hall in 1629–30, as the account books show.[23]

Most of Hilton's dialogues are contained in British Museum Add. MS 11608 (*P*), though, as we have just seen, it is also one of his which establishes the beginning date of the Bodleian manuscript as not before 1631. It is likely then that these other dialogues are later, and the general repertoire and palaeography of the British Museum manuscript confirm this. Therefore it seems reasonable to point to Ramsey as being earlier in the field as a composer of dialogues than Hilton, though perhaps not by much. Yet if he did provide the models for Hilton it is the younger composer who has the more old-fashioned style. Ramsey often comes close to true recitative without quite being able to keep the bass still enough to achieve real declamatory freedom. The result is often an uneasy compromise between recitative and two-part counterpoint aggravated by chromaticisms which are rarely very effective. Hilton, on the other hand, achieves a more homogeneous style by being less declamatory. The function of treble and bass is better balanced; the movement of each is more consistent within itself and with the other. In general terms, of course, their styles are similar, but a comparison of Ramsey's 'Howl not you ghosts' (*L*) with Hilton's 'Rise princely shepherd' (*P*) indicates that Ramsey is the more experimental if less successful practitioner.[24] The same conclusion is more clearly drawn from a comparison of their solo settings of Herrick's 'Thou may'st be proud' (Ex. 16).[25]

This is not to deny the dramatic effectiveness of Hilton's

dialogues. Particularly in the exchanges between the two har-
lots in *The Judgement of Solomon* an exciting effect is achieved
through the rapid alternation of the voices and the repetition of
the phrase 'It's mine!' progressively higher (Ex. 17).

After Ramsey and Hilton, this type of dialogue declined,
although it did not die out. Indeed, Ramsey's 'In guilty night'

Ex. 16a 'Thou may'st be proud' (Herrick)   Robert Ramsey (*L*)

Ex. 16b 'Thou may'st be proud' (Herrick)   John Hilton (*N*)

appears later in the century in two manuscripts erroneously
ascribed to Lanier (or perhaps with the bass modernized by
him) while Purcell, no doubt familiar with this version, reset
the whole thing in his own incomparable way.[26]

One mythological incident in particular continued to interest
composers—the 'Charon Dialogue'. Of the eight that survive in

Ex. 17 from 'When Israel's sweet singer slept' *(Judgment of Solomon)*   John Hilton (P)

musical settings dating from the first half of the century, three are earlier than 1620.[27] How the vogue rose is difficult to say. The point of each is, of course, a request addressed to the infernal ferryman to be carried over the River Styx. Sometimes the suppliant is a mythological character such as Orpheus; sometimes merely a spirit killed by unrequited love. Without doubt the supernatural element appealed, and the dramatic situation was much intensified by contrasting the bass Charon with the higher voice, tenor or treble. This may be the clue to

2 Henry Lawes 'Aetat. Suæ. 26. 1622'
(Choir Room, Salisbury Cathedral)

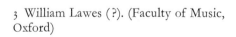

3 William Lawes (?). (Faculty of Music,
Oxford)

4 John Hilton the younger, 'Aetatis 50 Sept. 30th 1649' (Faculty of Music, Oxford)

5 John Wilson, 'D: Musica: Aetat: Sua. 59. 1655' (Robert Fisher. Faculty of Music, Oxford)

6 'Chloris sigh'd' by Alphonso (?) Bales (ornamented treble in Trinity College, Dublin. MS. F.5.13, c. 1617)

7 'O that mine eyes' by Thomas Brewer (British Museum, London. Add. MS. 10337, c. 1656)

its popularity, for it offered an opportunity for rich characterization by a bass in the 'horrific' role of Charon, as also in
biblical subjects where, again, there was a supernatural element
—the dead Abraham in *Dives*, Samuel's ghost in *Saul and the
Witch of Endor*, Satan in *Job*, etc. Heroic roles such as Paris,
Vulcan and King Solomon also gave a bass singer an opportunity to show his histrionic skill. Eerie subject matter vividly
portrayed in terms primarily of contrast between a bass (the
characterization of which the declamatory style was able to
exaggerate) and a suppliant high voice, are a common feature
of these dialogues, and no doubt an essential element in their
dramatic effectiveness.

No sooner had declamatory elements appeared in the songs
of the court masque than they began to emerge in playsongs. At
first it might be thought that such a sophisticated style could
have no place in the rough and tumble of the theatre, but the
character of the theatre itself was changing. In 1609 Burbage
and the King's Men took over the 'private' theatre at Blackfriars; an enclosed hall measuring only 66 feet by 44.[28] In
using it for his winter quarters, Burbage was doing more than
bringing the drama in out of the rain. The Globe Theatre had
been much larger and open to the sky. It catered for all classes
of society and gave them drama larger than life, broad comedy
and bloody murder. At Blackfriars the audience was smaller,
more select. It cost more to get in and, in general, conditions
approached those of the masquing hall rather than the public
theatres. And as playhouse and masquing hall came closer, so
did playsong and masque song—technically at any rate, although the different levels on which they functioned prevented
a complete merger of their styles.

In the masque, music was a means of magnifying the theme
of majesty, creating an aura of solemnity and splendour.
Through it reality was suspended and a world of symbolism
conjured up. Everything became possible, except (paradoxic-
ally) those particular effects which song could produce within
the context of spoken drama. Thus in this magical world, its

power to create atmosphere, to delineate character and to express feeling was diminished simply because song, as such, was no longer used as a special effect. But in the play its role was to deepen, not suspend reality; to make certain things more credible within the human situation.[29]

The playsongs surviving from the period 1609 to 1629 show that first Robert Johnson then John Wilson were employed as composers for the King's Men.[30] Johnson's indenture to Sir George Carey in 1596 doubtless facilitated his entry into the world of the theatre, for almost immediately Carey succeeded his father (Lord Hunsdon) in the office of Lord Chamberlain. He thus became patron of the Lord Chamberlain's Men, the theatrical company otherwise known as Hunsdon's Men and after 1603 called the King's Men. Of immediate interest are several of Johnson's songs written for the company between 1609 and 1617. Those for Shakespeare's *Tempest* (1610)—'Full fathom five' (*W1660*) and 'Where the bee sucks' (*Ibid.*, also *L*) are after the tuneful manner of Campion or Jones, and his beautiful song 'Away delights' (*R*) from Beaumont and Fletcher's *The Captain* (*c*.1612) would do honour to any composer. But mere tunefulness Johnson was willing to sacrifice in the cause of expression and characterization. The song 'Care charming sleep' (*G,L,P*) from *Valentinian* (*c*.1614), sung to soothe Valentinian dying of poison, is perhaps the best example of his expressive use of the early declamatory style, while his special talent for depicting the horrific and bizarre is well illustrated in his eerie setting of 'O let us howl some heavy note' (*J,K,M*) from Webster's *Duchess of Malfi* (*c*.1613).

Ex. 18 'O let us howl some heavy note' (Webster: *Duchess of Malfi*, c.1613)

Robert Johnson (*J*)

O let us howl some heav-y note, Some dead-ly dog-ged howl [etc.]

To the lute

54

This song is intended by Ferdinand to torment the Duchess before her murder, though ostensibly it is sung to cure her melancholy. The fact that it forms part of a Masque of Madmen adds to the grisly effect, and among other sinister touches are chromatic slidings between major and minor thirds found in the older versions.

Other 'characteristic' songs include 'Come away Hecate' (*G, J,*) from Middleton's *The Witch* (*c.*1616), borrowed for later performances of *Macbeth*. But perhaps his most remarkable playsong is 'Arm, arm! the scouts are all come in' (*M*), a description of a battle sung in Fletcher's *The Mad Lover* (1617) to cure the mad Memnon. The opposing armies are described, then with drums sounding the battle is joined, and the first blood shed. It is the nearest thing to *stile rappresentativo* in English music of the period, though it falls a long way short of Monteverdi's *Combattimento di Tancredi e Clorinda*. But for all its naivety, something of the excitement and confusion of battles comes across, and even pathos in the defeat of the enemy (Ex. 19).

Although Johnson's 'characteristic' songs are a remarkable feature of his output from the technical point of view, his sterling worth as a song writer is best seen in his 'straight' songs. Leaving aside the exquisite setting of Ben Jonson's 'Have you seen the bright lily grow?' (*Add. MS 15117, E,H, J,K,R*) which may or may not be his, there are at least half a dozen serious songs which are among the best of their time: 'Away delights' and 'Care-charming sleep', already mentioned, would certainly merit inclusion.

John Wilson's playsongs display less versatility. He could write a good straightforward tune; indeed, he had the common touch, and some of his songs may easily be mistaken for genuine ballads. In more sophisticated vein he could occasionally handle the declamatory style effectively, but he lacked Johnson's ability to explore deeper levels of character and feeling. After what may have been a period of collaboration he seems to have taken over from Johnson in the role of prin-

Ex. 19 from 'Arm, arm! the scouts are all come in' (Fletcher: *The Mad Lover*, c.1616)

Robert Johnson (M)

cipal song writer for the King's Men about 1617, continuing in that capacity for a dozen years or more.[31] Whether he may be identified with the 'Jacke Wilson' mentioned in the 1623 folio edition of *Much Ado About Nothing*—that is, as Balthazar, the singer of 'Sigh no more ladies'—is uncertain, but more than probable. There is, after all, no need to assume that this mention must refer to the first performance of the play in 1604 (when Wilson would have been too young for the part), merely to some performance prior to 1623, the period of Wilson's known association with the King's Men.[32]

Evidently he made his mark early, for his song 'Kawasha comes in majesty' belongs to the *Masque of Flowers* (1614). True, more remarkable achievements have been recorded by young men of 18, but he seems to have received further recognition almost immediately for his earliest playsongs date from about this time. Beaumont and Fletcher's *Valentinian* cannot be later than 1614, and if the songs bearing Wilson's name were written for the first performance then they must mark the beginning of his association with the King's Men. The contrast between his songs and Johnson's for this play may be taken as typifying their musical proclivities. On the one hand is 'Care-charming sleep', infused with melancholy, expressive and subtle; on the other, Wilson's 'Now the lusty spring is seen' (*W1660, S*)—a seduction song with the refrain 'Ladies, if not plucked, you die'—and 'God Lyaeus, ever young' (*Ibid.*), a drinking song. They are tuneful and popular in style, possessing a certain four-square vigour, which, however, does not prevent them from rambling. This frank ballad style is seen at its best in the setting of 'In a maiden time professed' (*B,R*) from Middleton's *The Witch* (Ex. 20).[33]

Here the tune fits the simple eight-line stanza very well, but in certain other songs the verse structure is too elaborate for the music, particularly when the poet is Fletcher. Wilson's tuneful style needs metrical regularity, and prefers alternating or couplet rhymes within short, symmetrical stanzas. Theoretically the declamatory style should be able to accommodate itself to a varied poetic pattern, nevertheless Wilson allows himself to be thrown out by changes in metre and rhyming scheme too easily, and cannot really hold interest beyond a six or eight line stanza. One of his best songs in the declamatory idiom is 'Take, O take those lips away' (*P1652, B,M,P,R, Ch.Cb 434*)— Shakespeare's (?) first stanza lifted from *Measure for Measure* and furnished with a second to do duty as an erotic song in Fletcher's *The Bloody Brother* (*c.*1617).[34] Given a simple lyric with no formal complications Wilson responded with more grace and loving care than usual. Declamatory and melodic elements merge easily, and the stanza is short enough to prevent the material becoming too digressive. The final cadence is

Ex. 20 'In a maiden time professed' (Middleton: *The Witch*, c.1616)   John Wilson (*B*)

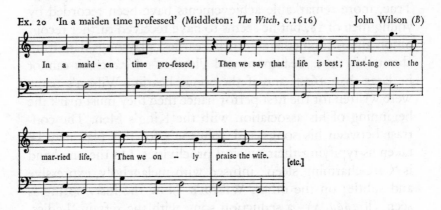

something of a cliché (but beautiful nevertheless), and we may note also one of Wilson's stylistic finger-prints—the interrupted cadence at the end of the first line. The song is well enough known not to need quotation. Instead, the opening of 'Turn thy beauteous face away' (*W1660,B,S*) from *Love's Cure* (*c.*1625) by John Fletcher may be given as an example of Wilson's declamation at its most commendable (Ex. 21).[35]

In the line of Johnson's supernatural and mad songs are Wilson's 'characteristic' songs such as 'Will you buy any honesty' (*W1660,S*) from *The Loyal Subject* (1618) and Higgen's songs in *The Beggar's Bush* (1622). Those sung by Constance in Brome's *The Northern Lass* (1629) are also worthy of note, as they provide a parallel with Ophelia's mad songs. At first glance they seem inept, vague in melodic outline and harmonic progression. It has been suggested that in this way Constance's deranged state of mind is conveyed: alternatively, that Wilson adopted a North Country folk-idiom appropriate to the character.[36] Indeed, the effect does suggest that he was attempting some such device of characterization.

With few exceptions Wilson's playsongs offer little evidence of refinement; plenty of a frank, unsophisticated melodic gift, carelessly applied. In the next chapter we shall observe how these qualities carry right through his creative output. To be

Ex. 21 'Turn thy beauteous face away' (Fletcher: *Love's Cure*, c.1625)   John Wilson (*B*)

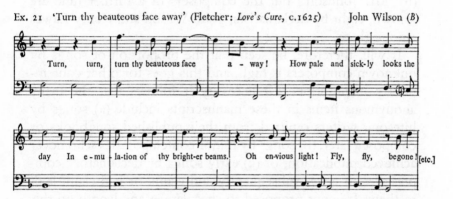

sure, they reflect the man, who, despite (or because of) them became successively city wait, court musician and Professor of Music at Oxford!

Beyond the range of masque and theatre songs the declamatory element was somewhat slow in becoming established. It hardly makes an appearance in the works of the lutesong school down to 1622, and among manuscripts dating from before 1620 or thereabouts only those at Tenbury (*Tenb*), Dublin (*E*) and Cambridge (*G*) contain an appreciable number of songs in a more advanced style. Soon after 1620, however, declamatory songs are more frequently encountered in the sources, which include manuscript collections made by two ladies, Elizabeth Davenant (*H*) and Anne Twice (*J*), and smaller books in the Bodleian Library (*I*) and the British Museum (*K*).

Only a very few items in these sources are ascribed. As we shall see, some are known from later sources to be by Robert Johnson, Nicholas Lanier, John Wilson, Henry Lawes and William Webb, but apart from these (and those by lutesong writers which are also identifiable) a high proportion are by unknown composers. For example, all 76 songs in the Dublin manuscript (*E*) are anonymous, though 42 are by known lutesong writers and four by later declamatists. Similarly, of the 28 songs surviving in Anne Twice's Book, only one is ascribed (to 'Mr. Johnson') but the composers of a further nine are known, eight by declamatists, John Wilson and Henry Lawes among them.

It will, therefore, be seen that the proportion of songs by unknown composers is high, and this goes for other contemporary manuscripts. Of necessity it follows that the many anonymous items in these manuscripts include (a) songs by lutesong writers omitted from their published songbooks or composed later, (b) songs by minor contemporaries who never achieved publication, or (c) early songs by declamatory composers who never subsequently laid claim, or had claim laid, to them. It is not proposed to speculate at any length on this matter, but the possibility should be borne in mind that among the run of songs by Campion and Jones in the Dublin manuscript may be some not previously known to be by them: 'Must your fair inflaming eyes' would be a candidate.[37]

Although not numerous, there are enough songs by later composers to show that not only Lanier and Wilson, but Henry Lawes and—rather surprisingly—William Webb were active before 1620. The following songs by these composers are found in early sources.

Lanier — 'I was not wearier' (originally in *J*)
(?) 'Like hermit poor' (originally in *J*)[38]
'Weep no more my wearied eyes' (*E,G*)[39]

Lawes — 'Hence vain delights' (*G*)
      'I'll tell you how the rose' (*J*)
      'Like to the damask rose' (*H,J*)
Webb — 'As life what is so sweet' (*H,K*, originally in *J*)[40]
      'Let her give her hand her glove' (originally in *J*)
Wilson — 'Cease, O cease this hum of grieving' (*H*)
      'Go happy heart' (*G,H*)
      'Sleep, sleep fair virgin' (*H*)
      'Virtue, beauty, forms of honour' (*E*)
      'Wherefore peep'st thou' (*J*)[41]

These in turn may be used for dating other songs by Lawes and Wilson since their presence in the early pages of the song collections of these composers (*A* and *B*) suggests, as does other evidence, that songs associated with them are also early. In the case of Wilson, the dates and position of his playsongs is a factor to be considered, and, weighing all the evidence, it would seem that most of the songs contained in the first 40 folios of the Bodleian song book may be dated prior to 1620 or so, though not necessarily in the form they take in the manuscript which was compiled about 1656.

However, the significance of this chronology in relation to the individual style of these composers and their development will be considered later. For the moment we will turn to the anonymous items for a representative view of English song round about 1620.

Disregarding frankly old-fashioned songs such as 'Like as the lark within the marlion's foot' (*E*), which probably dates well back into the sixteenth century though it maintained sufficient lease of life to be included in Forbe's *Songs and Fancies* (1662) and associated Scottish sources, there are others whose style is that of the lutesong. 'Venus went wand'ring' (*J,K*) for example, mixes common and triple time and displays imitation between treble and bass. Word repetition is also a feature, either as an element in melodic balance, or even as a relic of imitative texture (Ex. 22).

Then there are songs like 'Must your fair enflaming eye' (*E*), with simple, straightforward yet by no means unsophisticated melodies.[42] Another pleasing example is a setting of 'Wrong not dear Empress of my heart' (*J*) showing a fine sense of rhythmic and melodic balance. The dactylic chanson rhythm (♩ ♩♫) gives cohesion to the song, while the tonal design matches a dominant tendency in the first half with a sub-dominant tendency in the second half. Not everything is sym-

Ex. 22 'Venus went wand'ring' Anon. (*K*)

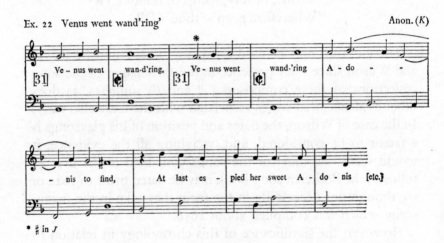

* ♯ in *J*

metrical however. After the parallelism of the first and second lines, the third moves away from the pattern already set, and the fourth fragments the phraseology with close motivic imitations between treble and bass, ending with an echo of the central cadence. One wonders just who the composer of this charming song was (Ex. 23).

Obviously songs of this kind are closer to the lutesong than to the declamatory ayre, but others hover between the two rather uncomfortably. 'Eyes look off' (*Tenb, K*) begins like Campion or Rosseter with neatly balanced phrases delicately syncopated, but continues like Ferrabosco with a wide-ranging

Ex. 23 'Wrong not, dear Empress of my heart'   Anon (J)

Wrong not, dear Em - press of my heart, The mer - its of true pas - sion;

By think-ing that he feels no smart Who su -eth for no com - pas - sion;

Since, that my plaints do not ap -prove The con - quest of your beau - ty,

It comes not from the ef -- fect of love, But from ex -cess -- ive du - ty.

vocal line rhythmically exaggerated and bass reduced to harmonic support pure and simple (Ex. 24). This latter characteristic is a noticeable feature of 'If when I die' (I,H) though the overall style is consistent.[43] Here we find traits of the declamatory ayre such as the rhythms ♩♪♪ or ♪♪♪ deriving from the ubiquitous ♩♫ or ♪♪♪ phrase-beginnings of so much renaissance vocal music. The final cadence of this song, too, is typical of the declamatory ayre, with the last line opening out and rising to a sustained high note tied over into the next bar while the bass maintains the movement. In this way a melodic climax is achieved, for which purpose, imitations, sequences and word repetitions may often be introduced in the final bars of the song.

Ex. 24 'Eyes look off, there's no beholding'   Anon. *(Tenb)*

Eyes look off, there's | no be - hold - | ing Where is | no ob - tain - | ing; What pre -

- vails the heart's | un - fold -ing And | no hopes re - | main - ing.

Two of the most interesting in this group of anonymous songs form a nice contrast with each other, reflecting on the one hand the rather dry declamatory idiom of Ferrabosco and Lanier, and on the other, the richer manner of Dowland and Johnson. Despite the fact that it is a serious song, 'Eyes gaze no more' (H,I) eschews the minor key and pathetic touches, making up for it by the energy and truthfulness of its declamation. The stanza is a single sentence running to eight lines, but instead of cadencing every two lines, the music runs on with the verse, pausing so as to underline, not destroy, the sense.

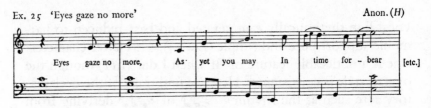

Ex. 25 'Eyes gaze no more'   Anon. *(H)*

Eyes gaze no | more, As yet you may | In time for - bear | [etc.]

'Down, down afflicted soul' (J,K) is rather different. The key is F minor, a not uncommon key for the more doleful songs of Johnson and Wilson (there are aspects of the song which recall both composers). Again the lines of the poem run on, and the music matches their rise and fall as well as their mood. The opening section setting the first four lines is sustained and melodic despite the assymetical structure which the words dictate, while the next section adopts a more urgent tone.

Ex. 26 'Down, down afflicted soul'   Anon. *(K)*

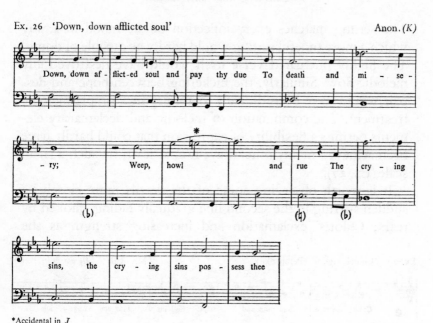

Down, down af - flict -ed soul and pay thy due To death and mi - se -

- ry; Weep, howl and rue The cry - ing

sins, the cry - ing sins pos - sess thee

*Accidental in *J**

It is tantalising not to know the authors of these songs. Presumably they belong to the transitional generation of Robert Johnson; indeed, one might guess Johnson for 'Down, down afflicted soul' and Lanier for 'Eyes gaze no more'. But they are just as likely—more likely, in fact—to be by lesser contemporaries. Even the author of one of the most famous songs of the period, 'Chloris sigh'd' is known only as 'Mr Balls', and that through a single attribution.[44] And whether it was Richard Bales or Alfonso Bales (or some other) is doubtful: Alfonso's claim is perhaps the stronger. Whoever it was, it is easy to see why it was so popular. Chloris, imagining her lover Amintas dead, laments and dies of grief. (A second verse found in some sources tells how Amintas returning, finds her dead then dies himself.) Sentimental though it is, it is difficult not to be touched by the final couplet:

> *And there she stopped, and thus she cried,*
> *'Amintas! Amintas!' and so she died.*

The setting matches every inflection of the mood in a way which a more tuneful setting would hardly be capable of doing. The highly puctuated verse itself would have destroyed any melodic flow. Similarly, the flickering between hope and despair would have been difficult to convey in a simple melodic treatment. The combination of melodic and declamatory elements permits a flexibility of expression that could hardly have been achieved in any other way; not, at least, on such a small scale (Ex. 27).

It is worth observing some of the details more closely: a sudden stirring in the second line gradually fading, choked by tears; Chloris' exclamation and increasing strength as she

Ex. 27 'Chloris sigh'd' (Pembroke) "Mr. Balls" [*Alfonso Bales?*] (H)

fondly remembers Amintas ('How sweet, how full of majesty'), then a reversal and falling away; her last pitiful cries of 'Amintas!'

But perhaps the most powerful expressive agent in this song is the ornamentation. All six manuscripts in which it occurs ornament it to some degree; two of the earliest (*E,H*) profusely (see Plate 6). The method of ornamentation employed is of the renaissance 'division' type, and similar passages are found in nearly all the manuscripts mentioned so far.[45] In most cases the rhythmic notation of these florid passages is inexact though the pitch contour is fairly precisely indicated. It is clear that their performance must have involved considerable distortion of the basic pulse, for there are just too many notes to sing otherwise. Of course, the declamatory style was ideally suited to *rubato* treatment, since the music itself lacks a marked sense of pulse.

Florid passages were not only fitted to words (such as 'awakes') where the illustrative function is obvious, but also to neutral words, thus colouring the prevailing sentiment and increasing the expressive effect of the song as a whole. Needless to say it was a matter left largely to the singer, for different sources of the same song do not agree as to the manner of embellishment. Nor can the absence of any written indication be taken as precluding ornamentation, for it was regarded as essential to the pathetic style betokening, moreover, fashionable acquaintance with Italian vocal techniques.

Two composers whose songs show transitional features are Robert Ramsey and John Hilton, already noticed in connection with their dialogues. Indeed, a case might be made out for Ramsey as an innovator, since his declamatory song 'What tears (dear Prince) can serve' (*L,P*) is usually taken to refer to the death of Henry, Prince of Wales, in 1612.[46] Certainly it is not impossible; nevertheless from the stylistic point of view 1612 or 1613 seems too early for the song in question, and we have seen that its earliest source (*L*) cannot be earlier than 1631. It therefore seems possible that it may be a companion piece to another song in the same manuscript commemorating the death of Charles I's eagerly awaited first-born son on 13 May 1629, after living only a few hours, ('How short a time of breath'). Be that as it may, it has to be admitted that though Ramsey's style is hardly ingratiating it has its effective moments, and he is able to sustain a phrase beyond the end of a line eloquently (Ex. 28).

There is a more tranquil quality in the songs of John Hilton, even the suspicion of Elizabethan temper and technique. He is, of course, better known as the composer of *Ayres or Fa-las* (1627) and editor of *Catch that Catch Can* (1652), but if we depended on Playford for our knowledge of him as a song writer we should know next to nothing about him. For the only solo song that ever seems to have come out in print was the rather poor and not at all typical 'Well, well, 'tis true, I am now fall'n in love' (*P1669*, *P,R*). Yet certain manuscripts represent him quite strongly, especially British Museum, Egerton MS 2013 (*N*) and Add.MS 11068 (*P*), and show him to have written some of the best ayres in the transitional style.

Ex. 28 from 'Go perjured man' (Herrick)   Robert Ramsey (*L*)

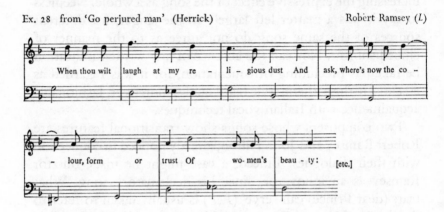

When thou wilt laugh at my re - li - gious dust And ask, where's now the co - lour, form or trust Of wo- men's beau - ty: [etc.]

At first sight one would judge that they were fairly early, for the lutesong idiom is heavily upon them. But this is more likely attributable to his own conservatism, for the sources themselves date (probably) from the 1630's, 40's and 50's and he is totally unrepresented in the earliest manuscripts. A dozen or more of his songs are extant and they betray a fine literary taste. In addition to Donne's *Hymne to God the Father*, Wotton's *On his Mistress the Empress of Bohemia*, and two Herrick settings (not surprising in view of their Cambridge connections) we find among the anonymous verse some lovely poems: 'Arise, arise fair sun', 'Hang golden sleep', 'If that I for thy sweet sake' and 'Love is the sun itself'.[47] They indicate a pre-Cavalier taste and some common ground with the lutenists. The Egerton manuscript probably contains the older songs which mostly occur in the opening part of the book. Unfortunately this manuscript is unreliably notated and certain points of detail

68

must remain doubtful in the absence of corroboration from other sources. Even so, we can see enough to deplore the fact that though his fa-las and catches achieved print, these songs did not. In this same manuscript we find such songs as Herrick's 'Thou may'st be proud' which Robert Ramsey set too, but whereas Ramsey adopts the newer declamatory technique, Hilton preserves the melodic flow of the serious lutesong.[48] Another Herrick setting, 'Am I despised' (*L,V*) also contrasts with a declamatory setting of the same words by Henry Lawes (*L1653, A,L*).[49]

This manuscript contains, in addition, Hilton's simple and unaffected setting of Donne's *Hymne to God the Father* ('Wilt thou forgive the sin'), though it is no match for the gravity of the poem.[50] It is more like one of Campion's 'moral' songs, yet as this is the only musical setting of these words that has survived contemporary with Donne himself there is a strong probability that it is the one to which Izaak Walton refers in a famous passage:

> I have the rather mentioned this *Hymn*, for that he caus'd it to be set to a most grave and solemn Tune, and to be often sung to the *Organ* by the *Choristers* of St. *Pauls* Church, in his own hearing; especially at the Evening Service, and at his return from his Customary Devotions in that place, did occasionally say to a friend . . . O *the power of Church-musick! that Harmony added to this Hymn has raised the Affections of my heart, and quickned my graces of zeal and gratitude;* and I observe, *that I always return from paying this publick duty of* Prayer *and* Praise *to God, with an unexpressible tranquillity of mind,* and a willingness *to leave the world.*[51]

Still in the same manuscript we have the song 'Hang golden sleep', the opening phrases of which reveal a breadth and unruffled beauty matched only by the best songs of the lutenists.[52] Unfortunately it is spoilt by increasing diffuseness of the musical material towards the middle, and rather conven-

Ex. 29 'Hang golden sleep'   John Hilton (N)

Hang gol - den sleep up - on her eye - lids fair, And fill the air With

mur - murs soft: let all the winds be still, And to her will

Fan - cies and dreams be rea - dy to o - bey. [etc.]

Ex. 30 'If that I for thy sweet sake'   John Hilton (?)

If that I for thy sweet. sake, Should my - self thy vas - sal make;

And at length dis - dain - ed be, As un - wor - thy to love thee;

In faith it shall not trouble me much, For my heart it shall not touch.

tional imitative treatment in the final line. This is hardly a continuo song at all; it seems to call for a full-flowing accompaniment throughout (Ex. 29).

As a source of Hilton's songs Add.MS 11608 (*P*) is probably much more reliable and the frequent occurrence of his songs in it (including the dialogues already mentioned) suggests an origin close to the composer. They show a greater addiction to the declamatory technique and may thus be later. Most of them are weaker as a result, but 'If that I for thy sweet sake' manages to combine elements of old and new, introducing triplet rhythms (*a*) into an otherwise square-cut phrase structure (Ex. 30).[53]

Taking his songs as a whole one forms the impression that Hilton belongs to the transitional phase which Lawes and Wilson outgrew, where tuneful and declamatory elements mingle, where melody has a life of its own and the bass (apart from the cadences) is still fairly free of the pull of fixed harmonic relationships. The fact that each song seems flawed in some way is perhaps the inevitable result of being a transitional composer—owing to the difficulty of satisfying different sets of criteria and lacking genius enough to establish new ones—or the versions as they survive may be corrupt. Even so, the blemishes hardly obscure the emergent picture of Hilton as an important song writer of the first half of the century, making one regret keenly that he did not prepare his own songs for publication.

Part two

The
court ayre

1 Henry Lawes' 'tunefull and well measur'd song'

The 'New Men' were becoming established in the 1620's. Lanier, in fact, was made Master of the King's Musick in 1626, and in the same year Henry Lawes became a Gentleman of the Chapel Royal. And although no court post came Wilson's way until 1635, he had already made his mark as a song writer with the King's Men and earned a place among the London waits in 1622—his candidature powerfully backed by Viscount Mandeville and the King's favourite Buckingham.

Each reveals a different musical character in his songs. Lanier is somewhat aloof; elevated in serious vein, yet he can be charming in a rather old-fashioned way, expecially in lighter songs. He shows a penchant for lyrics which, for all their 'lily whites' and 'blushing reds', are quite colourless. Wilson is more robust; a 'hit or miss' composer given to quirkishness when not being downright popular. Lawes is different again. His lighter ayres are stylish, and he uses triple-time dance measures in a more 'modern' and elegant way than either Lanier or Wilson. But it is his serious songs which demonstrate his superiority. His sensitivity to nuances of diction and feeling in a poem result in a richness compared with which the style of the others seems arid. It is he, really, who defines the declamatory ayre, and against whom the rest are measured.[1] As Milton wrote in the preface to Lawes' (*Choice Psalmes*, 1648):

75

Harry, *whose tunefull and well measur'd song*
First taught our English Music how to span
Words with iust note and accent . . .[2]

Over 430 of his songs survive, three-quarters of them in the autograph collection now in the British Museum (*A*).[3] It was probably begun in the mid-1630's, but there is some evidence to support the view that the earliest portion, the first 35 or so folios, includes much of his output up to that time arranged roughly in chronological order. We certainly notice a gradual transition from the grave, studied and rather stiff manner of the earlier songs to an easier, altogether freer declamation with wonderfully flexible vocal line and greater subtlety of feeling. These are the songs of his maturity, and they may be dated from the years following his appointment in the King's Private Musick in 1631.

Lawes himself probably recognized the immaturity of the early songs with their rather unsophisticated solemnity. Very few of them were included in the three books of *Ayres and Dialogues* which he published in the 1650's and the fact that they are rarely found in other manuscripts points to a restricted circulation and the possibility that they were composed in some isolation. For the most part the poems are by unknown authors and lack the polish of those by the court poets he set in the 1630's.[4] A favourite key is C minor, and the mood is often deep despair. 'O! where shall I lament', (*A*) is virtually a compendium of these and other features of the early songs. The morose tone of the verse is typical, and expressive devices include the affective use of the diminished fourth, false relations and freely treated dissonances (note especially, 'that I may die', 'what then remains', 'that from this loathsome life', etc.). The opening declamatory motif is used several times during the course of the song, but so far the characteristic rhythm ♩ ♩ ♩ ♩ has not given place to the later ♩ ♪ ♪ ♪. Rests and broken phrases do not yet play the role they assume in his mature songs. The repetition of the phrase 'weep, weep

more mine eyes' towards the end at a higher pitch is also a relic of an older style (Ex. 31).

Even so, there is obviously a clean break with the lutesong tradition. This is clear when we compare his settings of 'Sweet stay awhile' and 'O sweet woods'—both early songs—with Dowland's.[5] A fundamental difference, of course, is that Lawes' are continuo songs; comparisons of texture are therefore not strictly possible. But it is plain that the character and function of melody and bass is different. The opening of Dowland's 'O sweet woods' shows that the vocal line is truly melodic

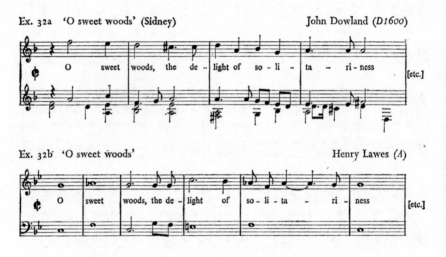

Ex. 32a 'O sweet woods' (Sidney)   John Dowland (D1600)

Ex. 32b 'O sweet woods'   Henry Lawes (A)

with a life and shape of its own, whereas Lawes' is, in itself, unmelodic and purely expressionistic. Its unequal rhythms exaggerate the accentuation and syllabic quantities of the verse, in contrast to the smooth flow of Dowland's. Compare, especially, the phrase 'the delight of solitariness' in both. There is an obvious contrast too in the function of the bass. Dowland's moves more or less in step with the melody as a counterpoint. The rate of harmonic change is thus quicker than Lawes' and a greater variety of chords is employed. On the other hand, Lawes' is clearly a continuo bass providing harmonic foundation in support of a vocal line strikingly differentiated in

78

character. Though unfigured the thorough bass would normally have been realised on some such instrument as the theorbo according to the Rule of the Octave whereby the third, sixth and seventh degrees of the scale and all sharp notes were treated as sixth chords; the others as fifths.[6] Cadences too received stereotyped treatment involving 4–3 suspensions and sometimes 7–6 progressions as well.

It is certainly true that Lawes' setting is the more rhetorical, though as yet his declamatory technique is undeveloped. Tentative the style may be, but the direction in which he is moving is clear. It is away from musical self-sufficiency towards a mode of expression which is dependent on the words themselves for rhythm and melodic detail.

Oddly enough, G minor (and to a lesser extent D minor) seems to have supplanted C minor in the composer's favour during what we may assume was the period of his early maturity. His entry into the King's Musick brought him into contact with the circle of court poets, Thomas Carew especially, whose work he was to set more frequently than any other. The new environment produced a more refined musical sensibility. The verse itself was more sophisticated of course, but not on that account more suitable for musical treatment. For metaphysical verse tends to be unmusical. The language of philosophy, theology or science is not suited to music, and thus the elaboration of a conceit is nothing more than misplaced ingenuity in a song, for music is a language of the emotions not of verbal ideas. Furthermore, colloquial diction and irregularities of metre, phrase and verse structure make poetry less suited to music. All this we find increasingly in the poetry of the first half of the seventeenth century, even in lyric verse.

As an example of the effect of this mannered versification on music we may examine Carew's well-known piece *To an inconstant Mistris*, and Lawes' setting of it.

When thou, poore excommunicate
From all the joyes of love, shalt see

The full reward, and glorious fate,
Which my strong faith shall purchase me,
Then curse thine owne inconstancie.

A fayrer hand then thine, shall cure
That heart, which thy false oathes did wound;
And to my soule, a soule more pure
Than thine, shall by Loves hand be bound,
And both with equall glory crown'd.

Then shalt thou weepe, entreat, complaine
To Love, as I did once to thee:
When all thy teares shall be as vaine
As mine were then, for thou shalt bee
Damn'd for thy false Apostasie.

A religious metaphor is used: constancy in love is like constancy in religion. The poet's own 'strong faith' will bring him everlasting happiness; his mistress's 'apostacy' will bring her everlasting torment. It is a conceit to the taste of a court that found religious controversy an intriguing diversion, but it is one to which music can add little or nothing since it is purely intellectual. It is through 'wit' that the point is made; there is little or no 'feeling' to communicate. One smiles in amused admiration of the poet perhaps and goes back to the second verse to work it out more carefully. It is a poem which needs to be read and unravelled rather than sung, and music can only serve to make the words audible and convey the general mood. The irregular phraseology is itself antimusical. Each stanza is a sentence too complex for straightforward setting, and the subordinate divisions avoid the regular and symmetrical cadencing typical of music, or, for that matter, of conventional lyric verse where line and couplet are natural breaks. Moreover, this element in the structure differs from verse to verse, making strophic treatment impossible if the sense is to be respected.

In setting the poem Lawes omitted the second verse as being dispensible to the argument, and treated the two remaining stanzas as halves of a through-composed song. Cadences coincide with punctuation marks (not necessarily with the ends of lines) and consequently phrase lengths are uneven. Structure like this is clearly dependent on the words. Like punctuation marks the cadences indicate the comparative completeness of each phrase. Thus, each stanza concludes with a full close, the first in the relative major key of B flat, the second in the home key of G minor, while each phrase ends with a half close. The arrangement below sets out the poem according to its phrase-sense, not verse-form (which has just been given). The length of each line is indicated in musical terms (i.e. bars), and it will be seen how the organization of cadences corresponds with the verbal syntax. Also marked are the musical stresses which result from syllables falling on the strong beats (first and third in a bar) or syncopated high notes. If the poem is then read aloud stressed and measured in this way, some idea of Lawes' sensitive response to the rhetorical qualities of the poem will be gained; still more when sung, for then musical rhythms, rests and inflections come into play.

When thóu, póor excommúnicate from áll the jóys of lóve
    (4½ bars: half-close in G minor)
Shalt see the fúll rewárd, and glórious fáte, which my strong fáith hath purchased mé,
    (5 bars; half-close in G minor)
thén curse thine ówn incónstancy.
    (2½ bars; full-close in B flat, i.e. relative)
For thou shalt wéep, entréat, complain to lóve, as I did ónce to thée[1]
    (4½ bars; half-close in G minor)
When áll thy téars shall be as váin as mine were thén,
    (3 bars; half-close in D, i.e. dominant)
for thou shalt bé dámned for thy fálse apóstasy.
    (4½ bars; full-close in G minor)

Ex. 33 'When thou, poor excommunicate' (Carew)   Henry Lawes *(A)*

The rise and fall of the voice in each phrase follows closely, in fact exaggerates, the inflection and emphasis of declaimed speech. Notice especially the contour of the opening of each section, and the build-up of such passages as 'shalt see/The full reward, and glorious fate/Which my strong faith', and 'When all thy tears shall be as vain/As mine were then' culminating in the final anathema of each verse. The nuancing of certain words and phrases—'excommunicate', 'reward', 'complain to love'—also show a subtle appreciation of rhythm and inflection. Rests, as always with Lawes, play their part in the delivery of the words (e.g. 'For thou shalt weep, entreat, complain/To love').

So far as the expressive treatment of the text goes certain obvious devices are employed, such as the augmented chords under 'entreat', 'once' and 'false', the false relation at 'vain as mine', the sharp to convey the idea of 'strong', and so on. In addition, certain words—'joys', 'glorious', 'complain'—are ornamented in the printed version of the song so as to add colour to their meaning.[8]

Compared with his contemporaries, Lawes' declamation is much more pliant in rhythm. Naturally the flexibility of true speech rhythm is impossible in this kind of music since the ratio of one duration to another is bound to be simple. (Thus ♪♪ may be too even for certain pairs of syllables, but ♪.♪ too uneven.) Even so, Lawes approaches closer to the ideal es-

Ex. 34a 'Weep not my dear, for I shall go' (Carew)

Henry Lawes (P*1669*)

Weep not my dear, for I shall go [etc.]

Ex. 34b 'Weep not my dear, for I shall go' (Carew)

John Wilson (B)

Weep not my dear, for I shall go [etc.]

pecially in his use of uneven rhythms to differentiate the longer and more emphatic syllables from the shorter and lighter ones. Compare, for example his setting of the opening line of Carew's 'Weep not my dear' (*P1669*, *A,V*) with Wilson's rather similar one (*B*) (Ex. 34).

In particular one cannot help noticing the way Lawes has caught the colloquial tendency to pronounce the line thus: 'Weep not, m'dear, and I sh'll go,' lightly touching the unstressed syllables with their indeterminate, almost non-existant vowel sounds, with the shortest note value available. This kind of subtlety is still more obvious if we compare his setting of Killigrew's 'Come thou glorious object of my sight' (*L1653*, *A,M*) with Lanier's (*N*). The latter's is stiff and ungainly by comparison. We have only to pronounce the phrase 'thou glorious object of my sight' first according to Lawes' rhythm and then Lanier's to see how superior the former is. (And note again Lawes' use of rests: it is a hall-mark of his style.) (Ex. 35).

Another aspect of his declamatory writing deserving atten-

Ex. 35a 'Come thou glorious object of my sight' (Killigrew)   Henry Lawes (*A*)

Ex. 35b 'Come thou glorious object of my sight' (Killigrew)   Nicholas Lanier (*N*)

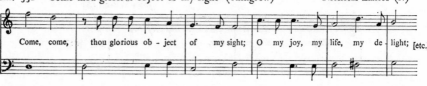

tion is the employment of discords almost as accidents of verbal delivery. Thus in the course of "'Tis but a frown' (*A*) we find the unorthodox use of the fourth ('whilst it gathers'), seventh ('with that same comfort') and ninth ('I beg but this').[9] Examples might be multiplied a hundredfold from his output.

Ex. 36a from "'Tis but a frown'   Henry Lawes (*A*)

Which, whilst it ga-thers com-fort

b (*Ibid.*)

With that same com-fort

c (*Ibid.*)

I beg but this of thee

False relations and melodic progressions such as leaps of diminished fourths and sevenths are also very common—they are, after all, natural to the minor key. One even finds the diminished octave at the end of 'Sweet stay awhile' (*A,V*).[10]

In most cases these idioms serve expressive purposes, as of course they do in the works of his contemporaries. But it is the

Ex: 37 from 'Sweet stay awhile' (Donne)   Henry Lawes (*A*)

And pe-rish in their in-fan-cy.

subtlety and truth of his declamation which makes him pre-
eminent. In it the ideals of Baïf's *Académie* and the Florentine
Camerata fuse and find a practical application consistent with
the character of English verse. It is not quantitative theory but
the actual rhythm and inflection of speech which are the deter-
minants. True accent and quantity are observed without recourse to a classical theory of longs and shorts, which even
Edward Filmer had to acknowledge as incompatible with
English poetry in the preface to his *French Court-Aires* (1629).

From the days of Burney to the present, Lawes' declamatory
songs have received scant appreciation. Perhaps there is little
point in trying to defend him against the strictures of eight-
eenth- and nineteenth-century critics, whose criteria were
neither Lawes' nor ours. (And, in any case, he is vulnerable.)
Since his songs derive so much from qualities of speech it is
consequently in performance rather than on paper that the full
subtlety and refinement of his technique can be recognized.
This is something that critics have failed to grasp. They saw
that his style was neither that of recitative nor air but lay between the two. Lacking a name it almost had no business to
exist! Harmonically and melodically the idiom was perplexing
to them, but Burney, to be fair, concentrated his attention on
'just note and accent' since here, he felt, was common critical
ground: if excellence was not to be found there, it was not to
be found anywhere. Consequently the *Comus* song 'Sweet
echo' (*A*) came under rigorous scrutiny:

> I shall here present the critical reader with the song, as set by
> Lawes, and then refer to such places as seem indefensible,
> even on the side of *accent*, and *quantity*.
>
> The long note given to the first syllable of the word
> violet, to *sad* (sad *song*), *have* (have *hid*), *sweet* (sweet *queen*),
> *tell* (tell *me*), and the first syllable of the word *daughter*, on the
> *unaccented* part of the bar, are all inaccuracies of musical ac-
> centuation . . . I should be glad, indeed, to be informed by
> the most exclusive admirer of old ditties, what is the *musical*

merit of this song, except insipid simplicity, and its having
been set for a single voice, instead of being mangled by the
many-headed monster, Madrigal?[11]

But if we look at the music by no means all of these points can
be sustained. In fact, the first syllable of *'violet'* is correctly
accented as it stands; so is 'sad'. Both are perhaps prolonged
longer than is strictly necessary, either to allow for the addition
of characteristic ornamentation appropriate to the sentiment of
'the violet embroidered vale' and 'her sad song'. or merely to
give these images time to register in the mind. At first sight,
it is true, the accent on 'have' is misplaced; nevertheless, the
fact that it is immediately followed by a longer note tends to
subordinate its emphasis to the next word ('hid') which is as it
should be. Likewise because syncopated long notes, of their
nature, attract an accent in this kind of music, there is no
charge to answer in the case of 'tell' and *'daugh*ter'. The justification for accenting and prolonging the word 'sweet' (and for
the jump to the seventh above, which Burney also censures) is

Ex. 38a   from 'Sweet echo' (Milton)   Henry Lawes (*A*)

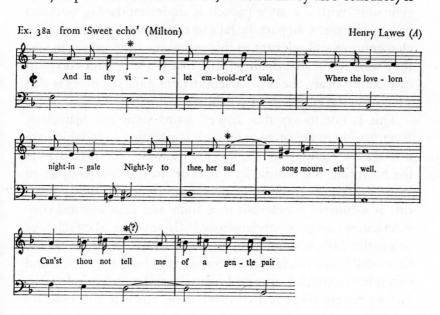

Ex. 38b *(Ibid.)*

entirely rhetorical: the 'Sweet Queen of Parley' is being addressed directly and the treatment seems peculiarly fitting. Indeed, the effect would have been feeble had there been no accent.

So, on closer inspection, Burney's strictures are found to be lacking in substance. On the contrary, we may conclude that Lawes' setting is finely adjusted to Milton's subtle handling of rhythm and stress. Burney betrays not only his own want of sympathy with the style (which is understandable), but also hasty judgement. In part, he fails to recognize that quantitative elements are still relevant to this technique of word setting (as they were to the madrigalists), and that while bar lines do indicate strong beats, the relative length (and pitch) of notes is also a factor in the emphasis of syllables.

This is not to say that Lawes' word setting is blameless. Even so, there are often extenuating circumstances which are not always recognized. Colles, for example, censured Lawes for accenting the words 'for' and 'of' in the final couplet of 'Sabrina fair' (*A*)—also from *Comus*—without noting that this is a tuneful conclusion to a song and thus musical considerations outweigh declamatory.[12] (If anything the fault was originally Milton's for allowing such words to occur on the first syllables of trochaic feet.) Similarly, a long note at the end of a line in a tuneful song will naturally fail to be entirely satisfactory where there is an enjambment, since it will hold up

88

what (from the literary point of view) ought to run on. But such things are to be expected in the circumstances. It would have been wiser if the poet in writing a song actually meant to to be sung had not run his lines on—that is, if he really thought it mattered. Pattison's criticism of Lawes' attractive setting of Suckling's 'I am confirmed a woman can' (*P1652, A, M R*) on this score is to object to its being a dance-tune rather than an art-song; in other words, for not being what it does not pretend to be (Ex. 41).[13]

Undoubtedly the rhythmic and melodic autonomy of purely musical composition will sometimes cut across the versification, and it is quite right that musical principles should take precedence, provided the result is not ridiculous. There is no reason why words should not sometimes take a back seat, and allow the music to go its own way when the tune is the important thing.

We can expect to find verbal misaccentuations in the tuneful songs of all composers. In Lawes' setting of Fletcher's 'Dearest do not now delay me' (*L1653, A,R*), for example, there is a symmetry of phrase which, line after line, throws into prominence the weak sixth syllable by drawing it over two beats and ornamenting it. Syncopations of this sort in triple time will inevitably do some sort of violence to trochaic verse, yet without them the musical effect would be limp. Short iambic verses are better served by courant and saraband rhythms, since they may actually allow an accented syllable to be emphasised by means of syncopation at certain places in the line. Thus in Herrick's 'Among the myrtles' (*P1652, A, L, R, U,*), which Burney called 'pleasing psalmody', the syllables 'as', 'en-' (of '*en*ter'), 'deep', and 'she-' (of '*she*pherdess') all receive stress though this gain is made at the expense of waiting longer than may be desirable in some cases on the previous accent.[14] Hemiola cadences are also able to reconcile verse accentuation with syncopated movement, Thus, in the second line of 'I am confirmed a woman can' (*P1652, A, M, R*) the word 'any' is correctly accented, though in the process 'or' has been over-extended.

On the whole though, the conflicting demands of music and poetry are quite well matched in these songs, and whatever may be sacrificed by way of prosodic nicety seems a small price to pay when the musical result is so attractive (Exx. 39–41).

The balletic quality in these dance-songs is obvious. It is the movement of the dancer not the poet that has determined its character. (But then, do not both move by foot?) We can see how close they are in a poem like Suckling's *Loose Sarabande* ('Aye me, the little tyrant thief' in *M*). Here, by the poet's ad-

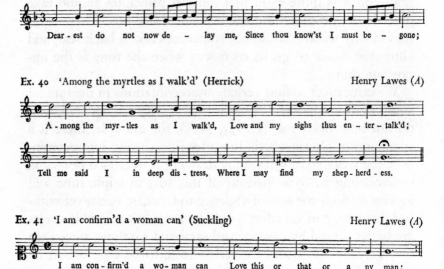

Ex. 39 'Dearest do not now delay me' (Fletcher)   Henry Lawes (*L1653*)

Dear - est do not now de - lay me, Since thou know'st I must be - gone;

Ex. 40 'Among the myrtles as I walk'd' (Herrick)   Henry Lawes (*A*)

A - mong the myr - tles as I walk'd, Love and my sighs thus en - ter - talk'd;

Tell me said I in deep dis - tress, Where I may find my shep - herd - ess.

Ex. 41 'I am confirm'd a woman can' (Suckling)   Henry Lawes (*A*)

I am con - firm'd a wo - man can Love this or that or a ny man;

mission, the verse reflects the characteristic rhythm of the saraband and naturally it is mirrored in Lawes' setting, particularly in the feminine cadences, the predominant harmonic rhythm (♩ 𝅗𝅥) and the ♩♩ . ♩ pattern of the melody. Likewise 'Begone, begone, thou perjur'd man' (*L1653 A*), is an unmistakable courant. The straightforward triplet movement of the jig and the country dance may also be seen in such songs as 'How happy art thou and I' (*P1652, A, P, R, U*) (Exx. 42–44).

Although a majority of Lawes' tuneful songs are in triple time, there are also many in common time. Among early songs 'Hard-hearted fair' (*A*) and 'Or you, or I, nature did wrong' (*A*) are redolent of the simple lutesong style.[15] Somewhat later, and truly representative of the boisterous cavalier spirit is the setting of Suckling's 'Out upon it! I have loved' (*A,M*), dating from the middle 1630's.[16]

Ex. 42 from 'Aye me, the little tyrant thief' (Suckling) Henry Lawes (*M*)

He snatch'd it up And flew a - way, Laughing at all, at all my pray-ing

Ex. 43 'Begone, begone, thou perjur'd man' Henry Lawes (*L1653*)

Be - gone, be - gone, thou per - jur'd man, And ne - ver more re - turn; [etc.]

Ex. 44 'How happy art thou and I' Henry Lawes (*A*)

How happy art thou and I that ne'er knew how to love; [etc.]

Ex. 45 'Go lovely rose' (Waller) Henry Lawes (*L1655*)

1. Go love-ly rose, Tell her that wastes her time and me
2. Small is the worth Of beau-ty from the light re - tir'd [etc.]

Songs such as these are naturally amenable to strophic treatment. But Lawes also wrote strophic declamatory songs, and this means that the music may not fit the second and subsequent verses with due attention to detail. For though less than satisfactory word setting may be justified in a tuneful song by claiming an over-riding musical authority, poor declamation can make no such appeal. It must be admitted that in this respect Lawes may be found wanting. The main trouble occurs when the stanzas do not maintain a parallel structure; when the punctuation and phrasing of one verse differs from another, or when the scansion of corresponding lines is at variance. Undoubtedly the opening lines of Waller's 'Go lovely rose' (*L1655*, *A*) are sensitively set, but what suits the first verse does not suit the second where we find a pause on 'worth' when it should run on, and undue prominence given to 'of' and 'from' simply because the accentuation of the line is not the same as the corresponding line in the first stanza (Ex. 45).

Ex. 46   from 'I rise and grieve'   Henry Lawes (*A*)

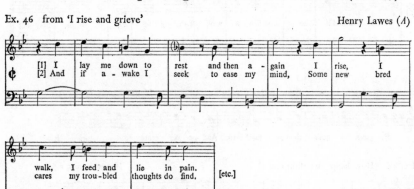

Not only is structural parallelism often lacking between stanzas; sometimes descriptive elements in the music which match the first verse are inappropriate or nonsensical when applied to other verses. For example, the setting of the lines—

> *I lay me down to rest, and then again*
> *I rise, I walk, I feed and lie in pain,*

in the song 'I rise and grieve' (*A*) is determined by the phrasing of the words and the physical ideas they represent.[17] But in the second verse both are different. The rest between 'seek' and 'to' is ridiculous, still more so between 'new' and 'bred', while the music originally set to the words 'I lay me down' reflecting a specific directional movement, now serves 'And if awake'— a contrary idea (Ex. 46).

Fortunately, this sort of thing is fairly rare. Lawes is more likely to give subsequent stanzas a varied strophic treatment, preserving the main melodic and harmonic features of the first stanza but modifying details to fit the changed circumstances of the verse. The setting of Suckling's 'No, no, fair heretic' (*A*) provides a good example.[18] The different 'flow' of the second stanza necessitates a number of modifications to both the vocal part as well as the bass, as the first few bars make clear (Ex. 47).

There is quite a large class of such songs, and though most of them remain in manuscript they are really the proof of Lawes' conscientious approach to word setting. (But when this

Ex. 47a 'No, no, fair heretic' (Suckling)   Henry Lawes (*A*)

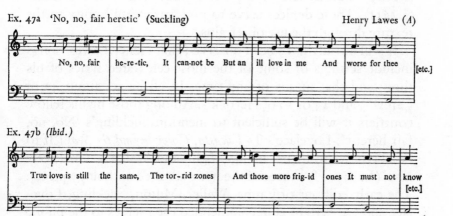

Ex. 47b *(Ibid.)*

song was published in *P1652* the music for the second verse was dropped, even though the words were printed. Presumably the singer had to shift as best he could in the circumstances.)

Usually, however, the verses of a through-composed song do not bear a variational relationship to each other. Instead, two or more stanzas relate to each other rather as do the 'strains' of an ordinary 'single song'.[19] We have seen one type of 'through-set' song in Carew's 'When thou poor excommunicate' where the two stanzas are complementary by virtue of their tonal reliance on each other, the first ending in the relative major key and thus demanding fulfilment or completion in the section to follow. But in others such as 'O! I am sick' (*A*) the stanzas depart from and return to the same tonic, which lessens the cohesion between them since they are now not so much interdependent as parallel—the relationship is merely an additive one.[20] Occasionally a change is made to triple time in a brief episode, (see 'Strike, sweet Licoris, the harmonious lute' in *P1669* which is possibly a late song in view of its absence from *A* and earlier prints), and, of course, concluding sections in triple time are common. Sometimes, too, a triple-time refrain recurs between verses, as in 'Farewell despairing hopes' (*P1669*—another late song possibly) and 'Now, now Lucatia' (*L1655*). These devices serve to give variety and unity to the texture through the use of refrains.

It will already have been observed that Henry Lawes' songs include settings of some of the most celebrated lyrics of his time; and that means of any time. In all he set about 40 of Carew's, and 14 or so of Herrick's. Among those by his fellow courtiers it will be sufficient to mention Suckling's 'No, no, fair heretic', Lovelace's *To Lucasta, Going beyond the Seas* ('If to be absent were to be' in *A, M, R*) and Waller's 'Go lovely rose' (*L1655, A*)—three of the most admired anthology pieces. The early editions of Carew, Waller, Milton, Suckling, Lovelace and Cartwright all recommended themselves to the public by mentioning (often on the title-page) that Henry Lawes had set their songs. Milton's famous sonnet in praise of Lawes is only one of many poetic eulogies extolling him.

His relationship with Milton was close, and indeed the poet seems to have begun rather as Lawes' protégé. Their friendship must have dated from the early 1630's if not before, for when Lawes had the job of arranging masques for the Egerton family on two occasions, he called upon the as yet unknown Milton for the text of *Arcades* and *Comus*. The Egerton children, whom Lawes taught, performed *Arcades* at Harefield House in honour of their grandmother Alice, Dowager Countess of Derby (perhaps on the occasion of her 70th birthday in

1629) and *Comus* was given at Ludlow Castle in 1634 in honour of their father the Earl of Bridgewater's installation as Lord President of Wales. The songs from *Arcades* have not survived, but those from *Comus* are extant (*A*).[21] When the text of the masque was published in 1637 it was edited by Lawes himself and dedicated to Viscount Brackly, Lord Bridgewater's heir.

During the early 1630's Lawes no doubt took part in many of the court masques for which his younger brother provided the music. In fact, Henry is often credited with having written the music for Carew's *Coelum Britannicum* (1634), though in the absence of the music itself or other direct evidence this contention rests on a doubtful reading of Carew's ambiguously phrased title-page of 1651: 'POEMS, With a MASKE, BY *Thomas Carew* Esq; . . . The *Songs* were set in *Musick* by Mr. HENRY LAWES Gent.' The separate title-page of the masque makes no mention of the composer, and a remark in the colophon of the early editions to the effect that 'The Songs and Dialogues of this Booke were set with apt Tunes to them, by *Mr. Henry Lawes*, one of His Majesties Musitians' almost certainly alludes to the Poems not the Masque—as does the wording of the title-page quoted above. He and his brother collaborated in Davenant's *Triumps of the Prince d'Amour* (1636), the songs and symphonies of which 'were excellently composed by Mr. HENRY, and Mr WILLIAM LAWS, His Majesty's servants'. Although some of William's music for this masque survives, only one item by Henry is known—the song 'Whither so gladly and so fast' (*P1669, A, V*).

In August 1636 the King and Queen visited Oxford where they were entertained by performances of William Strode's *The Floating Island* and William Cartwright's *The Royal Slave*. All the vocal music for these plays survives, that for the latter in a version (*M*, not autograph, but authoritative) which makes use of elaborate, masque-like settings for various solo combinations and a full chorus.[22] This was probably not Lawes' first collaboration with Cartwright. He had also provided the songs for *The Ordinary* (1635), or so it may be supposed since a setting by him of 'Come, O come, I brook no stay' (*P1659*, *A, R*), one of the songs from the play, is extant. But his most important Cartwright setting is his long Ariadne recitative, which he later printed at the beginning of his first book of *Ayres and Dialogues* (1653) with a lengthy preamble giving 'The Story of *Theseus* and *Adriadne*, as much as concerns the ensuing Relation'.[23] The 'ensuing relation' is, in fact, the lament of Adriadne on Naxos deserted by Theseus, and her deliverance by Bacchus. The recitative cannot be dated with certainty, but between 1636 and 1643 (the year Cartwright died) seems likely—later rather than earlier. After the court's removal to Oxford in the middle of 1642, Lawes and Cartwright may often have been together, and it was probably then, during the last year of Cartwright's life, that he and the composer discussed the composition of the recitative. In all probability the initiative came from Lawes, who, partly influenced by Lanier's *Hero and Leander*, and no doubt aware of Monteverdi's *Lamento d'Arianna*, wished to attempt something of the same sort. As it happens, the work bears little affinity with Monteverdi's great lament, rather more with Lanier's though still not much. Neither here, nor in two further 'Chloris-recitatives' ('Help, O help, divinity of love' in *L1655*, *A*, and 'See, my Chloris comes in yonder bark', in *L1658*, *A*) could he measure up to Lanier's achievement. The event celebrated in both is the Queen's landing at Burlington (i.e. Bridlington) in February 1643 after a stormy crossing from the Low Countries to assist her husband in the Civil War. The date lends weight to the suggestion that 'Ariadne' also belongs about the same time, or a year or two earlier—a period when Lawes was evidently experimenting with recitative.

Once the Civil War was over, Lawes returned to London where he was much sought after as a teacher, and embarked on the publication of his songs. Playford lists him first among 'many excellent and able Masters . . . For the Voyce or Viole' in his *Musicall Banquet* (1651). Undoubtedly he was well patronized, particularly by blue-stockings. Lady Mary Dering had been a pupil of his since 1648, and under his tutelage developed a talent for composition.[24] Another gifted pupil, the singer Mary Knight refers 'To her most honoured Master, Mr. HENRY LAWES' thus:

> *If I have Art, it is from Thee:*
> *Others do teach, but (to be free)*
> *Experience told me thou art best,*
> *For I have learn'd of all the rest*
> *That Fame call's Masters, and have cause*
> *To sacrifice to none but LAWES.*[25]

Fashionable musicales were held at his house. The Duchess of Newcastle 'went with my Lord's brother to hear music in one Mr. Lawes his house, three or four times',[26] and Edward Phillips (Milton's nephew) records:

> *While brightest* Dames, *the splendour of the Court,*
> *Themselves a silent* Musick *to the Eye,*
> *Would oft to hear thy solemn* Ayres *resort,*
> *Making thereby a double* Harmony.[27]

Among the 'brightest Dames' were no doubt his two erstwhile pupils, daughters of the old Earl of Bridgewater, the Lady Alice, now Countess of Carberry, and Mary, Lady Herbert. To them he dedicated his first book of *Ayres and Dialogues* (1653):

> *most of them being Composed when I was employed by Your ever Honour'd Parents to attend Your* Ladishipp's *Education in* Musick.

Already in 1652 Playford had printed some of Lawes' songs in his *Select Musicall Ayres and Dialogues* without the composer's permission. This seems to have prompted Lawes to prepare an edition of his own songs for the press which came out the following year:

Therefore now the Question is not, whether or no my Compositions *shall be Publick, but whether they shall come from me, or from some other hand; and which of the two is likeliest to afford the true correct Copies, I leave others to judge.*

He goes on to promise that

if this First Book shall find acceptance, I intend yearly to publish the like; for I confess I have a sufficient Stock lying by me . . .

He certainly had sufficient stock lying by him; the autograph collection had hardly been touched. But yearly was perhaps an over-optimistic estimate of what the market could bear. However, further books followed in 1655 and 1658.

Their lengthy prefaces are much concerned with defending himself, and English composers generally, from the slights of fellow-countrymen who affected a taste for Italian music—good or bad—above everything. Even so, it was rather unfair of him to hoax them by setting the table of contents of Antonio Cifra's *Scherzi ed Arie* (1614) in the song 'In quel gelato core' (*L1653*), for it is a thoroughly enjoyable piece even if the words are nonsense. The second book (1655) he dedicated to Lady Dering, and included three of her ayres among his own—'*some which I esteem the best . . . were of your own* Composition, *after your Noble Husband was pleased to give the* Words'. One at least, 'In vain, fair Chloris, you design' was good enough for Playford to reprint in his next edition of *Select Ayres and Dialogues*.[28] A sentence from the preface deserves to be quoted as putting in a nutshell Lawes' aim in setting verse:

the way of Composition *I chiefly profess . . . is to shape* Notes *to the* Words *and* Sense.

In 1656, Davenant's *Entertainment at Rutland House* and *The Siege of Rhodes* was performed. For *The Siege of Rhodes*, which was a proper opera with 'the Story sung in *Recitative* Musick', Lawes wrote the vocal music for the first and last entries, or acts. There were five entries in all, and the other composers of the vocal music were Captain Cooke and Matthew Locke. Unfortunately the music has been lost, and our only clues as to how Lawes may have set Davenant's text are recitatives like the Ariadne lament, and pastoral dialogues. The dialogues probably come closest to the style of Lawes' operatic writing.[29]

In addition to three books of *Ayres and Dialogues*, Playford published some more songs by Lawes posthumously in 1669 (1664?) *'transcribed from his Originals, a short time before his Death, and with his free consent for me to Publish them, if occasion offer'd'*. Even then not all his songs were printed. The total published in the seventeenth century is 240, out of a total of 434 known songs.

So far as the later development of his song-style is concerned, a falling off from his high seriousness is noticeable, and there is a tendency for the tuneful and recitative elements to separate themselves into songs that, on one hand, were strophic, definitely melodic and dance-like, on the other, through-composed and more or less purely declamatory. It was a time when lyric verse was loosing its strength of intellect and feeling, and Lawes' settings were likewise lapsing into insipidity. The last third of his autograph collection makes disappointing reading on the whole though it contains a few excellent songs and many which are pleasant enough. Compared with his earliest songs which, for all their lack of sophistication were full blooded, they are anaemic; compared with the refined eloquence of his maturer songs, they have run to seed. The years of Lawes' maturity were those he spent at court. From the court he had drawn artistic sustenance, and his songs—more than any of his contemporaries'—breathed its hot-house atmosphere. With the king dead and the court dispersed this environment ceased to exist. Its day was passed; so too was Lawes'.

2 Lanier, Wilson and the songs of some lesser composers

No consistent pattern of development is discernible in the songs of Nicholas Lanier. Despite his important innovations in English song he was mainly content to cultivate the light Elizabethan vein with its idyllic pastoralism and innocent view of life, or, more seriously, the declamatory idiom which he helped to establish. Within these two categories little progressive change is apparent. Unlike Henry Lawes, he was seemingly out of sympathy with the themes and ideals of Cavalier verse which he set rarely and then at its most conventional. Hilton apart, none of his contemporaries was more drawn to the Elizabethan poets: Campion's 'Thou art not fair for all thy red and white', 'Fire, lo here I burn' and 'Young and simple though I am', and Jonson's 'Though I am young and cannot tell' are among those which he set, and their tone is dominant throughout his output. Writing tunes for this kind of verse Lanier is successful enough. 'Young and simple though I am' (*P1652*, *P*, *U*), for example, is unpretentious and charming, and its simple diatonic chord progressions are typical of the composer (Ex. 48).

The declamatory style can bring nothing to this sort of lyric, for it is the wrong tool for the job. In fact, it represents a misunderstanding of the conventional relationship of music to light amatory verse; namely, that the music is more important than the words which exist primarily to be sung. We can see the extent of Lanier's offence in this respect if we compare his setting of 'Thou art not fair for all thy red and white' (*P1652, L, M, R*) with Campion's own (*R1601*), especially in the final couplet where, in Lanier's case we have little more than gabble, while in Campion's, poised and expressive line and movement (Ex. 49).

These deficiencies are less evident in more serious songs such as Raleigh's 'Like hermit poor' (*P1652, R, T*).[1] This is probably early and recalls some of the features of 'Bring away this sacred tree.[2] Compared with Alfonso Ferrabosco's setting of the same text (*F1609*) it provides a good example of the early declamatory ayre, though as yet the technique of declamation

Ex. 48 'Young and simple though I am'   Nicholas Lanier (*P1652*)

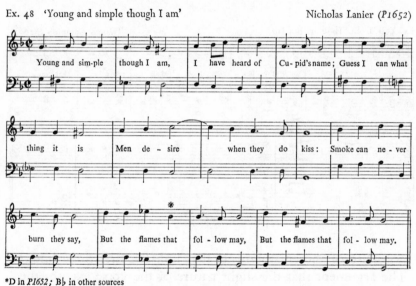

*D in *P1652;* B♭ in other sources

is practised for its own sake—as an effect in itself rather than as a means of interpreting the poem.[3]

Indeed, few of Lanier's declamatory ayres bear examination from the standpoint of the poem. Having secured a more or less correct accentuation of the text, he seems to have regarded his job as done. Consequently, the results, judged as word setting, are rarely satisfactory. The opening of Carew's 'Mark how the blushful morn' (*P1669, P, R*), for example, makes

Ex 49a from 'Thou art not fair'   Nicholas Lanier (*P1652*)

Ex. 49b from 'Thou art not fair'   Thomas Campion (*R1601*)

nonsense of the enjambments that link the first three lines.[4] The argument that the slight nature of the verse excuses the offence, or at least mitigates the ill-effect, would carry more weight if there were pronounced melodic qualities to compensate. Unfortunately this is only rarely the case, though as an example the wistful and rather fey 'Stay, silly heart' may be cited.[5] Already we have evidence of Lanier's lack of literary sophistication; here words and music take on an almost ballad-like quality. It reinforces the suspicion, already hinted at more than once, that for all his air of the Italianate courtier, this was only half the man.

Still, it is the more important half. For although the *Hero and Leander* recitative is not seminal in the sense that his early masque songs are, yet it is important both as a symptom and achievement in itself.[6] Presumably it dates from after Lanier's visits to Italy between 1625 and 1628, although we know little about his musical experiences there. He was at Venice and Mantua chiefly to buy the Duke of Mantua's pictures for the King, but his position as one of the Royal musicians was known to the Italians and some appreciative references to his musical ability are recorded. He travelled quite extensively over the north of Italy and as far south as Rome, and could hardly have failed to see and hear a great deal of music. But though Monteverdi was still living in Venice, there is no direct evidence that Lanier met him, or, for that matter, any other well-known Italian musician.[7]

It was Roger North who first suggested that Lanier's recitative was composed soon after his return from Italy, and it seems reasonable on the whole to date the piece from before 1630. What appealed most to North was that Lanier's recitative did not resemble the *recitativo secco* of his own day, which tried to express differing emotions without fully reflecting the difference in the music. There was variety in Lanier's declamation, and it was especially suited to the 'pathetick'. Quoting the opening bars in score, he continued:

> the rest expresseth passion, hope, fear, and despair, as strong as words and sounds can bear, and saving some pieces by Mr. H. Purcell, wee have nothing of this kind in English at all recommendable.[8]

The observation is largely true: the range of expression is extremely wide. First there is Hero's impatience and her growing suspicion that she has been forsaken by her lover (bb.1–66), a suspicion which overcomes her and rouses her to furious anger (bb. 67–88). Then a sudden reversal: she attempts to reassure herself that all is well; that Leander is, at this moment, swim-

ming across the Hellespont to her (bb. 89–109). She beseeches
the wind and waves to hold back until he lands, when they may
be as angry as they like so as to keep the lovers together (bb.
110–140). But a sudden storm springs up. The light she is holding to guide him on his course is blown out, and all her prayers
are in vain, for, though the sea is once more becalmed, there,
drowned on the shore is Leander (bb. 141–190).[9] Each of these
changes of mood is depicted in the music; the excitement, the
anger, the fickle sea—now calm, now stormy—the final tragedy. The whole piece is superbly descriptive of Hero's changing emotions and is perhaps worthy to be ranked among the
great laments of Monteverdi and Sigismondo d'India in the
breadth and intensity of its expression, and its psychological
truth. It is, indeed, an early *Erwartung*.

One element in its success is the fact that, though the poem
is long and written in rhyming couplets, few of the couplets are
stopped, so that it reads almost like prose. This assists the freedom and flow of the declamation, and leads to greater continuity. As an example the following extract has been set out as
prose with the result that it is quite difficult to discover the
rhymes.

O! But stay! What vain thoughts transport thee, Hero?
Away with jealous fury! Leander's thine, thou his; and the
poor youth at home lamenting is the wary eyes of his old
parents. Now steals from them apace unto the shore; now
with hasty hand doth fling his robes from him, and even now,
bold boy, attempts to swim, parting the swelling waves with
iv'ry arms; borne up alone by love's all pow'rful charms.

In comparison, Lawes' *Ariadne* lament is tame. Its movement is sluggish, and the obvious couplet division disruptive.
Cartwright is at fault here, for his lines are end-stopped, and
the mood predominantly lyrical and reflective. For once
Lawes' respect for the text is misplaced. His treatment of the
words is too detailed. In fact, his recitative differs little from

his normal declamation, and this is exactly the trouble; for what may be wonderfully effective in eight lines is just too much spread over 102. He has misjudged the nature of recitative. Even so, his contemporaries thought highly of *Ariadne*, and Milton, who knew enough about Italian music to make a sound appreciation of it, singled it out for mention in his sonnet to Lawes, through a footnote.

Further fruit of Lanier's Italian visits may be seen in his setting of 'No more shall meads be decked with flowers'—one of Carew's lyrics which Lawes did not set, perhaps because Lanier's setting was already well known.[10] This he treats as a ground, repeating a chaconne-type bass for four verses while varying the tune. (One literary source actually labels the poem *'Ciacono'*.) However, the formal significance of Lanier's song

Ex. 50 'No more shall meads'   Nicholas Lanier (Ground Bass - *P1669*)

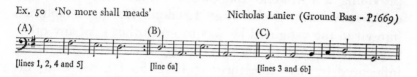

[lines 1, 2, 4 and 5]   [line 6a]   [lines 3 and 6b]

was probably not appreciated at first, for two manuscript sources (*N*, *P*) obliviously and independently of each other alter the bass during the course of the song, thus destroying its essential feature. It was not until Playford printed it after the Commonwealth (*P1669*) that the bass was restored to what must have been its original form, or something like it (Ex. 50).

Basically, the conventional tetrachord of the chaconne bass (A) is combined with a cadential progression (C). One full statement sets half the six-line stanza. Thus on the face of it, a simple repetition should suffice for the rest of the verse, but for some reason the last line is set twice, the first time by an interpolation (B) cadencing in A minor. This seems somewhat unnecessary although, musically, it creates a welcome diversion. However, the bass is ill-suited to the poem in other respects: the subdivision of the stanza into two threes is completely contrary to the rhyming scheme and structural logic which forms six lines by means of three couplets. The result is that the musical cadence occurs in the middle of the second couplet where there should be continuity, forcing the third line to join the first two and the fourth line to join the last two against the sense and form of the poem. Clearly Lanier has either the wrong bass for the poem, or the wrong poem for the bass—more evidence of a lack of discernment.

The contradiction in Lanier as a song writer begins to emerge. As early as 1613 his masque songs (see pp. 44–48) crystalize certain declamatory features already apparent in the songs of Dowland and particularly Ferrabosco, thus providing a decisive point of departure for a new type of song. The principal factor leading to this was Lanier's recognition of the new function of the bass, no longer a counterpoint to melody but providing a harmonic framework within which the voice could move with declamatory freedom. Having established himself in the vanguard he was to go further than any other English composer of his time in the direction of recitative, influenced by his experiences in Italy. So far, so good; his achievement is substantial and he gives the impression of a composer fully conscious of certain aims and the means of accomplishing them. Yet, one way or another, he shows incompetence, or, at least, misjudgment in his handling of words and a rather jejune taste. Unlike Lawes, he seems to have had little appreciation of the way musical declamation could convey the inner nuances of meaning and feeling of a lyric poem. Either he disregarded this aspect, or chose to set amatory verse of the lightest and most superficial kind where the necessity hardly arose. Yet he could create a dramatic effect. There is no disputing that 'Bring away this sacred tree' is perfectly attuned to the heroic ceremonial of the masque, and that 'Hero and Leander' is a superbly dramatic soliloquy.

But a final judgement on Lanier must be reserved, since many songs have been lost. This fact in itself should make us cautious in assessing what are clearly only the remnants of a larger output. Even so, it would seem that the younger John

Donne was over generous when he said that Lanier 'by his great skill gave a life and harmony to all that he set'.[11] We may perhaps prefer to shelter behind the ambiguity of Herrick's 'rare *Laniere*' which in one if not more senses may be closer to the truth.

'Rare' was the adjective Herrick applied to Lanier: 'curious' the one he applied to John Wilson, implying 'subtle' rather than 'odd' presumably.[12] Yet oddities there certainly are among his songs; subtleties—unless so subtle as to escape detection—very few.

We have already noted Wilson's early rise to fame as a composer of playsongs for the King's Men (pp. 55–59). It was as a forthright melodist that his reputation was acquired in his own

Ex. 51 'Since love hath in thine and mine eye' John Wilson (B)

Since love hath in thine and mine eye Kind-led a ho - ly flame, [etc.]

day and survives into ours, thanks chiefly to the contents of *Cheerfull Ayres or Ballads* (1660). Songs like 'From the fair Lavinian shore', 'In a season all oppressed' and 'In the merry month of May' could hardly fail to attract; they were copied from manuscript to manuscript and printed over and over again.[13] There is an apparent affinity with Campion and Jones though his style is less sophisticated and rather four-square. On the other hand, few songs of the period have such flexible and beautifully shaped lines as the opening of 'As tuned harp strings sad notes take' (B), or the first couplet of 'Since love hath in thine and mine eye' (*W1660, B,P,S,T*).[14]

Sometimes, perhaps, the four-squareness is due to the fact that in preparing his songs for publication (or, equally, for inclusion in B) Wilson up-dated the style in conformity with the idiom of the 1650's.[15] Many may therefore have been closer to the lutesong idiom than appears from these later sources. The setting of Donne's 'Wherefore peep'st thou, envious day' (*W1660, B, J,L,S*) could be such a case, for if the earliest version (*J*) is not a complete travesty, a comparison between it and Wilson's version 30 years later (*B*) reveals a marked change towards a more regular style of melody, simplifying many of the rhythmic subtleties which characterize the former[16] (Ex. 52).

One finds, too, traces of imitation at the beginning of some songs, which in itself is an old-fashioned trait. The opening of 'Hither we come unto this world of woe' (*B*) is of this type and contrasts with the more monodic approach of Lawes (Ex. 53).

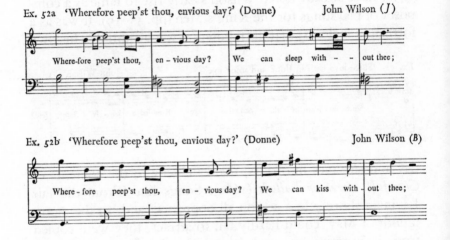

Ex. 52a 'Wherefore peep'st thou, envious day?' (Donne)　　　　John Wilson (*J*)

Ex. 52b 'Wherefore peep'st thou, envious day?' (Donne)　　　　John Wilson (*B*)

Normally Wilson adopts the declamatory style in setting serious verse, but his approach was more full-blooded than Lawes'. Subtlety, either in the rhythmic treatment of the text or in the expression which lay behind it, is rarely evident. Instead he is liable to seize upon certain key words and illustrate them boldly, either by chromaticism or some form of word-painting. This, of course, was a well-established practice, but side by side with progressions which are admirably effective—the opening of 'Languish and despair, my heart' (*B*) for instance, with its diminished intervals, madrigalisms, and (even) the treatment of 'howl' towards the end—we find passages which are merely arbitrary.[17] The following excerpt from 'Sleep in your lids' (*B*) is by no means exceptional (Ex. 54):

Too often Wilson puts his trust in a bass which moves by step, ascending or descending, chromatic or diatonic, leaving the upper part to shift as well as it can. At cadence points this tendency leads, when the movement is upwards, to a marked fondness for the interrupted cadence instead of the expected tonic-dominant close, and when the movement is downwards it leads to a phrygian cadence.

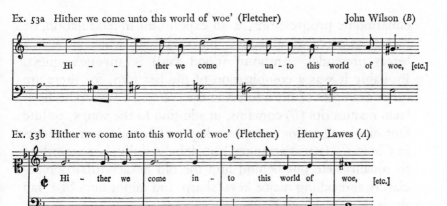

Ex. 53a Hither we come unto this world of woe' (Fletcher)   John Wilson (*B*)

Ex. 53b Hither we come into this world of woe' (Fletcher)   Henry Lawes (*A*)

More than any of his contemporaries, Wilson is a composer whose harmonic language belongs to the unsettled early Baroque and suffers for it. He has forsaken the modes but is not yet at home in the tonal system. There are, in fact, experiments which explore the system itself, such as the song 'Beauty which all men admire' (*B, M* also *Ch.Ch.17*). Taking the hint (possibly) from hexachord fantasies by Bull and Ferrabosco, the first six lines of the poem rise through all the chromatic degrees of the scale, from G to C, line by line (Ex. 55). The next four recapitulate the progression diatonically before finally cadencing on G. Whether this was intended as an exercise to practise the accompanist in all the keys, to test the singer's intonation with

Ex. 54 from 'Sleep in your lids'   John Wilson (*B*)

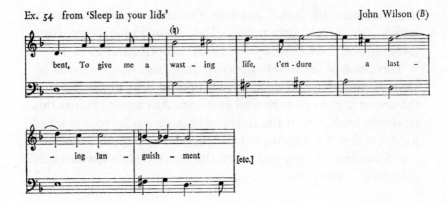

enharmonic progressions, as an experiment in modulation, or merely as piece of Wilsonian bufoonary (to which he was a 'great pretender' Anthony Wood said) is anyone's guess. Probably it was a combination of the last two, for there are other examples of his interest in the system of keys. The Bodleian manuscript (*B*) contains, in addition to the songs, 30 lute fantasies in all major and minor keys, while the list of contents in *Cheerfull Ayres* is arranged not alphabetically, but according to tonality. He put behind him the old hexachordal nomenclature and calling major keys 'sharp' and minor keys 'flat' ran the gamut from G to F (Ex. 55).

It is all too easy to regard Wilson as a bungler whose successes owe more to luck than judgement. True, his ballads show that he had a pleasing melodic gift, popular in character and undeniably attractive. But with a few exceptions his declamatory ayres are dull and spoiled by awkward passages that now seem inept. However, his tablatures demonstrate that he was far from being technically incompetent.[18] These contra-

Ex. 55 'Beauty which all men admire'   John Wilson (*B*)

dictions are difficult to resolve. We may put them down to un-disciplined talent; prolific, careless and uncritical. One suspects that it goes deeper than that, to a lack of sensibility—a de-ficiency of what are called 'fine feelings'. There is little or no response to the noble and pathetic in his music; delicacy and even charm elude him. Perhaps his character was too extrovert to appreciate these things. There was little that was fastidious or refined about him, and judging by the poems he set, his literary taste was second rate. As against numerous settings of Thomas Stanley, Henry King, Owen Felltham and many worse, he set only a handful of lyrics by poets of the front-rank. Had his temperament been more reflective we might have had more songs like 'Wherefore peep'st thou, envious day' and 'Take, O take those lips away'.[19] By the same token, we might have been deprived of those frank and honest 'Cheer-full Ayres' which Wilson himself recognized as being more truly representative of his genius.

William Lawes has more in common with Lanier and Wilson than his elder brother. Although we know little enough about any of them, one detects something of Lanier's well-bred air and Wilson's geniality both in his character as a man and in his songs. It is not surprising then that he should succeed the former as chief composer for the court masques, and the latter as song-writer for the King's Men at the Blackfriars Theatre. He seems to have been a more glamorous personality than his brother; his urbanity won him wide affection during his life and universal sorrow at his untimely death from a stray bullet at the siege of Chester in 1645. First and foremost he was a composer of instrumental music. His songs are fewer than his brother's or Wilson's, and, on the whole, inferior—to his brother's any-way.[20] Certainly some were popular in their day, above all his setting of Herrick's 'Gather ye rosebuds while ye may' which is found in at least eight manuscripts and was reprinted more than 20 times in the seventeenth century.[21] But his declama-

tory ayres lack flexibility and subtlety. Even when the externals
are there, as they are in 'Amaryllis, tear thy hair' (*B1678, C* and,
significantly, misattributed to Henry in *P1669*), one is aware,
nevertheless, of a certain dry quality which contrasts with the
soft and gentle pathos of his brother's best songs. Rather, it is
Lanier who comes to mind, with whom he shares a well-
developed sense of tonality and an almost classical diatonicism
oddly contrasting with the harmonic daring of some of his
string music.

The difference in style between the two brothers may be
seen in comparing their settings of Thomas Carey's 'Farewell,
fair saint'. Henry's treatment is noticeably more pliable from

Ex. 56a 'Farewell, fair saint' (Cary)   Henry Lawes (*P1669*)

Ex. 56b 'Farewell, fair Saint' (Cary)   William Lawes (C)

the rhythmic point of view, and melodically more polished. Out of 20 syllables in the first couplet there are only two pairs of equal notes, whereas there are seven pairs in the younger brother's setting (Ex. 56).

William's strength as a song writer lies elsewhere. His style is more suited to extrovert, heroic matter; a good example is his setting of Tatham's verses 'Upon my Noble friend, Richard Lovelace Esquire, his being in *Holland*, an Invitation'—'Come Adonis, come again [away]' (*P1659*, *M*).[22] Presumably it was written between 1643 and 1645, and its forthright diatonicism and swagger, give us a foretaste of the Restoration. But he is at his best when he allows his melodic gift free rein. Inevitably, these are his lighter songs, and, of course, the one which springs to mind immediately is 'Gather ye rosebuds', though probably the words more than the rather stodgy tune gave this song its wide circulation. Elsewhere one finds a natural gift of melody linked with a feeling for the rhythmic ambivalence of 3/2 and 6/4, especially in approaching a cadence. These hemiola rhythms are everywhere and proclaim the link with the dance, a link which in the case of 'O my Clarissa, thou cruel fair' (*P1652*, *M*, *P*, *R*, and *U*) is explicit since this popular song occurs as an instrumental saraband in Playford's *Court-Ayres* (1655) and in Lawes' Harp Consort No. 4 (Ex. 57).

Ex. 57 'O my Clarissa, thou cruel fair'   William Lawes (*P1659*)

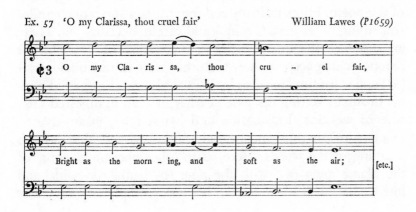

It is the movement and rhythm of the saraband which under-
lies most of his tuneful songs in triple time. The characteristic
rhythms ♩ ♩. ♪ and ♩ ♩ are common, so are hemiolas. Not
surprisingly verbal accentuation often suffers when it does not
coincide with the rhythmic characteristics of the dance. The
hemiolas in 'Faith, be no longer coy' (*P1652*, *C*, *R*), for example, make nonsense of the natural movement of the verse.[23]
Again, it has to be recognized that in such songs the tune is
more important than the words. For the most part we find
regular and balanced phrases, and correspondingly a much
more modern, architectural sense of tonality, for the musical
self-sufficiency of the dance carries over into these dance-
songs. As such, we may perhaps call them 'ballads', though in
this rather literal sense they relate to a courtly rather than a
popular dance tradition. They do not betray the earthiness of
Wilson's tuneful ayres but remain courtiers' songs—gallant
and sophisticated.

One might have expected Lawes to have adopted this tuneful
style in his playsongs, but with one or two exceptions his playsongs are declamatory.[24] It is not easy to generate much enthus-
iasm over any of them, and even when the lyric has real literary
merit the settings tend to be cold and perfunctory. The two
songs in Suckling's *Aglaura* (1637)[25] are probaby the best of
this kind, yet despite some attractive details 'Why so pale and
wan, fond lover' seems laboured and misses the wry cynicism
of the poem. Flippant irony and the anti-romantic tone require
something other than C minor and careful declamation. There
are more glaring inadequacies in the setting of 'No, no, fair
heretic' which accompanies the other song in one manuscript
(*M*) and is presumably also by William Lawes. Compared with
his brother's setting discussed earlier, it is an ill-digested mixture of wooden declamation and hymn tune, insensitive to
nuances of rhythm and verbal inflection, and thus to the
meaning of the words. Here, as in other playsongs, some of
the blame must rest with the poet for being too witty and
intellectual, instead of casting his lyrics simply and regularly

for musical setting. This song, with its elaborate structure further subtilized by run-on lines makes life unnecessarily difficult for the composer. On the other hand, when the playwright supplies simple verses and short lines, as Davenant did in 'O draw your curtains and appear' (*C,M, B1678*) from *Love and Honour* (1634), Lawes' style lapses into aridity.

The weakness of his playsongs, which stems from a basically anti-lyrical make-up as a composer, becomes a strength when composing vocal music for the court masque.[26] For, like Lanier, his musical ear responded to euphuistic verse. Expressive subtleties were not required. What was needed was music that was bold and extrovert, that gave the illusion of magnificence to verse that was merely magniloquent. His diatonicism and developed sense of tonality were well adapted to this as was his unaffected declamatory style, for it was not details so much as the whole heroic spectacle that needed illumining. A fair amount of vocal music survives for Shirley's *The Triumph of Peace* (1634), Davenant's *The Triumphs of the Prince d'Amour* (1636) and the same author's *Britannia Triumphans* (1638). The contrast with his brother's songs in *Comus* is striking. Henry's gifts were as right for Milton's concept of the masque as William's were for Davenant's. One is pastoral, an exquisite poetic creation graced by songs which, for all their undoubted merit are incidental to the artistic design; the other is heroic ritual, music and dance, speech and spectacle combining together to celebrate the Divine Right of Kings. As with Lanier, the musical expression is externalized: there is panache but little passion. Undoubtedly William Lawes had a talent for the lighter kind of song, tuneful and elegant; but tenderness—to go no deeper—eluded him. Had he lived he would have been as much an ornament of Charles II's court as he was of Charles I's whereas his brother would have been a fish out of water.

If William Lawes points forward to the Restoration, Charles

Coleman does so even more. Certainly it comes as a surprise to discover him listed among King James's musicians as early as 1625, still more to discover that he took the part of Hymen in a masque of 1617, though possibly as a treble. His surviving songs are not numerous and none occurs in early manuscripts. A songbook once belonging to Lady Anne Blount (O), now in the Library of Lambeth Palace, contains the only songs not also found in print, and it may be that Coleman was music master to Lady Anne for a time—until she eloped with (or was abducted by) Tom Porter the playwright in 1655. His earliest datable song is the dialogue 'Did not you once, Lucinda, vow' (*P1652*) from *The King and Queenes Entertainment at Richmond* (*1636*) and it provides us with some characteristic glimpses of his style.[27]

More than any of his contemporaries he provides well-figured basses, otherwise rare in the songs of Lanier, Wilson and the Lawes brothers. More than theirs too, his harmony has a dynamic quality which derives from a strong sense of tonality. This awareness he shares with William Lawes, but his harmonic language is richer and more expertly handled. In minor keys especially his chord progressions are particularly effective—in fact, he fully recognizes the harmonic minor. His

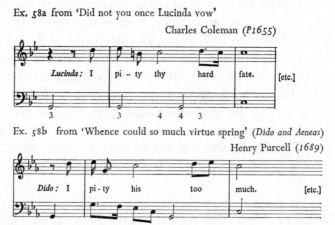

Ex. 58a from 'Did not you once Lucinda vow'

Charles Coleman (*P1655*)

Ex. 58b from 'Whence could so much virtue spring' (*Dido and Aeneas*)

Henry Purcell (*1689*)

declamation is frequently characterized by false intervals and free discord treatment such as we associate with Locke, and there are pre-echoes of Purcell (see Ex. 58).

His least impressive songs recall the rather trite, strophic, semi-declamatory ayres of Henry Lawes *Ayres and Dialogues* (1658)—'When, Celia, I intend to flatter you' (*P1653*) is a fair example.[28] But his best songs leave Lawes a good way behind stylistically, and undoubtedly 'Wake, my Adonis' (*P1652*) is foremost amongst these.[29] It is a lament of Venus for her lost Adonis, and is presumably the original playsong from Cartwright's *The Lady Errant*, thought to have been performed privately, possibly at Oxford early in the Civil War (*c.* 1642). What is so remarkable about this song is the range of tragic feeling it displays, and for its time it may only be compared with Lanier's *Hero and Leander*, though it is much shorter and the style rather different. The emphasis and inflection of Venus's opening entreaty is poignantly conveyed. Her distraction is expressed through urgent, disjointed phrases, jerky in rhythm, jagged in contour, pointing the antitheses between 'looks and wiles', 'frowns and smiles'. A pause—then she realizes that she calls in vain, and this brings partial acceptance of the tragedy and temporary resignation. But her agitation revives with the recollection of certain ill-omens; a vision of her lover's ghost, the uprooting of a myrtle tree in her grove, and it is not until the third part of the song that she finds consolation in the thought that since she, Venus, must always love, she will love her grief:

> *Sorrow shall to me*
> *A new Adonis be.*

A final section objectifies the moral in an heroic couplet, rather spoiling the effect so far achieved by lapsing into a triple-time dance measure (Ex. 59).

For all the differences that are immediately apparent, this song points to Purcell's *Blessed Virgin's Expostulation*. The

Ex. 59a from 'Wake my Adonis, do not die' (Cartwright: *The Lady Errant*)

Charles Coleman (*P1652*)

dissimilarities, which need not be dwelt on, are of physical and emotional scale rather than kind, and though the comparison may seem flattering to Coleman it confirms the impression that not only was he the most modern in style of the court song-writers, but that his gifts—especially his dramatic gift—were such that, had the times been other than they were he might have been the founding father of English Opera. This, of course, is speculation. Taken as a whole his songs are few and uneven; they offer hints rather than proof that he had the talent for such an undertaking. Even so, he stands in the direct line that leads from Lanier to Purcell.

There are, in addition, a number of less important composers whose songs merit discussion in the present context. As we have already seen (p. 60) some of William Webb's seem to have been among the first declamatory songs to achieve popularity. He appears on almost equal footing with Lanier, Wilson and Henry Lawes in pre-1625 manuscript song collections, but as a song writer his reputation failed to keep pace— or rather, it took another direction, for his inclination lay in the direction of the tuneful partsong. Most of Webb's printed songs are of this type, and they are among the best of their kind.

One song, 'Let her give her hand or glove' was among those now missing from Anne Twice's Book (*J*) and must therefore be early.[58] The melody is attractive in a plain, straightforward way, and shows no trace of the declamatory principle. 'As life what is so sweet' (*H. K. R.*, also missing from *J*) offers a specimen of his more serious style.[31] It was evidently highly admired in view of its presence (originally) in at least three early manuscripts. A mild declamatory tendency may be detected here, but one or two later songs like 'Go and bestride the southern wind' show an altogether greater commitment.[32] So too in 'Come noble nymphs' (*P1659*, *L*), written (presumably) in the first place for Jonson's masque *Neptune's Triumph* and intended for performances on Twelfth Night, 1624, but not performed because of a squabble between the French and Spanish Ambassadors. Jonson was able to use the song a year later in *The Fortunate Isles*.[33]

Despite the popularity of some of his songs and the attractive quality that recommended them to Playford, Webb's other songs did not achieve a wide circulation. Two manuscripts represent him strongly: Don.c. 57 (*L*) with six songs, and John Gamble's manuscript with nine (*R*). Between them they contain all but one of the manuscript songs. The relationship with Gamble is interesting and probably points to personal acquaintance, for Gamble was a London wait, as Webb had been, although their periods of service did not overlap.

Associated with Webb are two other composers of about the same age who were on the fringe of the court in the 1630's— Simon Ives (a wait like Webb) and William Caesar, *alias* Smegergill. Both wrote pastoral dialogues in the declamatory

manner, but in addition they were attracted to the tuneful partsong or glee, and are well represented in contemporary catch
books. Each has one or two pleasant songs to his credit. In
lighter vein, Ives's 'Will Chloris cast her sun-bright eyes'
(*P,U,V, P1667*) moves in an elegantly syncopated triple
rhythm, as does Caesar's 'If any live that fain would prove'
(*P1652*)—which reverses the more usual practice by changing
from triple to common time in the final couplet.[34] A more
serious song is Ives' 'Go bid the swan in silence die' (*S*).[35] Why
such a charming piece should have failed to achieve a wider
circulation, or even print, is mystifying.

Ex. 60 'Go bid the swan in silence die' Simon Ives (*S*)

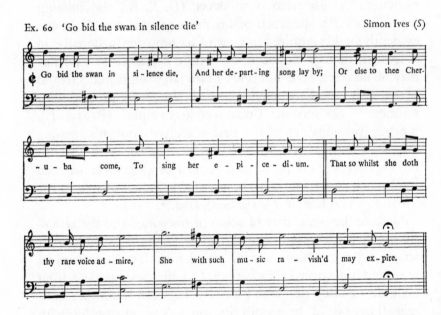

Thomas Brewer is another composer whose name appears
frequently in the catch books. His serious songs are of more
than average interest and reveal a passionate nature which
sometimes gets the better of him, as in the opening of 'Tell not
I die' (*P1653*, R). G minor juxtaposed with B minor is perhaps
what might be expected from a minor Italian monodist of the
early seventeenth century.

Ex. 61 'Tell not I die'   Thomas Brewer (*P1653*)

Better and more controlled is the remarkable song 'O that mine eyes could melt' (*P1664*, P,*Q*,R), a meditation on the passion, thoroughly counter-reformation in its imagery and feeling, reinforcing suspicion of Brewer's Italian sympathies.[36] Two of the three manuscript versions of this song are profusely embellished and, significantly, it is this song that Playford chose to include in his Introduction to the Skill of Musick as an example of an English song suitable for ornamentation 'after the Italian manner'.[37] Actually, the printed version marks only a few crosses where the *trillo* may be sung, but the manuscripts supply trillos, relishes, backfalls, beats, etc., as well as elaborate divisions. Normally, of course, this type of ornamentation would have been performed extempore, but many examples survive written down either as models for students or aids to memory.[38] Occasionally the exact meaning of some of the symbols used is uncertain since they do not conform to those listed by such authorities as Playford and Simpson. But this matters little as the haphazard way they are used shows that they imply general rather than specific types of embellishment. In doubtful cases the shape of the signs employed often suggests the way they should be interpreted. Thus a group of dots denotes some kind of shaked ornament (relish), a comma or slanted stroke before a note indicates an appogiatura from above (backfall) or below (beat or forefall) depending on the direction of the stroke, while an upward stroke above or after a note designates some kind of échappée effect (springer). But a too scrupulous approach to ornamentation is to be avoided. A few bars from 'O that mine eyes' gives an idea of the sort of thing that was widespread, as many sources attest especially in 'Passionate Musick' (Ex. 62, see also Plate 7).

Ex. 62   from 'O that mine eyes'   Thomas Brewer   (ornamented cadence).

Evidently the interpretation of such music in strict tempo was impossible, as we are informed in the *Synopsis of Vocal Musick* (1680):

> the ordinary measure of Time is here less regarded, for many times is the value of the Notes made less by half, and sometimes more, according to the conceit of the words, with a graceful neglect.[39]

'A graceful neglect' is the operative phrase when it comes to performing such passages as the above. According to Playford, writing in 1666—

> singing after this new method by *Trills, Grups* [relishes], and *Exclamations* . . . have been used to our *English* Ayres above this 40 years and Taught here in *England*, by our late Eminent Professors of *Musick*, Mr *Nicholas Laneare*, Mr *Henry Lawes*, Dr. *Wilson* and Dr. *Colman*, and Mr. *Walter Porter* who *30* years since published in Print Ayres of 3, 4, and 5, Voyces, with the *Trills* and other Graces to the same.[40]

Certain ornaments, such as the *trillo*, were no doubt new, or fairly new, then. But it was the end more than the means of ornamentation that had changed. In practice, divisions were still the main device employed, but now more for their pictorial and emotional effect—their swooping and swooning— rather than as colouring of a particular line. Likewise, it was the dissonant element of the appogiatura type of ornament, beats and backfalls, that applied; the throbbing passion of the *trillo*, the thrill of the exclamation (which today we would hardly regard as an ornament, being merely 'a slackening of the voice to reinforce it afterwards'). It need hardly be pointed out that the declamatory ayre was well suited to this kind of interpretation for the vocal line was of a type that could bear distortion of the basic pulse.

John Atkins was a composer who achieved a pleasing effect in a few songs. Eleven out of a total of 12 are found in Drexel MS. 4041 (*M*) a fact suggesting a close relationship between the scribe and the composer. Surprisingly, not one song was ever printed under his own name, though Playford published 'I can love for an hour' (*P1653*, R) attributed to William Lawes, and 'Wert thou yet fairer' (*P1652*, M,R) to Wilson.[41] Both are attractive triple-time ayres of the saraband type, but he could also manage the declamatory style, as in 'This lady ripe' (*M*) from Davenant's *The Just Italian* (1629), though spoiled by its lame ending.[42]

John Taylor is also well represented in Drexel MS. 4041, which contains six out of his seven songs. Playford printed a catch 'Then let us be friends' (*P1663*) and his best known song 'Lay that sullen garland by thee' (*P1652*, M,T)—a declamatory ayre with closing couplet in triple time.[43] Also successful is his setting of Tatham's 'Tell me not that I die' (*M*) though it lacks the impact of Brewer's setting, adopting instead a less dramatic mode of expression.[44]

Here, if anywhere, is the place to deal with John Gamble, since he seems to belong to the generation of such men as Atkins and Taylor, and to their milieu. Extraordinary is perhaps the only word to describe him, since, for all his industry both as a composer of more than 230 songs and indefatigable anthologist of other men's work, he came as close to writing musical nonsense as any of his contemporaries. His intentions were good. Clearly he aimed to out-Lawes Lawes in matching 'just note and accent', but in fact his declamatory style is more like Wilson at his worst, with rambling basses and undisciplined chromaticism in the vocal part.[45] It may even have been this resemblance that won Gamble 'a great name among the musitians of Oxon. for his book before publish'd, entit. *Ayres and Dialogues . . .'.*[46] Nor were there lacking writers of laudatory verses. Thomas Stanley and Richard Lovelace, both of whom seem to have been related to Gamble, as well as a number of other Oxonians, each contributed their encomiums. Oxford and musical style apart there is another link between Gamble and Wilson through Stanley, many of whose lyrics Wilson set, as did Gamble in his first book of *Ayres and Dialogues* (1656, also 1657). In his second book (1659) he seems to favour the London poet Thomas Jordan—that is, if Gamble's attentions may be regarded as a favour. There is a third collection of ayres still in manuscript, and likely to remain so.[47]

However, posterity can only be grateful to him. His Commonplace Book (R) provides a vast conspectus of songs from the period 1620 to 1660, many of which do not survive elsewhere.[48] It was probably completed about 1659 and is the largest collection of its kind.

Sometimes the initials 'J.G.' are attached to songs in Playford's publications, but they indicate John Goodgroome rather than John Gamble. Here we have another puzzle, for though he appears as a composer of quite pleasing songs in the 1659 and 1669 editions of *Select Ayres and Dialogues*, there is no evidence that he composed any songs at a later date, even though he apparently lived on until 1704! It seems strange that having shown some talent he should have dried up almost completely during the last 40 years of his life. His songs include a setting of Suckling's exquisite lyric 'Dost see how unregarded now' (*P1659*, U) with some touching moments achieved largely through a happy conjunction of eloquent line and unforced asymmetry of phrase.[49] There are blemishes certainly, even so the song creates a charming effect poised between aristocratic restraint and natural feeling.

Edward Coleman, the son of Charles, is a similar type of composer. His setting of Cotton's 'Why, dearest, should you weep'(*P1653*) is one of those gently affecting semi-declamatory ayres that so many composers seem to have been able to produce at least once.[50] But his renown, such as it is, is based on the fact that he set Shirley's 'The glories of our birth and state' (*P1667, O,U,V*).[51] Undoubtedly it is the poem which has carried his name to fame, for the music is hardly remarkable. In its original version it seems to have been sung as a solo at the end of *The Contention of Ajax and Ulysses* (1658), but a note in the printed edition of the play states:

This was afterwards sung in parts, the Musick excellently composed by Mr. *Ed. Coleman.*

'Afterwards sung in parts' may mean immediately afterwards as a sort of Finale to the play, or it may mean some time after the play had been performed. (It may even imply that the song itself was not sung in the play at all, but that Coleman later set it to music.) The most likely inference would seem that it was sung at the end of the play first as a solo then repeated by the chorus. Certainly, it was the partsong arrangement that subsequently became popular, though all of Playford's three versions differ from each other. The original version is thus obscure, but a manuscript copy in Lady Ann Blount's song book (*O*) may have some claim to authority, owing to the fact that the manuscript is a good source of his father's songs. It gives an ornamented common-time solo version of the 'verse' breaking into three time for the 'chorus'.

Far from being an ill-defined group of composers writing songs indistinguishable from each other, these men—Lanier, the Lawes brothers, Wilson and Coleman anyway—emerge as distinct musical personalities, their songs clearly differentiated in style. There is, of course, a common denominator; nonetheless, certain individual traits stand out. It is evident that the 'main stream' flows from Ferrabosco, through Lanier, William Lawes and Coleman, to pass at the Restoration—as we shall see—to Pelham Humfrey. It is a classical line (somewhat analogous to the school and successors of Ben Jonson in poetry), characterized by unaffected, though by no means unsophisticated, melodic and declamatory writing, and increasingly by a tonally directed harmonic idiom. Their work tends to be conventionally lyrical and extrovert in character, while the pathetic has little appeal. Taken as a whole it represents the tradition through which we may trace the main evolutionary trend of English song during the first half of the seventeenth century.

John Wilson and Henry Lawes in their different ways are off-shoots of this line. As against the Tribe of Ben they may be compared with the School of Donne. They are romantics, they dwell on details, and indeed it might be said that their expressive devices provide a musical parallel to metaphysical wit. As romantics they are individualists. Wilson is a mass of contradictions: part balladeer, part sonneteer. Many of his early playsongs and 'cheerful ayres' are robust and tuneful, of a kind that could have been written almost any time betwen 1550 and 1750. Yet his serious songs for the most part are contorted and contrived. The declamation is arid, the bass ill-directed, and both are liable to be spoilt by excessive and irrational chromaticism—not all, fortunately, but too many to make a more favourable generalization.

The field of the serious declamatory ayre is dominated by Henry Lawes. His tuneful songs are charming enough, though perhaps not so fresh as his brother's. But, in general, no other composer can approach him when it comes to matching words and music in terms of poetic diction and feeling. He sought the best poets and they sought him, and this mutual respect and admiration provided the basis of a marriage of voice and verse. Perhaps Lawes moved further in the poets' direction than they did in his; yet it was not only a matter of 'just note and accent'.

It is the sum, not the parts, which makes the work of art: the technique and feeling of the poem and music must be one. It is appropriate to quote Francis Sambrooke on his 'worthy Friend (and Countriman,) Mr. Henry Lawes.'[52] Using a metaphor to describe how inseparable the Lawes brother had been, he symbolizes also the complementary relationship of verse and music in Henry's finest songs.

> *Such numbers does the soule consist of, where she*
> *Meeting a glance of her own harmonie,*
> *Moves to those sounds she heares: and goes along*
> *With the whole sense and passion of the song;*
> *So to an equall height, two strings being wound,*
> *This trembles with the others stroke; and th' sound*
> *Which stirr'd this first, the other does awake,*
> *And the same harmonie they both partake.*

Part three

Interlude
and
interregnum

1 The catch and the glee

With the Court in exile, church music silenced, and theatres closed, the social organization of music during the Commonwealth was completely disorientated. Many of the King's musicians turned to teaching while others availed themselves of offers of patronage. Enterprising musicians organized music meetings. Anthony Wood has left us an account of those which flourished at Oxford, especially the ones at the house of William Ellis, which Wood attended and at which John Wilson presided.[1] In effect, meetings such as these were informal concerts, and the profits from Ellis's meeting were enough to keep him and his wife in a comfortable condition. Another Oxford musician, Edmund Chilmead, dispossessed of his petty-canonry at Christ Church, moved to London and set up a music meeting at the Black Horse in Aldersgate, prior to his death in 1651. Somewhat later we read of 'the musick house at the Miter, near the West end of St. Paul's Church' where the most famous catch club of the day met. It was for this meeting, later at Old Jewry, that Playford published his *Musical Companion* (1667).[2]

The shift, then, in social orientation was towards the middle class. Professional men, merchants and shopkeepers paid the piper and called the tune. It would be rash to generalize about their taste, but Playford seems to have sized it up thoroughly. He and his son Henry dominated the publishing scene in the second half of the century. It is fair to say that he was inspired by something more than pecuniary gain. He was an enthusiast, a musical amateur who composed a little, and represented in himself the public for which he catered. Not only did he satisfy the needs of amateur and professional musicians by supplying instrumental and vocal music in print, but he took steps to expand the market by issuing instruction books for the lyra viol, cittern, etc., and many editions of his *Introduction to the Skill of Music* (from 1654) so that musical literacy might increase.

His most important song collection was the *Select Ayres and Dialogues* series, started in 1652 with further volumes in 1653, 1659 and 1669.[3] (The first two issues were titled *Select Musicall Ayres* etc.) All were folio volumes in three sections; the first containing songs printed on two staves 'for one and two Voyces, to sing to the *Theorbo, Lute,* or *Basse Violl*' (there was no tablature); the second, pastoral dialogues for two voices and continuo; the third, three-part ayres or glees. The collection grew by addition, and once a song had been included it tended to remain there. The 1652 edition included 67 by Wilson, Coleman, Henry Lawes and William Webb (mentioned on the title page) as well as by William Caesar (*alias* Smegergill), Johnson, Lanier, William Lawes, Robert Smith and John Taylor. The next edition contained 80 songs and added Thomas Brewer, Edward Coleman, Jeremy Savile and others to the list of composers. Subsequently, Lady Dering (wife of Sir Edward Dering and a pupil of Henry Lawes), John Goodgroome, Simon Ives, John Jenkins and Playford himself were included (125 songs in 1659), and Thomas Blagrave, William Gregory, Roger Hill, John Hilton and Alfonso Marsh (124 songs in 1669). Of these, songs by Henry Lawes outnumbered all the rest.

The question arises as to how reliable Playford's versions are. He himself wrote (*P1659*):

my care, pains, and charge hath not been small, by procuring
true and exact Coppies, and dayly attending the oversight of the
Presse, as no prejudice might redound either to the Authors
or Buyer: And herein I resolve to meet with those
Mistakers, *who have taken up a new (but very fond) opinion,*
That Musick cannot as truely be Printed as Prick'd,
(*and which is more ridiculous*) that no Choice Ayres or Songs

are permitted by Authors to come in print, *though 'tis well known that the best Musicall Compositions, either of our owne or Strangers, have been and are tendered to the World by the Printers hand; To convince the former, and to testifie my Gratitude to those Excellent Masters, from whose owne hands I received most of these Compositions; doe I say thus much, that this my present Endevor and care in the true and exact publishing this Book will redound to Publick Benefit, and the Authors Reputation . . .*

Playford was certainly well placed to secure authentic versions, especially from composers still living and, in particular, fellow Londoners. And although Henry Lawes complained (*L1653*) that Playford was less likely to print his songs correctly than he himself, he did not actually accuse him of inaccuracy. Experience shows that Playford is less reliable when it comes to the songs of Lanier, Wilson and William Lawes, and that even when a song was set-up again for a new edition only rarely were mistakes in the old edition corrected. Furthermore, his lists of corrigenda are far from complete.

Except for the dialogues, nearly all the ayres in the first two editions are strophic and non-declamatory, with a large proportion in three time. This suggests that Playford thought he could sell more copies with ear-tickling ayres than with the other kind. It is obvious that the collection did not represent a cross-section of the songs then in existence, for triple-time ayres are in a minority in most manuscripts. But later editions make a broader selection, and by 1669 the proportion of one sort to another seems to correspond with that typical of the majority of manuscripts. Rather than reflecting a compositional trend, the apparent increase in declamatory ayres may be seen as rectifying the imbalance caused by the predominance of the more tuneful type of song in the first two books. The series is, after all, basically retrospective, and may be taken as indicating the taste of the period 1630–60, rather than plotting a stylistic development between 1652 and 1669. This being so, it is worth noting the extent to which more or less declamatory songs dominate the repertory; indeed, tuneful triple-time ayres do not amount to more than a third—a startling contrast with what was to be the Restoration taste.

In 1651 John Benson and John Playford published as the third part of the *Musicall Banquet* the first catch book since the days of Ravenscroft's *Pammelia* (1609), *Deuteromelia* (1609) and *Melismata* (1611). The following year a new series entitled *Catch that Catch Can* began under the editorship of John Hilton, and underwent a further five or six enlarged editions and a change of title during the next 20 years. It was not until metamorphosed into *The Musical Companion* in 1667 that glees were admitted to the collection. These short tuneful partsongs represent another level of musical taste which Playford catered for in the third section of his *Select Ayres and Dialogues* series; Lawes, too, in his own *Ayres and Dialogues*. The entire contents of Wilson's *Cheerfull Ayres or Ballads* (1660) were published in the same form. The preface makes clear how these songs could be sung:

> *CANTUS PRIMUS* is a compleate Book of it selfe, carrying the principall Ayre to Sing alone with a through Base. *CANTUS SECUNDUS* and *BASSUS* are also printed singly to make two, or three Parts, as shall be requisite for the Company that will use them.

Playford and Lawes also stipulate that their part-songs 'may either be sung by a Voyce alone, to an Instrument, or by two or three Voyces', but instead of providing separate partbooks they printed the treble and thorough bass together on two staves at the top of the page, and below, separate parts for secundus and bassus (the former printed upside down so that it could be read from the opposite direction). The idea was obviously derived from the lutesong publications of the earlier part of the century, though now a single page sufficed, songs rarely spreading over a double opening. Composers of these 'Short Ayres or Balads' include the Lawes brothers, Lanier, Wilson, Webb and Ives.

It is necessary to look at the literature of catches and glees rather more closely. Playford's terminology of song types is very free and though he defines a catch as 'a Song for three Voyces, wherein the several Parts are included in one; or, as it is usually tearmed, Three Parts in One',[4] yet some pieces which he calls catches are merely part-songs—Henry Lawes' 'Man's life is but vain' (famous through *The Compleat Angler*) is called 'The Angler's Catch' in *The Musical Companion* (1667) though there is nothing canonic about it. Nor does he distinguish between the terms Round, Canon and Catch though canons often involve imitation at intervals other than unison, and the voices tend to enter closer together than in rounds and catches. If anything, their meanings are differentiated more by their character. Christopher Simpson points out that catches and rounds are 'of less dignity' than canons. He goes on to explain how simple it is to write one:

> if you compose any short strain, of three or four Parts, setting them all within the ordinary compass of a Voyce; and then place one Part at the end of another, in what order you please, so as they may aptly make one continued Tune; you have finished a Catch . . .[5]

If anything then, a catch tended to be humorous or bawdy, a canon moral and sober, while a round might have a folk or traditional origin. This, at least, is the implication of general usage. The catch often had a non-musical point, either punning, programmatic or otherwise descriptive, while the round and canon were of musical interest only.

Similarly, there seems to be no technical distinction implicit in the terms glee, ballad and ayre, all of which are applied to freely composed partsongs in from two to four voices. But again one detects a difference in character. Most glees (so-called) are light-hearted and 'gleeful', ayres are usually more serious and ballads have a traditional 'folk' flavour.

As has already been observed, the spate of catch books began in 1651 with *A Musicall Banquet*, and continued through several editions of Hilton's *Catch that Catch Can*. Almost every songwriter of the time is represented in these collections (not Lanier or Charles Coleman, however), but the most prolific catch writers were Hilton and William Lawes, while certain otherwise negligible composers such as Cranford, Ellis, Holmes, and Nelham seem also to have been popular. The 1658 edition of *Catch that Catch Can* (also the 1663, which was virtually a reprint) even drew on a few old favourites from *Pammelia* and *Deuteromelia*. Some are ascribed to a Mr. White—author of such famous rounds as 'Great Tom is cast' and 'My dame hath a lame tame crane'—others are anonymous, including 'Three blind mice'. A new series of *Catch that Catch Can* was started in 1685, changed its name to *The Pleasant Musical Companion* a year later, and continued to be printed over and over again into the eighteenth century.

Catches were written on all subjects; religious, serious, humorous, bibulous, amorous or scurrilous. Conviviality is the prevailing mood and drinking catches outnumber all the others. As an example of the learned type of canon John Cobb's setting of 'O pray for the peace of Jerusalem' (*H1652*) may be quoted. Described as '*A Canon in the 5. above, & 4. below. a Sembreeffe after one another*', it is quite a neat piece of counterpoint for all its brevity and reliance on sequences (see Ex. 63).

Most catches are for three voices, and the title page of *Catch that Catch Can* shows three men sitting round a table with a book open upon it. Unlike most of the rounds which have remained popular to this day, catches were usually composed of long lines and the resulting texture when all the voices were participating was quite elaborate—not merely a simple succession of chords. As has been observed already, there was usually some 'point' to a catch over and above the canonic element. In Hilton's 'Oyez, if there be any man can

Ex. 63 'O pray for the peace of Jerusalem'   John Cobb ⟨H1652⟩

tell' (*H1652*) the point is the imitation of the town crier. There is no hidden meaning in the words, merely a drunken clamour. Sometimes personal references occur, and it is tempting to identify these with known catch-men. It is quite probable that the Simon mentioned in Hilton's 'Let Simon's beard alone' (*Ibid.*) and William Howes' 'Good Simon how comes it your nose looks so red' (*Ibid.*) is Simon Ives, while frequent mention of Harry in other catches may refer to Henry Lawes. We may wonder, too, whether Hilton's 'We three Wills' (*Ibid.*) alludes to William Lawes, William Ellis and William Cranford—three inveterate catchers—and the Jack to John Wilson, the George to George Holmes (or Jeffreys), all of them in Oxford during the civil war. This particular catch, though not dependent on punning, does not get its full message across until all voices are singing. Then the second and third combine to give the following:

> *Will boy, fill boy, swill boy, till boy,*
> *The ground turns round like a mill boy—good boy!*

One imagines a hiccup or belch before the final 'good boy', then back to the start again and another jug of ale.

Ex. 64 'We three Wills'   John Hilton *(H1652)*

The *double entendre* was the favoured device in the bawdy catch. The aim was for two or more lines to come together during the course of the song so that, by means of judiciously placed rests in one or other parts, indelicate or obscene phrases otherwise unsuspected would emerge. William Cranford's 'Here dwells a pretty maid' (*Ibid.*) provides an example, and again it depends on the conjunction of the second and third lines. Cranford had quite a talent for this sort of thing, though this was the Hyde-side of him, apparently. He appears as Jekyll in old Lord North's description:

> Mr. Cranford, whom I knew, a sober, plain-looking Man: his pieces mixed with Majesty, Gravity, Honey-dew Spirit and Variety.[6]

Perhaps we may take the following as a specimen of his honey-dew spirit!

Ex. 65   'Here dwells a pretty maid'   William Cranford (*H1652*)

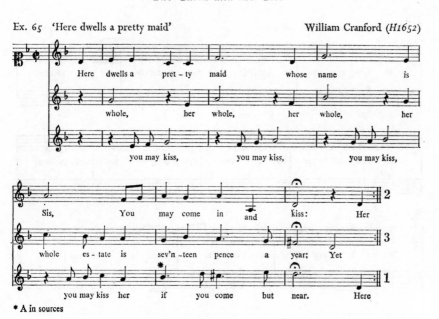

* A in sources

Glees were the lineal descendants of the three- and four-part ayres of Campion, Jones and other Elizabethan songwriters. Most were adaptations of solo songs, the actual process of adaptation rarely being a sophisticated one. The top part usually remained undisturbed, unless to permit some slight independence of movement in the other parts, in which case rests might be introduced or notes lengthened. Sometimes the style was simplified in order to bring it into line with the *cantus secundus*. Henry Lawes' partsong arrangement of 'If my mistress fix her eye' (*L1653*) shows modifications along these lines when compared with the manuscript solo version (*A*). Though a few of the differences may, in fact, represent an updating of the style—the F sharp in the first bar of the bass in the 1653 version, for example—others are clearly the result of converting a solo song into a partsong. The solo version's subtler declamation of 'ruder lines of mine' (bb. 3–4) has been ironed out in the interest of equality between the voices, half a bar's rest has been inserted between the lines of the final couplet (b. 10) to permit an anticipatory imitation of the phrase

Ex. 66a 'If my mistress fix her eye'   Henry Lawes (♩)

Ex. 66b 'If my mistress fix her eye'   Henry Lawes (*L1653*)

'can release', and the final cadence has been expanded by half a bar, partly to readjust the rhythmic structure as a result of the previous interpolation, and partly to make a more impressive end, with 7–6 and 3–4–3 progressions suited to a three-voiced texture. The singing bass mostly follows the thorough bass, dividing the bass simply according to its verbal rhythm, but sometimes ornamenting it with passing notes, as at 'on those ruder' and 'how I lie' (Ex. 66).

This is as much, if not more modification than is usual, especially in triple-time ayres or straightforward ones in common time. For, in general, elaborate imitative writing was entirely absent from the glee. Tuneful homophony prevailed and the *secundus* part moved for much of the time in parallel thirds, sixths or tenths with one of the other parts. Ungainly jumps in the inner part were by no means uncommon, as were consecutive fifths and other progressions which would normally have been considered faulty. It should be remembered that few song writers of the mid-century had undergone rigorous theoretical training; they were first and foremost practical musicians and no doubt effective performance justified a good deal of careless writing. Even in the case of a skilful polyphonist like William Lawes there is little or no contrapuntal interest in his glees.

There is, however, a species of imitative partsong deriving from the madrigal rather than the ayre that does not conform to the general style of the glee. Settings of sacred lyrics in manuscript (*Ch.Ch.736–8*) by Thomas Ford and John Jenkins have sufficient overlapping counterpoint from phrase to phrase not to require a continuo.[7] Similar secular pieces, such as Lanier's 'Sweet, sweet do not thus destroy me' (*Ch,Ch,17*) and Richard Dering's 'Sleep quiet Lee' (*Ch.Ch.747–9*) link up with the canzonet tradition (Ex. 67).

In contrast to this rather conservative technique Walter Porter's *Madrigales and Ayres* (1632) contains three-part continuo madrigals with the baroque idea of paired high voices over a continuo very much in evidence.[8]

Ex. 67 'Sweet do no thus destroy me'   Nicholas Lanier (Ch.Ch.17)

Comparatively few secular pieces seem to have been written in this style in England during the first half of the seventeenth century, though the metrical psalm settings of John Wilson, and Henry Lawes are influenced by it. Sacred or secular, they provide evidence of the current declamatory principles applied to contrapuntal writing. Sometimes rapid parlando gives way to more sustained vocal writing, just as violinistic passage work changes to broader movement in the varied texture of the early seventeenth-century sonata. Indeed, we find the sonata's sectionalization in such songs as William Caesar's 'Welcome, welcome, to the grove' (*P1653*) or 'Musick, thou queen of souls' (*Ibid.*). (Perhaps for that reason they should be called cantatas, though the term will be reserved for sectionalized solo vocal works.)

'Musick, thou queen of souls' starts with all three voices in broad homophonic style later breaking into simple imitations in which the *cantus primus* leads the other two voices. Were it not for the words it could well be the opening section of a canzona by an early Baroque composer (Ex 68a). The next

Ex. 68a 'Music thou Queen of Souls' (Randolph)   William Caesar (P1659)

Ex. 68b (Ibid.)

Ex. 68c (Ibid.)

section is in concertato style, much more varied in texture (Ex 68b). Then each voice has a solo. The final chorus is closely imitative, but at the words 'strike a sad note' (marked '*Slow*') the expression becomes affective, though decorum is re-established for the final cadence (Ex 68c).

Evidently this kind of duet (or trio) takes itself a good deal more seriously than the glee, and its appeal must have been limited. It did not have many practitioners immediately after the Restoration, though some of Henry Bowman's *Songs* (1677) are of this type. But the technique continued in the duos and trios of verse anthems and court odes, and towards the end of the century the form was revived by Purcell and Blow—to what good effect may be judged by instancing Purcell's 'Elegy on the Death of Queen Mary' ('*O dives custos*').

As a compendium of the popular partsong repertory during the Commonwealth and early Restoration period, the 'loose Papers' thrown before the Old Jewry Music Club (and the store from which the second part of *The Musical Companion* was culled) are extremely interesting.[10] They comprise four part-books (*primus, secundus, bassus* and *continuo*) containing in all 100 surviving items. The most frequently represented com-posers are Henry Lawes (13), Playford (11) and Wilson (8), with Isaac Blackwell, Thomas Brewer, William Caesar, Ed-ward Coleman, Richard Dering, John Goodgroome, George Holmes, Simon Ives, John Jenkins, Nicholas Lanier, William Lawes, Matthew Locke, Thomas Pierce, Ben Rogers, Jeremy Savile, Thomas Tempest and William Webb each with two or more items. (Playford's disproportionate representation is explained by the fact that he was a member of the club and the compiler of the manuscript; other members included Savile and Tempest.)

Some of the pieces are described as Hymns—Blackwell's '*Laudate Dominum*', Brewer's '*Gloria tribuatur Deo*', and Locke's 'Behold how good a thing' and 'Praise our Lord'. Others, such as Morley's 'Now is the month of maying' and Campion's 'If love loves truth' go right back to the early part of the century.

Dering's five partsongs are also characteristic of an earlier period, and are, in fact, versions of Italian *canzonette* which he published in Antwerp in 1620.[10] Some of the songs are royalist in sentiment while others cover all moods and tastes from the debauched to the exquisite.

A few have remained popular to the present day. 'Man's life is but vain' and 'Gather ye rosebuds' by the elder and younger Lawes brothers respectively are quite well known, and Edward Coleman's 'The glories of our birth and state' likewise survives on the strength of its poem. But for a last look at the repertory we may turn to three songs actually composed by members of the Club. Playford's 'Comely swain' at once echoes the fa-la's of a bygone age and even retains a certain freshness while showing the decline, especially in technique, which such writing had suffered.

Ex. 69 'Comely swain why sit'st thou so'   John Playford (*U*)

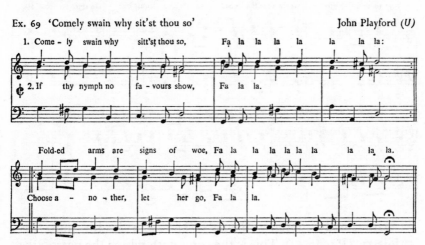

Beside this may be set a serious piece by Thomas Tempest. Despite a certain awkwardness (such as coming back to G minor at the start of each couplet, thus seeming never to get anywhere) 'Sweet Music' has some feeling and even Purcellian turns of phrase to recommend it. The dependence on progressions of thirds between the upper parts characteristic of the glee is here clearly seen, and serves to underline the essentially tuneful nature of the form and the dispensibility of the secundus part.

Ex. 70 'Sweet music'   Thomas Tempest (*U*)

And finally, Jeremy Savile's 'Here's a health unto his Majesty' (*P1667, U*). This is the song with which the partbooks of Playford's Club begin, and thus it may have served as a kind of anthem or loyal toast at meetings even before the Restoration. Among the list of members written in the bass part is 'Mr. Jeremy Savile Gent', but his absence from the list printed in *The Musical Companion* (1667) suggests that he may have died the previous year in the plague. For the record here is Savile's original version as found in the opening pages of the manuscript.

Part four

Songs
of the restoration court
and stage

7 Ayres and songs sung at court...

King Charles II was restored to the throne and the theatres officially reopened in 1660. One company was under the patronage of the King (and managed by Tom Killigrew); the other was under the patronage of the Duke of York (and managed by Will Davenant). Both found it difficult to fill their theatres. For Restoration Drama lacked the strong popular support that the Elizabethan and Jacobean theatre had enjoyed. In comedy and tragedy it catered for an aristocratic audience, for the world of fashion, wit and gallantry.[1] Nothing apparently could commend a new collection of songs better than '*BEING* Most of the Newest SONGS sung at *Court*, and at the Publick *THEATRES.*'

This, in fact, is the subtitle borne by Playford's *Choice Songs and Ayres*, begun in 1673 and continued in five books up to 1684. (The first edition was revised and enlarged in 1675 and 1676; thereafter each book contained a new selection of songs.) Playford gives an interesting running commentary on the hopes and disappointments attendant on the series in his prefaces. In the end 'Age, and the Infirmities of Nature' compelled him to hand over to his son Henry, who (with Richard Carr at first) took up the torch in *The Theater of Music*, four books appearing between 1685 and 1687. Then in 1688 began *The Banquet of Musick* with six books issued up to 1692. Meanwhile John Carr (with Samuel Scott) launched his own series: *Comes Amoris* (five books between 1687 and 1694) and *Vinculum Societatis* (three books between 1687 and 1691). Yet another publisher, John Hudgebut, entered the market in 1693 with *Thesaurus Musicus* (five books up to 1696). Not to be outdone,

Henry Playford returned to the field with an altogether superior collection of songs entitled *Deliciae Musicae* (two composite volumes, 1695–96). Another series, *Mercurius Musicus*, appeared monthly between 1699 and 1701.[2]

As a reflection of the prevailing taste and the way it changed, the *Choice Ayres* series may be followed through successive issues spread over more than a decade—a decade in which Purcell entered the arena and participated in the change that came over English song. During the 70's the triple-time air, modelled on the rhythm and form of the dance, reached the peak of its popularity. By then the tuneful song in common time had been largely emancipated from declamatory bondage; soon it moved from a position of marked inferiority in comparison with the triple-time air to one of superiority. *Choice Ayres* confirms this trend, for triple-time songs outnumber those in common time by roughly four to one in the 1676 edition, whereas by 1684 there are half as many more in common time than triple time. Apart from the fickleness of taste the explanation may lie in the fact that by then triple time had served its evolutionary purposes, for through it the rhythmic, periodic and harmonic organization of dance music had been carried over into vocal music, in due course establishing autonomous principles of musical composition. Thus the stylized rhythms, symmetrical phrasing and harmonically ordered cadences that are the substructure of binary dance music came to provide a musical rather than a literary basis for song setting, whether in triple or common time.

The formalistic nature of the Restoration lyric was itself conducive to this development. For the age of Dryden was a classical period in which polished regularity became one of the principal technical aims of poetry. This new ideal found its most typical expression in the heroic couplet, rhyming and stopped; a powerful vehicle for lofty or satirical themes but ill suited to song. As a result, artificiality of feeling affected lyric forms so that correctness and ornament replaced the fervour and metaphysical conceits of an earlier generation.

The Earl of Rochester alone came closest to equalling the best of Charles I's court poets. But of verses with a claim to literary merit, Dryden's outnumber the rest when it comes to musical settings. Day and Murrie list 62, mainly playsongs.[3] Playsongs also account for a high proportion, and sometimes all, of Shadwell's (40), Settle's (38), Lee's (23) and Tate's (19), while the courtier poets, Etherege (16), Rochester (15) and Sedley (13) lag behind. Even then, most of Etherege's and a handful of Rochester's and Sedley's were playsongs.

However, the distinction between songs set independently and for the theatre is artificial. Apart from the fact that play-songs were often furnished with instrumental ritornellos, there is virtually no difference between them on the technical level; simple metrical and rhyming schemes predominate in both, while on the expressive level pastoral symbolism served a universal purpose. Could anything seemingly be more ridiculous (and at the same time symptomatic) than Abdalla courting Lyndaraxa in Dryden's *Conquest of Granada, Part I* (1670), to the following song:

> *Wherever I am, or whatever I do,*
> *My Phyllis is still in my mind;*
> *When angry, I mean not to Phyllis to go;*
> *My feet of themselves the way find . . .*

(The setting is by Alfonso Marsh in *P1673a*).[4] That such piffle could be anything but incongruous in an heroic tragedy dealing with the struggle of Christians and Moors in Spain seems laughable now, but it testifies to the strength of the convention. Polish rather than passion was the aim, and reading through the poems of Rochester and his cronies, it is only too obvious how often their lovers are shepherds and shepherdesses (and how the moral tone of Whitehall seems to prevail in Arcadia too). No wonder Dorset objected:

> *Methinks the poor Town has been troubled too long,*
> *With Phyllis and Chloris in every song:*

By fools, who at once can both Love and despair;
And will never leave calling them Cruel and Fair.
Which justly provokes me in Rhyme to express,
The truth that I know of Bonny Black Bess.

This Bess of my Heart, this Bess of my Soul,
Has a skin white as milk, but hair black as coal;
She's plump, yet with ease you may span round her Waste,
But her round swelling thighs can scarce be embrac'd:
Her belly is soft, not a word of the rest;
But I know what I mean, when I drink to the best.

though no doubt it was all the same in the end whether Mrs.
Barnes was called Black Bess or Phyllis.[5]

One poet seemed to answer the need of those who desired
something more profound from the lyric muse, and though
'profound' is not perhaps the first word that springs to mind at
the mention of Cowley—still less of the aptly named Thomas
Flatman who also enjoyed some esteem—the contrast with
Rochester and his circle is obvious. True, Cowley belonged to
another generation, an older one; nevertheless he remained in
fashion a long time after the metaphysical school had been dis-
credited, and his 'Pindaric' vein appealed to those composers
who wanted verse they could get their teeth into. His lyrics
were, at least, of serious import, elevated in diction and
imagery. He is approached with reverential awe by almost
everyone, particularly, it seems, by a number of composers
living in Oxford, among whom William King (*K1668*), Henry
Bowman (*B1677*) and Pietro Reggio (*R1680*) published collections of songs almost exclusively devoted to his work. He was
by no means forgotten by Blow and Purcell; the latter setting
his verse on 16 occasions.

However tedious the pastoral convention of the courtiers, it
has to be admitted that their metrical regularity and super-
ficiality of sentiment are conducive to the emergence of the
purely musical (or abstract) qualities of song, in which bal-

anced and melodious phrase structure is all important. Obviously four or eight-line stanzas are prone naturally to binary
division, poetically and musically, and it is easy to see that the
prevailing four-foot line of English lyric poetry must accommodate itself naturally to the four-bar phrase.

It is equally obvious how close this symmetry of structure
brings us to dance music. Thus, it is not surprising that the
rhythms of popular dances like the courant, saraband and jig,
should affect vocal music. Without doubt their characteristic
rhythms are much in evidence among triple-time airs; the
hemiolas of the courant, the feminine cadences of the saraband,
and the lively triplet movement of the jig. Many examples
might be given, but the whole matter is made explicit in a song
cycle by William Gregory which actually takes the form of a
suite of dances. Under the title 'CORIDON *and* PHILLIS, *or
the* Cautious Lover' (*P1683*), the songs are labelled *Almain,
Courant, Saraband* and *Jigg* in order. Beyond a common tonality
there is no linking device between these four songs, but the
poems themselves describe successive stages in the courtship of
Coridon and Phyllis. In the almain ('To love and like, and not
succeed') the shepherd first becomes aware of his love for
Phyllis; in the courant ('At length in musing what to do') Love
instructs him; in the saraband ('Coridon met Phyllis fair') he
declares his love, while in the jig ('Then we'll join hand in
hand') the lovers celebrate their innocent delight in country
pleasures.

The almain is in declamatory style, and shows that even this
kind of vocal writing relates to the dance (Ex. 72a). The courant retains the rhythmic ambiguity of six beats to the bar,
divided sometimes into three and sometimes into two in a way
which imparts vigour though tending to maul the accentuation
of the verse (Ex. 72b). On the other hand, the saraband and jig
are rhythmically straightforward. Most triple-time songs of the
period approximate to one or the other; the more sentimental
to the saraband, the more lively to the jig. This is precisely the
case here; the blandly flowing air of the saraband subsiding in

feminine cadences (Ex. 72c), whereas the tune of the jig skips along matching triple-metre verse with triple-metre music (Ex. 72).

Ex. 72a 'To love and like, and not succeed'   William Gregory (P1683)
Almain.

To love   and like,   and not suc-ceed,   Such pas-sions in the mind do   breed; [etc.]

Ex. 72b 'At length, in musing what to do'
Courant. *Second Part:*

At   length, in mus - ing what to   do,   Love un- der   took to show the way to   woo; [etc.]

Ex. 72c 'Coridon met Phyllis fair'
Saraband. *Third Part:*

Co - ri -don met   Phyl - lis fair   close by   a   ri - ver-side   [etc.]

Ex. 72d 'Then we'll join hand in hand'
Jigg. *Fourth Part:*

Then we'll   join hand , in   hand,   and   walk o'er   the   down, [etc.]

Although these dance-songs are as idiomatic as one could find in any instrumental set, not every song can be related to a specific dance model. This said, however, the 'balletic' quality of many songs cannot be mistaken. Take away the words and what is left is dance music.

The dance, then, brought two principles of autonomous structure to English song in the Restoration period: 'strains' of regular length balancing each other and, underlying this formal articulation, a tonal scheme increasingly committed to the principle of tonic-dominant polarity and the circle of related keys and chords each separated from each other by a fifth. This was not entirely a new thing, of course, but by now the tonal system with its harmonic relationships defining key and modulation from one key to another had crystalized into its classical form. And since we find it at its clearest and simplest in binary dance movements, naturally we find it in songs which are related in style and form to dance music.

Isaac Blackwell's 'Give me thy youth' (*P1681*) comes to hand as a simple example of a song divided into two equal halves, with a dominant cadence in the middle. Indeed, it reflects many of the stylistic traits already noted, and can be regarded from all points of view as an average specimen of its type. The stanzas are composed of eight lines (86.86/86.86) rhyming alternately, with the main division occurring at the end of the fourth line, and sub-divisions at the end of the second and sixth. The melody is 16 bars long, the principal cadence falling at the eighth bar in the dominant, the other cadences (corresponding with couplets) at the fourth and twelfth bars—both half closes on the dominant. Regular phrase formation could hardly be more clearly demonstrated, and it is worth looking closer at the actual chords to see what an important part the circle of fifths plays in the harmonic structure. (In the example below, progressions with either the bass or the root falling a fifth are bracketed together.) The second half of the song in particular is seen to be absolutely dominated by this phenomenon (Ex. 73).

Longer and more elaborate stanza forms naturally lead to greater elaboration of phrase structure. Even so, two or three major divisions usually appear, sometimes displaying contrast of movement and metre between them. Frequently a third division, often in triple time, functions as a kind of chorus or

Ex. 73 'Give me thy youth'   Isaac Blackwell (P1681)

Give me thy youth, the time of love, The now that's in thy pow'r; I'll
fall on thee like migh - ty Jove, In love a nob - ler show'r. My
thoughts shall still be fix'd on thee, With love thy love re - ceive; Un - con - stant then, and
fic-kle be, If love will give you leave.

coda. Sectionalization such as this may be even more pronounced in non-strophic songs where an irregular almost
Pindaric verse structure requires the poem to be through-set.
In the repertoire of court and theatre there are comparatively
few of these, nevertheless occasional songs are encountered in
which semi-declamatory and tuneful triple-time sections are
placed in apposition, without showing quite that degree of
separation and contrast qualifying them to be regarded as
'recitative' and 'air'. This 'double-barrelled' form becomes
more common later in the century, Humfrey's 'Cupid once
when weary grown' (P1679)—to be examined more closely in
a moment—is an example. At a later date the sections may
increase in number, each assuming the proportions and structural features of short songs. The resulting chain may be

termed 'cantata' by analogy with the equivalent Italian form and its instrumental parallel the 'sonata'. In the works of Blow and Purcell we find a significant treatment of this type of extended vocal composition. So too with ground basses, examples of which are both rare and generally feeble outside the works of these two composers.

Blow and Purcell must indeed be considered apart from their contemporaries if for no other reason than to allow the minor figures to come out of the shadow. But before taking a closer look at them, it may be as well to summarize briefly the general development of English song during the 20-year Restoration period. At first, as we have seen, the triple-time song showing dance influence was dominant, as indeed it was in France and Italy at the same time. Charles II's own personal taste was *à la mode* in this respect and no doubt was influential. As North observed:

> and for songs he approved onely the soft vein, such as might be called a step tripla, and that made a fashion among the masters, and for the stage, as may be seen in the printed books of the songs of that time.[6]

But in the 1680's its supremacy was on the wane. For with principles of musical self-sufficiency established, new developments in melody could occur. Instead of relying on the pattern of words as a *raison d'être*, melodic composition was able to function on the basis of an underlying tonal structure. The old-style declamatory ayre did not survive the period of triple-time dominance; in its place emerged a robust forthright ballad style, as found typically in the songs of Thomas Farmer and many lesser composers (and, indeed, continuing right up to the time of Dibdin in the late 18th century and beyond). This rather blunt manner is well illustrated in some of Nicholas Staggins' songs; for example, 'As Amoret with Phyllis sat' (*P1679*) from Etherege's *Man of Mode* (*1676*).

Ex. 74 'As Amoret with Phyllis sat' (Etheridge)   Nicholas Staggins (P1679)

*Possibly C

Towards the middle of the 1680's a more graceful idiom
appeared, tending in one direction to the merely elegant (for
example, in the flowing quavers found in many of the songs of
Turner and King), in another to a more highly mannered
style, found in some of Hart's songs, for example and much
more strikingly in Blow's and Purcell's. Within a few years
the influence of Purcell himself was dominant. The opening
of Moses Snow's 'When you have broke that tender loyal
heart' (P1687) may be taken as typical of a vein which many
composers tapped again and again.

Ex. 75 'When you have broke that tender loyal heart'   Moses Snow (P1687)

The normal accompanying instrument for these songs was
the theorbo or theorbo-lute, though title-pages offer the bass
viol as an alternative and, increasingly later on, the harpsichord
(though Playford had included it as a possibility as early as
1652). The guitar, too, was popular and Pepys and Evelyn
refer to them all as accompanying instruments in their diaries.
It depended very much upon what was available and more
often than not this was some sort of lute. Mace observed:

the Theorboe-Lute is Principally us'd in Playing to the Voice, or in Consort; It being a Lute of the Largest Scize; and we make It much more Large in sound, by contriving unto *It a Long Head, to Augment and Increase that Sound, and Fulness of the Basses, or Diapasons, which are a great Ornament to the Voice, or Consort.*[7]

and went on to show how a bass could be realised, '*Amplifying* your *Play,* by *Breaking* your *Parts,* or *Stops,* in way of *Dividing-Play* upon *Cadences, or Closes*'.[8] The elaboration of a single bass line into a harmonic texture appropriate to the instrument was an ideal which perhaps not many attained to, but clearly it was not to be ruled out (see p. 216).

We are dealing with two generations, or waves, of composers. The first grew to maturity during the Commonwealth period and burst into print in the last of Playford's *Select Ayres* (1669) and the first of *Choice Ayres* (1673), actually called *Choice Songs and Ayres* for this single edition. It included such men as John Banister, William Gregory, the precocious Pelham Humfrey, Matthew Lock, Alfonso Marsh and Robert Smith. And while they held the stage, the next group—Thomas Farmer, James Hart, Robert King, William Turner, and, of course, John Blow and Henry Purcell—were coming up.

Probably the foremost song composer of the first group was Pelham Humfrey,[9] though his best known song, 'I pass all my hours in a shady old grove' (*P1673a*)—the words supposedly by Charles II, hence its reputation as a curiosity—is a very ordinary piece; no better and no worse than hundreds of other songs in triple-time written at this period. Smith and Marsh too were fluent song writers, though more limited in range. Banister, though he lacked their polish, made up for it with a more direct and homely style. Unfortunately his musical language is uncouth at times. In general, they were all addicted to the short, strophic, triple-time air, though not without a backward glance at the declamatory style of the previous generation in their comparatively rare common-time songs. We find the two styles side by side in Humphrey's 'Cupid once when weary grown' (*P1679*) which is in two sections; a declamatory opening followed by a tuneful conclusion. Cupid's complaint in the first part recalls the declamatory style of Lawes, especially the affected nuances and inflections of the vocal line, though the stronger tonal motivation in the harmonic treatment gives it a more up-to-date flavour. Then as Venus replies the music slips into a graceful triple time. All in all, the piece is quite delicious.

Ex. 76   from 'Cupid once when weary grown'   Pelham Humphrey (*P1679*)

Smith, Marsh and Banister are less accomplished song writers, and their work has a more popular air, which no doubt recommended it to theatre audiences. Their play-songs typify one aspect of their output; what, for want of a better word, may be called their 'galant' style—trifling triple-time airs. Marsh is at the same time the most polished and insipid composer of the three, and may be seen fairly typically in his setting of Dryden's 'After the pangs of a desperate lover' (*P1673a*)

Ex. 77 'Farewell fair Armida' (Dryden) Robert Smith (*P1676*)

from *An Evening's Love* (1668).[10] Smith can write as pleasingly, but he offers more life and variety too. Among his Dryden settings, for example, there is the ballad-like 'Farewell fair Armida' (*P1673a*), the saraband 'Long betwixt hope and fear' (*Ibid.*) from *The Assignation* (1672), and the declamatory epithalamium 'The day you wished arrived at last' (*Ibid.*) from *Amboyna* (1673).[11] The stylistic range here is quite wide, and because he attempts more than Marsh it is not surprising that

Ex. 78 'Dry those eyes which are o'erflowing' (Davenant/Dryden: *The Tempest*)

John Banister (*P1675b*)

Dry those eyes which are o'er-flow-ing, All your storms are o-ver blow-ing;

While you it this isle are bid-ing, You shall feast with-out pro-vid-ing:

Ev'-ry dain-ty you can think of, Ev'-ry wine which you would drink of,

Shall be yours; all want shall shun you, Ce-res bless-ing so light on you.

•.E♭ in source

occasionally he over-reaches himself, or does not quite get the effect he is after. Indeed, there are some of what Burney might have regarded as crudities in each of these songs; for example, the delightful slip to the key of the flat seventh in line six of 'Farewell fair Armida' spoiled by an awkward bar following (Ex. 77).

Much the same is true of Banister, a clumsier writer than Smith with more talent for instrumental than for song composition.[12] But there is no mistaking a vigorous musical personality in the courant-like 'Beneath a myrtle shade' (*P1673a*) sung in Dryden's *Conquest of Granada, Part I* (1670), though his lack of imagination is seen in the setting of 'Dry those eyes' (*P1675*) written for the 1667 version of *The Tempest*, which

Ex. *79* 'Oh! do not wrong that face' William Gregory (P*1683*)

does nothing to alleviate the rhythmic monotony of the verse (Ex. 78).[13]

Among the lesser song writers of this time a few others rate a mention, notably Roger Hill and John Moss, both of whom inherit the idiom of Henry Lawes and Charles Coleman, but cannot be completely dismissed as untalented imitators.

More interesting than most of those already mentioned is William Gregory, whose solo songs are particularly worth attention.[14] It is true that his tuneful airs are nothing out of the ordinary, but he does offer interest and variety in other directions. He seems to have had no association with the theatres whatever, and in his settings favoured Thomas Flatman more than any other poet. This is consistent with the impression we get of a worthy, yet trifle dull musician who probably disapproved of the thinly veiled (if not naked) eroticism that was current, though he was not above setting a drinking catch or the innocent 'Dear Jockey's gone to the wood' to 'A Scotch Ayre' (*P1679*)—one of the earliest in a vogue for 'Scotch' songs which gathered force in the 1680's. By contrast his sophisticated galant style is seen at its best in his setting of Flatman's 'O do not wrong that face' (*P1683*). It provides a good example of how triple time, syncopated after the manner of a courant or saraband, adapts to heroic couplets. By running two bars of 3/4 together and alternating 6/4 with 3/2 the first foot (with iambic stress often reversed) begins on the second half of a 6/4 bar, the ensuing accents falling on the strong-beats of a 3/2 bar, and the final stress on the downbeat of the next 6/4 bar—the next line taking over on the second half of the bar and the process repeating from there. Thus within a four-bar phrase we get three syllables to the bar without misaccenting alternate feet (Ex. 79).

It is an effect both simple and subtle, though this is not to deny that there are blemishes in the song. The new rhythm at the beginning of line four disturbs the established pattern a bit too radically perhaps, even though it is caused by a shift in the verbal accentuation. And the bass, though reasonably sound harmonically, clings too closely to the melody; it would gain in strength if it moved more independently. Yet there are some felicities of melody, harmony and rhythm, best illustrated by the eloquent last line.

At the other stylistic extreme we find him quite a polished declamatist. Certain other Flatman settings may be mentioned in this connexion. 'When Coridon a slave did lie' (*P1673a*) is one of those 'double-barrelled' songs that open with a declamatory stanza and close with a tuneful one. The contrast in mood between Coridon's melancholy in the first, and his light-heartedness in the second is nicely pointed in these parallel passages from each stanza (Ex. 80).

Other settings of the same poet include the Pastoral 'O Delia, for I know 'tis she' (*P1675/6*) which, apart from the concluding chorus, is declamatory throughout, and the elegy on the death of Pelham Humfrey ('Did you not hear that hideous groan' *P1681*). These and other works such as the 'Pastoral Song upon a Ground' ('Come, come away, let's to the maypole go', (*P1679*) and his song-cycle dance-suite already discussed, create an impression of a composer of

Ex. 80a from 'When Coridon a slave did lie' (Flatman)   William Gregory (*P1676*)

taste and talent, and somewhat aloof. He is versatile, and whether he writes gallant tuneful airs or pastorals in the declamatory style he shows refinement of sensibility as well as technique.

An even more isolated figure is William King, whose *Songs and Ayres*, mostly settings of Cowley, were published at Oxford in 1668. Bearing in mind the special character of Cowley's verse it is not surprising that this collection should be so different and eschew the tuneful influence of the dance almost entirely. Though settings are often strophic the style is declamatory, suggesting Purcell rather than Lawes however.

167

Ex. 81 'I wonder what those lovers mean' (Cowley)   William King (K1668)

The suppleness of his line seems to mark him off from his contemporaries and foreshadow the younger composer. Perhaps it is his integral use of ornament together with the device of syncopated underlay that brings such flexibility to his word setting. The opening of 'I wonder what those lovers mean' illustrates these points; with elevation and backfall on 'wonder' and underlay beginning the syllable before the musical stress—a madrigalist's device which Purcell made use of (Ex. 81).

Another feature of his declamation is his occasional willingness to expand on certain key words and vary the pace generally, thus bringing greater freedom to what otherwise would be a rigid declamatory pattern. Usually the words are those with pictorial connotations that translate easily into musical figures, and it was no doubt one of the attractions of Cowley as a poet that he often used them. The treatment is on the whole quite modest. From the opening couplet of the first song

Ex. 82 'No! to what purpose should I speak' (Cowley)   William King (K1668)

in the book, the phrase 'swell till you break' provides an
example, although there are others more extravagant (Ex. 82).
To the present group of composers we should also add

Ex. 83 from 'In a soft vision of the night' (Flatman)   Matthew Locke (*P1679*)

169

Matthew Locke, though if we come to Locke's songs expecting a wealth of great things we shall be disappointed. Indeed, he is hardly represented in the miscellanies at all. Even so, at least two items are notable—Marvell's dialogue 'When death shall part us' (*P1675*) and the recitative *Urania to Parthenissa* ('In a soft vision of the night', *P1679*). The latter is

Ex. 84   from 'When death shall part us' (Marvell)   Matthew Locke (*P1676*)

among the best specimens of 'Recitative Musick' before Purcell. In some ways it brings Lanier's *Hero and Leander* to mind, not so much the incident dramatized—Urania's vision of the dead Parthenissa in a dream—as the musical language itself. Considering how far the words are from having real dramatic power (Flatman again!) Locke brings intensity and something like true pathos to his setting (Ex. 83).

Other examples of recitative songs are few in this period, though Robert Smith demonstrates a modest talent in *The Storm* ('Hark, hark, the storm grows loud', *P1673a*) somewhat indebted to similar works of Henry Lawes. Outside opera it was in the pastoral elegy and dialogue that recitative was mainly used. So far as the pastoral dialogue went it was an enfeebled tradition, yet in 'When death shall part us' (*P1675*) Locke brings deep emotion almost for the first time to this species of song. So desirable does Elizium seem that the lovers Thirsis and Dorinda make a suicide pact in order to be together and taste its joys.

> *Then let us give Clorillo charge o' th' sheep,*
> *And thou and I'll pick poppies, and then steep*
> *In Wine, and drink on't even till we Weep;*
> *So shall we smoothly pass away in Sleep.*

There is more sentimentality than drama in the situation, yet Locke extracts what there is in the concluding dialogue of the lovers. Chromaticism and impassioned declamation make it truly affecting as the following exchanges show (Ex. 84).

This then is the first generation of Restoration song composers. Collectively they demonstrate some continuing attachment to the older declamatory idiom but a much greater predilection for the triple-time tuneful air. The influence of the dance is clear. Sentiments are gallant and expressed through pastoral symbolism; yet each cultivates the convention differently. Humfrey displays real feeling and refinement of taste; Gregory too, though in comparison his style is less polished. Among the men of the theatre Marsh can write an elegant tune and a competent bass without transcending the merely polite; Bannister suffers from the opposite complaint, yet for all his ungainliness makes a more positive impression. Smith combines the virtues and vices of both, and demonstrates a wider technical range. But each in his own way conforms to the current fashion. Locke, by ignoring it, stands out all the more strongly.

The next group of composers are contemporaries of Blow and Purcell. The leaders among them—Thomas Farmer, James Hart, Robert King and William Turner—were prolific and not without talent. Farmer, perhaps, is least interesting, Turner and King are agreeable melodists, while Hart is both less and more than that. His early songs are unremarkable and follow Humfrey and Smith in their preference for triple time. But gradually he broadens his range. Common-time songs become more frequent and we begin to get sectional through-set songs (cantatas) and idioms of harmonic and melodic progression that we recognize as Purcellian; for example, in the disjunct

Ex. 85   from 'While Chloe full of harmless thoughts'   James Hart (*P1679*)

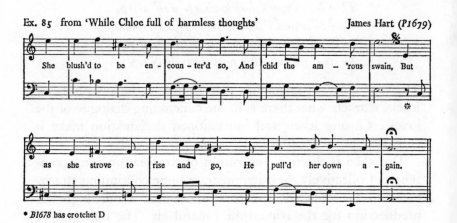

She blush'd to be en - coun - ter'd so, And chid the am - 'rous swain, But as she strove to rise and go, He pull'd her down a - gain.

* *B1678* has crotchet D

vocal line and frequent leaps of diminished intervals, as well as the false relations and dotted rhythms which characterize even a light song such as 'While Chloe full of harmless thoughts' (*B1678*) (Ex. 85).

In the 1680's Hart shows increasing interest in the sectional form of the cantata. The sections themselves are brief, and there is little or no attempt at recitative beyond a rather stiff, quasi-declamatory style. Thus, force of contrast between sections is lacking, and though he may alternate minor and major, common and triple time, this goes only a little way towards realizing and clearly defining the dramatic stages of a poem.

In 'How oft did love' (*P1687*) the argument—related as a monologue—concerns the revenge Love takes on Strephon for rebuffing him so often, and the Shepherd's subsequent discovery of the pleasures he has been missing. The crucial moment is thus the moment of Strephon's first experience of love, in effect, his seduction, yet the music at that point is utterly perfunctory (Ex. 86).

It is not difficult to imagine what Purcell would have made of these words, but Hart seems strangely impotent. It follows that with such a negligible emotional impact here, there can be no release in the concluding dance-like section and thus the inner necessity as against the outward convention of the cantata is utterly thwarted.

Ex. 86   from 'How oft did love assault'   James Hart (*P1687*)

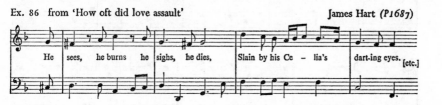

It is, of course, easy to criticize a composer like Hart using Purcell as a standard—easy and not particularly valuable. Looking at his songs as a whole (and at their own level) they show a certain individuality despite material which is in the common idiom of the day and could be by almost anyone, including Purcell. Even so, the impression which forms is of a composer less inhibited than most of his fellows. His melodic style is not so graceful, yet its harsher countours suggest a more vital appreciation of the expressive capabilities of the vocal line. This at least brings him closer to Purcell than the others we are considering.

Thomas Farmer forms a nice antithesis. He shows a penchant for sober common time and basically stodgy movement. He may be the more correct composer, but he is duller. His unsophisticated tunefulness reminds one of John Wilson, though even his playsongs are more like hymns than ballads. At his best one recognizes a certain grave simplicity that can be quite moving, but unfortunately this is a rare quality, and one which lies dangerously close to tediousness. A song like 'Phyllis whose heart was unconfin'd' (*P1683*) from Aphra Behn's *The Rover, Part II* (1681) illustrates his moderate virtues at the same time revealing his endemic rhythmic dullness (Ex. 87).

William Turner is a similar composer; musicianly but rather colourless. Unlike Farmer his vocal line is often smoothly

Ex. 87 'Phyllis, whose heart was unconfined' (Behn)   Thomas Farmer. (*P1683*)

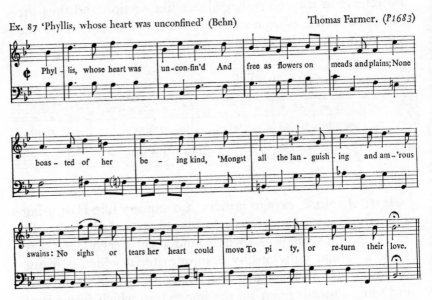

flowing and this gives a veneer of elegance, though his simpering quavers pall after a time. Still, this kind of song belongs to the same tradition as Purcell's second setting of 'If music be the food of love' (*C1693*); in fact, there are more than general resemblances between the two as the following excerpts make clear (Ex. 88).

Still more polished is Robert King, who must rank next below Purcell as a songwriter in this period. He is represented in the anthologies from 1684 onwards and is especially pleasing

Ex. 88a 'Ah! what can mean that eager joy' (Behn)   William Turner (*P1683*)

Ex. 88b 'If music be the food of love' (Hevingham) Henry Purcell (*C1693*)

Ex. 88c *(Ibid.)*

in the flowing common-time song of the sort we have just observed. With some reason he seems to have considered himself a cut above the usual run of contributors to the miscellanies. In order to do himself justice he had two books of songs engraved in 1692 and 1695 (?). As he stated in the preface to the first collection:

Haveing observ'd that most of my former Songs in the Common Printed Books about Town were not only imperfect but in a very bad CARACTER, feareing least these should meet with the same Fate, I was willing to publish them my self . . .

It contains songs for two and three voices as well as solos. In style they are smooth and elegant, tonally stable but rather

Ex. 89 'Die wretched lover, Damon cry'd'   Robert King (*K1692*)

anaemic. One of the best is the ground bass 'Die wretched lover, Damon cried' which begins very promisingly though it fails to develop as Purcell's do, by means of fragmenting the vocal line and phrase repetition. Despite its inhibitions it is a touching song nevertheless and suggests that King had some acquaintance with the suave *bel canto* of mid-century Italian composers. Indeed he says as much when he claims:

I have imitated the ITALIANS in their manner of ARIET-TAS; who for there EXCELLENCE in VOCAL MUSICK are (in my Judgment) the best PATERNS . . .

The contents of his *Second Booke of Songs* are a trifle more ambitious, and more florid in style. Among them is a Pastoral Elegy on the death of Queen Mary in several sections, including recitative, air and chamber duet. But even here there is surprisingly little deepening of the expressive language beyond conventional Italianate idioms picked up from composers such as Stradella.

Ex. 90a   from 'A PASTORALL ELEGY on . . . Queen Mary'   Robert King (*K1695*)

Ex. 90b *(Ibid.)*

177

What is so obviously lacking in the songs of King, as of the others, is fibre, strength and depth of feeling. In contrast, certain less technically competent composers offer more vigorous personalities, among them Isaac Blackwell and Nicholas Staggins. Blackwell shares some of Farmer's solidity. His tuneful style as at its best in 'Give me thy youth' (*P1681*) which has admirable strength and directness, and contrasts with the polite inanities of so much else (Ex. 73). Staggins, too, is redeemed by his robustness. Songs like 'As Amoret with Phyllis sat' (*P1679*—Ex. 74) or his setting of Dryden's 'How unhappy a lover am I' (*P1673*) from Part II of *The Conquest of Granada* (1670) would not be out of place in *The Beggar's Opera*, and it is to the popular ballad tradition that they belong.

There is, however, little to say in favour of Francis Forcer, whose numerous songs are among the feeblest written by any composer of the period. What slight melodic gift he has appears to best advantage in the popular type of song in triple time such as 'When first to Dorinda' (*P1679*). His '*NEW LOYAL SONG*' ('Hark how Noll and Bradshaw's head') written to celebrate the discovery of the Rye House plot '*and sung at the great Feast of the* Loyal Gentry *of the City of* Westminster, *in* Westminster-Hall, Thursday July 19.1683' is so awful that it must have made Whigs of any sensitive musicians present. Failure of the various anti-Catholic conspiracies produced a spate of 'loyal songs' at this time. Most belong to the broadside repertoire and are thus outside our present scope. However, some songbooks were more or less given over to them, the largest being *A Choice Collection of 180 Loyal Songs, All of them written since the Two late Plots (Viz.) The Horrid Salamanca Plot in 1678. And The Fanatical Conspiracy in 1683* (third edition with music, 1685). Perhaps surprisingly, the years immediately following the Glorious Revolution of 1688 cannot show an equivalent publication celebrating the triumph of the whig cause. In fact, the same collection was reissued in 1694 with a new title page omitting all reference to the plots but otherwise standing as a testimony to Jacobite feeling. Compared with Forcer, Louis Grabu was at least competent—though much abused, then and now. After only a year in England he had been appointed Master of the King's Musick, for which, no doubt, his French nationality and training recommended him even if his talents did not. Certainly he made a swift rise at the expense of Humfrey and Banister, hence

Ex. 91 'When Lucinda's blooming beauty'   Louis Grabu (*P1685a*)

When Lu - cin - da's bloom - ing beau – ty Did the wond - 'ring town sur -

- prise, With the first I paid my du - ty, Fix - ing there my wand' - ring

eyes: Her kind spring each hour dis - clo - ses Charms we no - where else can

trace, Gay - er than the blush on ros - es Are the glo - ries on her face.

their criticism. On the other hand, Dryden's estimate of him was too high. His mishandling of the English language to which Dent drew attention in *Albion and Albanius* (1685) is quite venial,[15] and in fact there is something to be said for his Lullian recitative.

As it is, Grabu makes only infrequent appearances in the

song-books, though when he does be betrays some worthy qualities such as a straightforward style of melody and an up-to-date harmonic idiom. 'When Lucinda's blooming beauty' (*P1685a*), a gavotte, shows a perfectly satisfactory regard for English rhythms and stress, and an air of sophistication into the bargain. It moves well, rhythmically, melodically and harmonically; only towards the end does it falter momentarily, at the words 'blush on roses', where the melody loses its sense of direction and the harmonic progression wavers (Ex. 91).

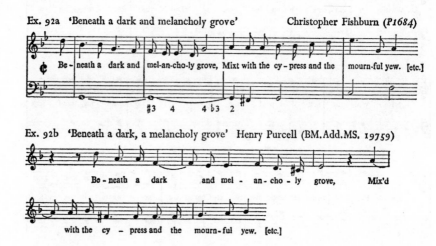

Ex. 92a 'Beneath a dark and melancholy grove'   Christopher Fishburn (*P1684*)

Ex. 92b 'Beneath a dark, a melancholy grove' Henry Purcell (BM.Add.MS. 19759)

Two song writers, part-time soldiers as well as part-time composers, were Simon Pack and Christopher Fishburn. Pack seems to have furnished songs for a number of plays in the early 1680's, and can show a spontaneous melodic gift. Fishburn, in addition, was a poet of sorts; the author (among other literary efforts) of 'Welcome to all the pleasures', the Cecilia Ode which Purcell set in 1683. It is interesting to note a resemblance between the opening lines of his setting of 'Beneath a dark and melancholy grove' (*P1684*) and Purcell's. Both date from about the time of their collaboration on the Ode, although Purcell's is incomplete (Ex. 92).

Ex. 93 'In the shade upon the grass'   Christopher Fishburn (P1684)

In the shade up - on the grass, Where nymphs and shep - herds lie,

Will was cour - ting of a lass, And Nell stood list - 'ning by: Quoth

Will, "You will not tar - ry Two months be - fore you mar - ry:" "Fie, no, fie, no,

ne - ver, ne - ver tell me so; For a maid I'le live and die:" Quoth Nell, "So will not I."

*♯ in P1684   † F in P1684   ‡

Ex. 94 'Why am I the only creature'   Christopher Fishburn (P1684)

Why am I the on - ly crea - ture, Must a ru - in'd love pur - sue;

2

O - ther pas - sions yield to na - ture, Mine there's no - thing can sub - due.

Not the glo - ry of pos - ses sing Mo-narch's wish - es gave me ease,

More and more the migh - ty bles - sings Did my ra - ging pains in - crease,

2

But in his own right Fishburn is an appealing melodist. 'In a shade upon the grass' (*Ibid.*) has a freshness and unaffected grace that recalls the Elizabethans (Ex. 93). On the other hand 'Why am I the only creature' (*Ibid.*) shows him completely at home in the late seventeenth-century idiom, particularly in his treatment of accented discords, his thoroughly resourceful use of harmony within the minor mode, and his well managed modulation (Ex. 94).

Others who, though not prolific as song writers show an attractive vein, include Thomas Tudway, Charles Taylor and James Paisible. Some of their songs are quite accomplished within modest limits. On the other hand the Italian Giovanni Battista Draghi (usually referred to as 'Senior Baptist') frequently exhibits a cramped and rather ungrateful style, which Playford further impairs by mangling the figured bass. (Being more harmonically venturesome than usual in songs of this type they are all the more vulnerable). Too often he seems to strive for effects which do not come off, yet he secures respect, not only for some gallant failures, but for touching songs like 'The pleasures that I now possess' (*P1685a*—Ex. 95) and some real successes, among which the ambitious setting of 'Where art thou God of dreams' (*P1686*) deserves to be mentioned.

Altogether inferior in quality are the songs of Moses Snow, John Roffey and Alexander Damascene, while Samuel Ackroyde and John Reading composed fluently but innocuously in a more popular style.

These then are the contemporaries of Blow and Purcell as they appear in the songbooks. Robert King is probably the most consistently attractive songwriter among them, then Hart and Turner, though sparks of promise are not lacking elsewhere. Indeed, it does not seem to have been beyond quite mediocre talents to produce one or two more than passable songs. But what sets them all apart from Purcell is their impoverished view of the art of song. Physically and emotionally their songs are puny; they attempt little and consequently achieve little. The terrible restraint of politeness was upon them. Although their songs were often well turned and graceful, sometimes mildly affecting even, they were rarely moving. As composers they were circumscribed by the conventions of gallantry and pastoral insipidity.

Perhaps this is unfair, for we are dealing with a type of music which in most cases aimed to please for the moment only. It would be unreasonable to expect more—were it not for the fact that Purcell had already raised our expectations.

Ex. 95 'The pleasures that I now possess'   G. B. Draghi (P1685a)

2 ...and at the publick theatres'

Song played an increasingly important role in Restoration drama until by the end of the century it was one of the chief attractions used to draw and hold an otherwise reluctant audience. During the reign of King Charles II the Duke's Company, first under Davenant then under Betterton, seems to have been a good deal more musical than the King's, for well over twice as many songs survive from their repertory as from the other's. It was this company too, which led the way with 'opera' (i.e. theatrical representations 'by vocal and instrumental music, adorned with scenes, machines and dancing', as Dryden put it), and which had at Dorset Garden from 1671 onwards the better theatre for this purpose. John Banister was most frequently employed to write songs for the company up to about 1675, with Robert Smith, Alfonso Marsh, Nicholas Staggins and Pelham Humfrey also in demand. In the next ten years a variety of more or less mediocre musicians was employed; Thomas Farmer and Simon Pack most frequently. From about 1685 Henry Purcell held sway, but among lesser mortals Samuel Ackroyde, Robert King and John Eccles were called upon quite often. From 1683 to 1694 the two companies united under Betterton but subsequently split again, Eccles maintaining his link with Betterton and Daniel Purcell composing for Rich's Patent Company.

Every play had to have its songs.[1] In Otway's *Friendship in Fashion* (1678) Saunter dislikes a play simply becuase 'there was never a song in it', appropriate or not. In Buckingham's *The Rehearsal* (1671) Smith asks Bayes:

How comes this song in here? for, methinks, there is no great occasion for it.

to which Bayes replies:

Alack, Sir, you know nothing: you must ever interlard your Playes with Songs, Ghosts and Dances.

In the early years it was fortunate that players such as Harris, Nell Gwynn and Moll Davies could sing so well. (Moll Davies, sang the part of Venus in Blow's *Venus and Adonis* after she had 'retired'.) Even so, a large proportion of songs were not sung by, but at the behest of, a character, usually a principal, who lacked skill in singing, or to whose role singing was inappropriate. A simple formula was then used to introduce a song, such as:

> *Boy, take thy Lute, and with a pleasing ayr*
> *Appease my sorrows, and delude my care*

in Otway's *Alcibiades* (1675), for example. In later years, however, song became such an important feature that the need was for actors who could sing, and singers who could act. In this latter category came Bowman, Freeman, Leveridge, and Reading among the men, and Mrs. Ayliff, Mrs. Bracegirdle and Mrs. Cross among the women. Lute or theorbo, sometimes guitar, were the accompanying instruments normally employed, but a consort was also used on occasions, providing symphonies and doubling voices in chorus.

An exhaustive study of the songs in Restoration tragedy supports the view that, in general, the writers 'consciously endeavoured to place their lyrics in natural relationship to the context of the play, and the content of the song . . . intimately related to the situation which it accompanied.'[2] Despite the prevailing classical aesthetic which, it might be thought, would militate against the use of song—solo song especially—these writers were by no means opposed to it even in their tragedies.

It is true that some of the best examples, such as Dryden's *All for Love* (1677) and Otway's *Venice Preserv'd* (1682), to name only two, renounce song entirely, but these are exceptional. It was probably Lee who grasped the potentials of the convention to the fullest, and made best use of song in his tragedies. There were, of course, no theoretical objections so far as comedy was concerned, and indeed song is frequently exploited as a device of comic characterization.

Ex. 96   from 'O Love! if e'er thou'lt ease a heart' (Crowne)   Pelham Humfrey (P1676)

Un - der thy shades I faint - ing lie; A thou-sand times I wish to die: But when I find cold death too nigh, I grieve to lose my plea - sing pain, And call my wi - shes back a - gain.

Song used for atmospheric effect in tragedy is common, particularly at the beginning of a play or act where it serves the double function of quietening the audience and helping to create the right mood. Draghi's 'Lucinda close or veil those eyes' (P1688b) sung to the lovesick king at the beginning of Mountfort's *The Injured Lovers* (1688) establishes the mood swiftly and economically; so too does Banister's song 'Lo behind a scene of seas' (P1673a) at the start of Crowne's *Juliana* (1671). Similarly, at the beginning of an act or the drawing of a scene: thus in the same author's *History of Charles VIII of France* (1671), Act IV Scene 2 begins with Humfrey's

Ex. 97a 'Ah! fading joy' (Dryden)   Pelham Humfrey *(P1676)*

'O love if e'er thou'lt ease a heart' (*Ibid.*) sung 'within', while Charles watches lovingly the sleeping Julia. The setting is a fine one. On the technical level it is thoroughly convincing considering the metrical irregularity of the verse, and from the expressive point of view the rise and fall in the last half of the stanza paralleling the lyrical development in each strophe is specially notable. (The triplet rhyme itself has a cumulative effect here.) The music mounts in the first line from E to A, in the second to D, in the third to F, only to subside gently during the course of the final couplet. Note too the treatment of 'pleasing pain' in the penultimate line, first by the major third to suggest 'pleasing' then by the minor third to suggest 'pain'. Yet it is not merely on account of details that this song makes its effect. Overall it shows the refined and sensuous qualities typical of the composer imparted to the dramatic context (Ex. 96).

Another excellent song of Humfrey's used to open a scene is 'Ah fading joy' (*P1675*) in Dryden's *Indian Emperor* (1665).[3] The Spaniards are resting in a grotto watching an entertainment. The mood is idyllic and contrasts the cares man takes upon himself with the contentment of nature. Suddenly Guyomar and his Indians rush out from hiding and capture the Spaniards before they can get to their swords. The mood is broken, and the reversal all the more striking because of the spell created by Humfrey's song. The opening, lamenting the transience of human joy, is in recitative. Here details *are* important: the expressive rise and sharp fall of a diminished fourth on the opening phrase, man's urge to self-destruction suggested by the plunging of two diminished fifths at the words 'And what too soon would die', the gradual mounting of the vocal line over the next three bars with rising chromaticisms leading to a climax at 'we seek out new'. Contrasted with this are the delights of nature expressed in tuneful triple time, and to close, a wonderfully atmospheric chorus, brief but touching in its evocation of idyllic contentment, peace and respite from the strife of war (Ex. 97).

As well as helping to set a scene, songs sometimes serve

other functions such as indicating the passage of time, or separating episodes in the same scene. An example is provided by Staggins' 'How severe is fate' (*P1679*) in Lee's *Gloriana* (1676) which interposes between Augustus's granting Caesario a reprieve and the latter's reunion with Narcissa dying for love of him. As with most playsongs it serves a dual purpose, for in addition to its structural function it has a descriptive role. It

Ex. 98 'How severe is fate' (Lee)   Nicholas Staggins (*P1679*)

prepares the audience for the changed situation and introduces a pathetic note. There is an old-fashioned, almost folk-like quality about it (significantly there is no F sharp in the key signature though the tonality is based on E), and despite certain modern turns of phrase tending to jar the overall impression it makes is one of tenderness and simplicity—rare qualities in the songs of this superficial and cynical age (Ex. 98).

The supposed curative, sedative and supernatural powers of music continue as important functions of Restoration playsong. Similarly its potency as an aid to courtship and seduction. A frequent role in tragedy was to alleviate melancholy and despair, and for this purpose Farmer's 'Bid the sad forsaken grove' (*P1681*) in Tate's *Brutus of Alba* (1678) is sung to calm the deserted Queen of Syracuse. The classical allusion here is the lament of Venus for her dead Adonis. The song itself is a rather uneasy mixture of declamatory and tuneful

Ex. 99 'Bid the sad forsaken grove' (Tate)   Thomas Farmer (*P1681*)

writing which never quite settles down as either, though it promises well at the beginning, moving into three time and out again with unusual ease for this composer. Unfortunately his modest talent for the square-cut tune cannot cope with the excessively irregular verse structure of this lyric. Nevertheless, the setting is genuinely affecting and is not unworthy of Tate's fine verse (Ex. 99).

Closely allied and often combined with the therapeutic function of song is its use as a sedative. In Rochester's adaptation of *Valentinian* (1684) Lucinia, sad at her separation from her husband, calls for his favourite song:

> Go, Marcellina, fetch your Lute, and sing that Song
> My Lord calls his: I'll try to wear away
> The Melancholy Thoughts his Absence breeds!
> Come gentle Slumbers in your flattering Arms
> I'll bury these Disquiets of my Mind . . .

The song, 'Where would coy Amintas run' (*P1684*) by Grabu begins attractively enough and confirms the composer's pleasing melodic gift, but owing to the fact that the stanza is composed of a large number of short lines and that the music fails to make use of repetition it looses direction towards the end. Later in the same play we find Rochester exploiting the erotic function of a song, as perhaps we might expect. Grabu's settings are included in his *Pastoralle* (1684); the dialogue 'Injurious charmer' being sung to assist the Emperor in his seduction of Lucinia, and the song 'Kindness hath resistless charms' as he makes love to the Eunuch.

Love songs used simply as serenades are very common. In the opening scene of Shadwell's *The Libertine* (1675)—a play on the Don Juan legend—Don Juan summons his 'fiddlers' and instructs them:

> Rank your selves close under this Window, and sing the Song I prepar'd.

The song is Turner's 'Thou joy of all hearts' (*B1678*) and a jaunty piece it is, though no '*Deh vieni*'.

Songs also function as epithalamia. Two by Farmer may be mentioned: his rather trite setting of Dryden's 'Can life be a blessing' (*P1681*) from *Troilus and Cressida* (1679),[4] and, more ingratiating, 'Blush not redder than the morning' (*Ibid.*) from Lee's *Caesar Borgia* (1679). Here he manages to disguise his normally somewhat heavy tread by the use of passing notes in the voice and flowing quavers in the bass (see Ex. 100).

Ex. 100 'Blush not redder than the morning' (Lee)   Thomas Farmer (*P1681*)

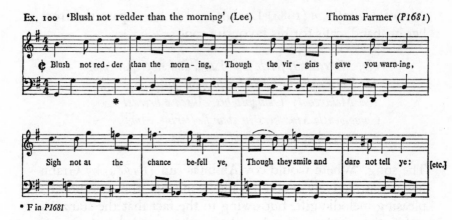

Blush not red-der than the morn-ing, Though the vir-gins gave you warn-ing,

Sigh not at the chance be-fell ye, Though they smile and dare not tell ye: [etc.]

* F in *P1681*

It has already been observed that songs play an important role in comedy as a means of sketching the character of fops and other types. Crowne's Sir Courtly Nice in the play of that name (1685) is a case in point. Making no claim to be a playwright ('that's Mechanick') he boasts nevertheless of having bestowed 'some Garniture on Plays, as a Song or a Prologue'. In Act V we are permitted to sample one such piece of garniture, a song 'As I gazed unaware' (*P1685b*) which he describes as a 'pretty Foolish soft Song, most Ladies are very kind to it'. It has a tune 'of my own composition' (actually Robert King's). Leonora, in whose honour the song was made, is not impressed, and in fact ridicules him, especially his singing of the last line. The peculiarity here he explains with the remark:

> I always humour my words with my Ayr. So I make the Voice shake at the last Line, in imitation of a man that runs after a Thief. (*Sings*) sto-ho-ho-hop Thief.

This song, then, is not to be taken quite seriously, but it is interesting for the fact that it points to the likelihood of composer and playwright having consulted together in order to make the most of the comic situation (Ex. 101).

In tragedy, song was often used to depict madness. Celania

Ex. 101 from 'As I gaz'd unaware' (Crowne)   Robert King (P1685b)

To my | ru - in and grief, Stop_____ thief, stop thief, stop thief, stop thief, stop thief.

*B in P1685b

(a part created by Moll Davies) in Davenant's *The Rivals* (1664) sings a sequence of mad songs, rather like Ophelia in *Hamlet*, including the well known 'My lodging is on the cold ground' to a tune, which, if it was not then a ballad tune soon became one.[5] As with the Ophelia songs, madness is conveyed not through any bizarre quality of words or music but through pathetic incongruity. Their simple and artless style and the overt sexuality of their content, is so disturbing in a normal context that this indecorum is taken as a reflection of a mind no longer in control of itself. Here also we find the common device of singing incoherent snatches of song used as a sign of madness.

Song also plays an extremely important supernatural role, especially in incantatory or ritual scenes. Spirits give objectified expression to dreams through songs in several plays, which are thus highly integral to the plot since a character's subsequent actions are often determined by what has been revealed to him in this supernatural manner. Farmer's 'Awake, O Constantine, awake' (*P1685a*) in Lee's *Constantine the Great* (1683) is in this category (Ex. 102). In a solemn section Constantine is presented with a vision of his future:

> *This Emblem of a bleeding Love*
> *Shall both thy Cross and Triumph prove.*

At first the music matches the awesome occasion very well; what follows is bathos. Constantine must purge his past sins by a period of torment, but the music seems to treat this impending ordeal as no more than a mild discomfiture already successfully overcome and lapses into a complacent triple time. At root the trouble is caused by the verse itself moving into triple metre here, a palpable miscalculation on the part of

Ex. 102 'Awake, Oh Constantine! awake' (Lee)   Thomas Farmer (1685a)

the poet whether or not he realized it, for music tends inevitably to exaggerate the levity of this measure:

> *For alas! 'tis decreed by the Heavenly Doom*
> *To purge thy past crimes there's a Torment to come.*

The various revivals of *The Tempest* which were put on at the Duke's Theatre during the second half of the seventeenth century provide an interesting sample of songs used for purposes of supernatural effect. There is no need (for the present) to consider the later version which Purcell is presumed to have written but those of 1667 and 1674 in which Shakespeare underwent a 'sea-change' at the hands of Davenant, Dryden and Shadwell, and for which songs by Banister, Humfrey, Reggio and Hart are extant.[6] Which of the surviving songs belongs to which version is a problem that has received some attention,[7] but the following seems the simplest interpretation of a rather confused situation. Banister was employed to set Davenant's (or Dryden's) additional lyrics for the 1667 adaptation, as well as to provide new versions of 'Full fathom five' (*P1675b*) and 'Come unto these yellow sands' (*Ibid.*). (Probably Johnson's 'Where the bee sucks' continued in use, for it was current in Playford's collections up to 1673 though ascribed to Wilson.) By 1674 Banister was out of favour and Humfrey was asked to provide the music for two additional masques at the end of the second and fifth acts, the instrumental music being assigned to Locke who published it as an appendix to his vocal music in *Psyche* the following year. By this time too, Johnson's 'Where the bee sucks' was well over 60 years old and was probably felt in need of replacement, so Humfrey wrote another setting. Otherwise Banister's songs from the 1667 production were retained.

So far, so good; but one or two points have yet to be explained; for example, the reasons, for Reggio (not Humfrey) setting 'Arise ye subterranean winds' (*R1680*), and the inclusion of Hart's 'Adieu to the pleasures and follies of love' among 'ARIELS SONGS *in the play call'd the* TEMPEST' (*P1675b*) although its text does not occur in the quarto. It is, of course, possible that these two songs belonged from the first to the earliest performances given in the spring of 1674, though it is difficult to see why Humfrey did not set them. Conceivably Humfrey was too ill to complete the task assigned to him (he made his will on 23 April 1674, a week before the probable date of first performance). Hart's song may have been an *ad hoc* interpolation since it was never absorbed into the printed text of any edition of the play.

Banister's treatment of Shakespeare's lyrics is predictably straightforward. It cannot be pretended that he actually improves on Johnson's 'Full fathom five'; nevertheless his setting is quite an atmospheric piece and, like Johnson's, makes use of a peal for the burden 'Ding, dong, bell'. 'Come unto these yellow sands' has no earlier setting with which to compare it. It begins with an attractive one-and-a-half-bar phrase effect, nicely balanced then contrasted with a more regular period. However, the movement is disrupted towards the end by a new metrical pattern in the verse which throws Banister out, and the song ends lamely.

Of the non-Shakespearean songs in the 1667 version, Ariel sings 'Dry those eyes' by way of reassurance to Alonzo, Antonio and Gonzalo following their tribulations in Act II (see Ex. 78, p. 164). It is a pleasant enough song and adequate to its purpose, but rhythmically stiff and repetitive thanks largely to the monotonous octo-syllables and feminine rhymes of the verse. The Echo Song 'Go thy way' between Ferdinand and 'invisible' Ariel certainly impressed Pepys, who on one occasion attempted to copy the words down in the theatre while they were being sung, only to find when he came to look at them afterwards that they were illegible.[8] Actually, instead of just echoing the endings the whole of each line is sung as an echo, that is, as a canon two in one. It is of no great technical accomplishment, but on the stage it is easy to see how it could prove effective (Ex. 103).

Ex. 103 'Go thy way, why should'st thou stay' (Davenant/Dryden: *The Tempest*)

John Banister *(P1675b)*

Apart from an extremely attractive setting of 'Where the bee sucks' *(P1675b)* Humfrey's additions for the 1674 adaptation comprise music for the Masque of Devils in Act II and the Masque of Neptune and Amphitrite at the end of Act V.[9] But the most interesting song from this production is Reggio's 'Arise ye subterranean winds' (Ex. 104). It alone of all the vocal music of the play has dramatic force. The opening gives some idea of the strength and vigour of the piece, which, of course, needs compelling delivery to bring off, while the conclusion catches a true vein of heroic excitement. At any rate, the public found it—indeed, the opera as a whole—excellent fare. As John Downes reports in *Roscius Anglicanus*:

> all things perform'd in it so Admirably well, that not any succeeding Opera got more Money.

When we look at the songs in these semi-operas we realize that there is little to distinguish them from the general run of

Ex. 104a 'Arise, ye subterranean winds' (Shadwell) Pietro Reggio (R*1680*)

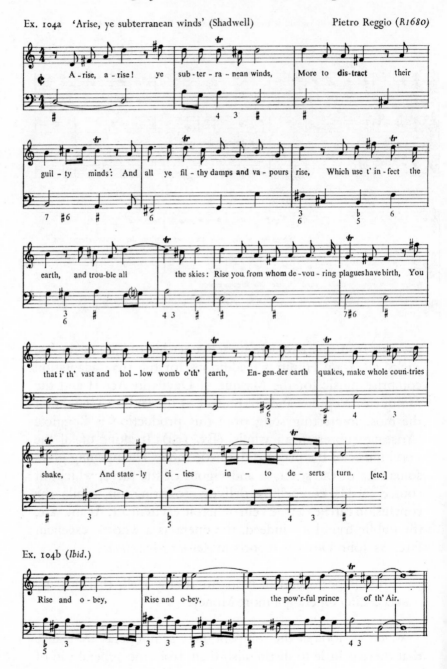

Ex. 104b (*Ibid.*)

songs in the miscellanies. Those in Locke's *Psyche*, for example, are mostly in the vigorous, tuneful, triple-time vein currently popular, and the dialogue in the same sort of recitative as the pastoral dialogue employed.[10] There were, of course, choral movements too, and instrumental symphonies and ritornellos linking the various items together. In his preface to the score Locke, characteristically, was rather proud of the variety he offered:

> you have from Ballad to single Air, Counterpoint, Recitative, Fuge, Canon, and Chromatick Musick: which variety (without vanity be it said) was never in Court or Theatre till now presented in this Nation: though I must confess there has been something done, (and more by me than any other) of this kind . . .

There are a few isolated songs in the work, two of which, 'All joy to fair Psyche' and 'The delights of the bottle' were printed by Playford (*P1683*) as simple strophic songs.

The most remarkable passage in the opera from the point of view of musical expression (if not of dramatic relevance) is the scene between 'Two despairing men and two despairing women' ('Break distracted heart'); a dialogue in which they debate the suffering caused by love. This is one of the scenes which Shadwell commented on in his preface to the printed text:

> *I believe, the unskilful in Musick will not like the more solemn part of it, as the Musick in the Temple of* Apollo, *and the Song of the* Despairing Lovers, *in the Second Act; both which are proper and admirable in their hands, and are recommended to the judgement of able Musicians; for those who are not so, there are light and airy things to please them . . .*

Nevertheless, it is a fine example of Locke's declamatory and expressive technique and shows a subtle handling of equal and unequal rhythmic quantities; words such as 'nothing', 'molify', 'passion', 'misery', 'oppresses' being carefully reproduced in accentuation, length and inflection of syllables. Moreover the rhythm and contour of each line as a whole is moulded faithfully to the words.

Ex. 105a from 'Break, break, distracted heart' (Shadwell)   Matthew Locke *(L1675)*

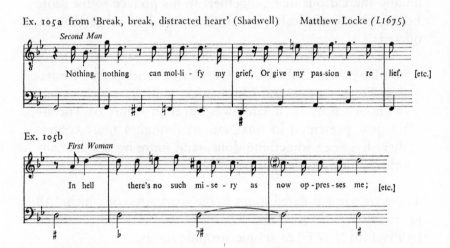

These brief excerpts only hint at the intensity of expression that Locke was capable of. At other times augmented chords, false relations, leaps of diminished intervals and chromatic progressions bring him close to an irrational harmony—or rather, one whose rationale is expressive rather than purely musical. To some extent it was self-defeating, for music has a logic of its own which needs to be observed if expressive devices are to be fully effective. Purcell alone was able to reconcile the two. From Locke, he inherited a penchant for extravagant progressions and gained an insight into their expressive power; his development as a song writer shows the path he took to realize this potential to the full in terms of a viable musical language and structure.

Part five

Orpheus Britannicus and Amphion Anglicus

1 Henry Purcell's development as a songwriter

By and large, the songs of the Restoration court and theatre took the trivial view of love and life. But deeper emotions stirred even in that cynical age; emotions that neither the lyrics of the courtiers nor the tunes to which they were set were altogether capable of expressing. It is the songs of Purcell and Blow, principally, that penetrate beyond such gallantries. True, there are many short, dance-like songs by both composers that are hardly distinguishable from those of their contemporaries; yet, in general, if we compare their songs with those we have been considering we can hardly fail to notice certain quite striking differences, particularly the increased scale—physical and emotional—of many of them.

So far as the tuneful style is concerned, it becomes more abstract and self-sufficient musically. There is less dependence on dance forms and rhythms; instrumental idioms are incorporated, and the result is that fewer and fewer words suffice for more and more music. On the other hand, declamatory writing becomes more varied. In place of the comparatively stiff recitative of Locke and Humfrey there is more flexible movement, often involving changes in the speed and style of the declamation, repetition of certain words and phrases for dramatic effect, and frequently an exaggerated attention to descriptive details translated out of the literary into the musical medium.

Overall it represents a change from a fairly restrained to a more flamboyant, rhetorical style.

It appears that this was virtually Purcell's single-handed achievement. The tentative recitatives and songs in the court odes of Cooke, Locke and Humfrey, and the early ones of Blow, show just how tremendous was Purcell's emancipation after 1682.[1] Of course, something from nothing is impossible, yet the most important ingredient in this development was his own genius brought to bear on musical materials already at hand. Just as in his instrumental music he set out to graft the Italian sonata style on to the English fantasy, so in his vocal music he tried to do the same. An over-simplification perhaps, since neither in his instrumental nor in his vocal music did he desire to cut himself off from the native English tradition—or from the French for that matter. But in both the significant developments are almost wholly attributable to a desire to learn from the Italians, translating the lesson into English and specifically Purcellian terms.

The years round about 1680 were crucial so far as the formation of his mature style was concerned. It was a time when Italian rather than French influences were ascendant. In fact, the King had maintained a band of Italian musicians from the early years of the reign.[2] Giulio Gentileschi and Tom Killigrew were encouraged to start up Italian operas soon after the Restoration and for this purpose Italian musicians were imported. Apparently the King was prepared to spend £1,700 a year on their salaries, and though no operas were forthcoming, Vincenzo and Bartolomeo Albrici were already in service by 1665, and three others—of whom Giovanni Sebenico is the best known—were engaged the following year. In due course Giovanni Battista Draghi arrived, and the castrato Girolamo Pignani. It was he who dedicated a collection of Italian songs to the Duke of Norfolk in 1679 entitled *Scelta di canzonette Italiane* (published by Playford and Godbid) containing pieces by such famous masters as Carissimi, Cesti, Pasquini, Luigi Rossi and Stradella among others, as well as fellow country-

men in England—Bartolomeo Albrici, Draghi and Matteis—
not forgetting Pignani himself.

Many of these composers are strongly represented by secular
vocal works in contemporary English manuscripts, particularly Carissimi, with whom Vincenzo Albrici had studied, and
Rossi. Pietro Reggio, another Italian musician resident in
England, compiled at least one such collection of pieces by
Carissimi, Cavalli, Cesti and Rossi, as well as Albrici and himself in 1681 (BM Harleian MS 1501). To the English their style
was characterized by one outstanding feature, a vocally brilliant yet expressively detailed setting of the text. For when it
came to pastiche it was *coloratura* that turned an English
declamatory song into an Italian one—or so 'Seignior *William*
in *Northampton-Shire*' thought when he set 'See how Thames's
silver streams' as '*A Song after the* Italian *Mode*' (*B1678*). So
important was the vocal line that he neglected to provide a
bass to the song! Of course, intentionally or not, the song is a
joke, but even so it gives an indication of what Italian vocal
music stood for in the minds of Englishmen, and the vogue it
was enjoying.

Ex. 106   *A Song after the* Italian *Mode*   Seignior *William* in *Northampton-Shire* (*B1678*)

Pietro Reggio was probably the most influential of these
immigrant musicians. Like the Albrici brothers and other
Italian musicians he had been in the service of Queen Christina

of Sweden before 1654, moving on after her abdication and working for a while in Germany, eventually coming to England in 1664.[3] Pepys called him a 'slovenly and ugly fellow' but was very impressed with his singing, as was Evelyn. In 1678 he published a book called *The Art of Singing*, a treatise on vocal ornamentation which no longer survives, and two years later his *Songs set by Signior Pietro Reggio* (R*1680*) came out dedicated to the King. In the preface he adopts a defensive tone, anticipating the charge that as an Italian he could not set English words well. Playford, was indeed to make this charge (in P*1681*), though it does not seem particularly well-founded. Nevertheless, it has to be confessed that, on the whole, they are rather unexciting settings of rather unexciting poems— mostly (and significantly) by Cowley. Predictably, three-time ayres are predominant, though instead of being simply strophic there is a tendency to treat successive verses as variations. There is, however, only one ground bass ('She loves and she confesses too') and it is worth noting that Purcell was to use the same words and the same bass in his own rather more animated setting of a year or two later.

The songs in part two of the collection are larger and altogether less inhibited in style. There is a stronger ring to the settings of 'I'll sing of heroes' and 'Awake my lyre', and it is instructive to compare his version of the latter with William King's (K*1668*). Although Reggio's is through-composed and King's strophic, the former's freer and bolder handling cannot be attributed to that cause alone. The vigorous opening, for example, contrasts markedly with King's almost introspective beginning. The Italian gives happy expression to the idea of 'gentle thoughts' which King overlooks, and points the antithesis

Though so exalted she and I so lowly be

better, not only by means of high and low but by melodic parallelism too. Reggio's last line makes a more climatic (and descriptive) effect, whereas King's is without panache (Ex. 107).

Ex. 107a 'Awake, awake my lyre' (Cowley)   Pietro Reggio (*R1680*)

Ex. 107b 'Awake, awake my lyre' (Cowley)   William King (*K1668*)

A number of English songs by Reggio survive in manuscript also, though they do not materially alter the impression left by his published collection. One or two are on a large scale, and in his setting of Cowley's 'The big-limbed babe' we see him fully extended (BM Add. MS 33234). Unfortunately he cannot stand such prolonged exposure, and it becomes abundantly clear that while he may not be an incompetent composer, he

is, sad to say, a quite unmemorable one. He continually promises more than he can deliver. There is little melodic gift to
speak of, his coloratura is mechanically patterned and his
harmony is pallid. But he does open up a wider perspective.
Word and phrase repetitions in his music may still be rare,
nevertheless he shows the alternative to the cramped underlay characteristic of English and French vocal music; he shows
that words, to be intelligible and expressive, may move both
quickly and slowly within the same song; that certain words
need to be lingered over—the poetry as well as the singer must
be allowed to breathe. It is this that makes him an important
forerunner of Henry Purcell.

The corpus of Purcell's songs is very extensive and not easily
delimited, for it includes songs from plays and operas as well
as those with no theatrical connections, and even items from
occasional pieces such as Odes, Birthday and Welcome Songs.
Moreover, to exclude from the arena songs for two or more
solo voices, songs with chorus, songs with instrumental
ritornellos and obbligato accompaniments, would be to force
an unnatural division and produce anomalies. In fact, we may
allow Widow Purcell to define the field, for these were all
types of song which she included in *Orpheus Britannicus*.[4]
So far as solo songs (with or without concluding chorus)
are concerned, Zimmerman catalogues 107 of these extant,
while Westrup and Meltzer list a further 148 songs for the
theatre.[5] In all there are some 65 strophic songs; the rest are
through-composed in some way—single movements such as
recitatives, ground basses, etc., paired and multiple movements
(cantatas) in two or more distinct sections. In addition, there
are 20 sacred songs and duets. Grove lists the theatrical and
non-theatrical songs in chronological order based on the date
of publication of the song book or the date of production of
the play in question. Although these are only terminal dates,
in the case of independent songs it seems likely that an overall

sequence of earlier followed by later songs emerges. So too in the case of playsongs, though in some instances it is uncertain whether they were composed for the first performance or a revival; or, if the latter, which revival.[6] Even so, the general perspective is certainly reliable. It is possible then, to view Purcell's development as a song writer chronologically over the 20 years or so of his activity.

Unconsciously realized perhaps, he seems to have had one end in view; the attainment of an expressive language of song that could match the transcendental ideal of the late Baroque. Emotional range and physical size were inextricably mixed in this as cause and effect, and the overall pattern of his development illustrates their interaction. He starts with the polite limitations of his contemporaries. True, he was never able to reject the superficial verse of his time just as he never renounced the light dance-songs which were its musical counterpart. But about 1683 his aims become more serious, and he begins to probe beneath the surface in settings of Cowley and other poets with Pindaric tendencies. Recitative by itself and within the context of the sectional cantata was the vehicle through which he chose to explore this new territory. Yet developing the expressive potential of recitative on the dramatic side still left the problem of large-scale lyric form to be solved. In the years up to 1688 or so, he found a solution in the ground bass—a vocal form theoretically capable of infinite extension—and with increasing freedom in the handling of the bass, all the more resourceful. From then on he turned more and more to the binary and *da capo* aria forms of the Italians, in which abstract and fundamentally instrumental techniques were employed in the creation of sizable and musically self-sufficient structures.

Whether or not the earliest songs attributed to Henry Purcell are, in fact, by him is doubtful. 'When Thyrsis did the splendid eye' in *P1675* which bears the name 'Mr *Pursell*' may well be by his father or uncle, judging by its old-fashioned style. Also doubtful are the six songs printed in *B1678*, one of

which ('Sweet tyraness, I now resign') is in any case a solo
version of a glee printed in *P1667* and unlikely to be the work
of an eight-year-old. One cannot be dogmatic, but it seems that
the plentiful use of ♩ ♪ ♪ ♪ rhythms at the beginning of lines
is an obsolete trait pointing to a composer of the older generation.[7] It may be, of course, that this is evidence of Purcell's
immaturity, but the contrast with songs published only a year
later is striking. Compare, for example, 'I saw that you were
grown so high' (*B1678*) with 'Amintas, to my grief I see'
(*P1679*). The structure of the stanzas is identical, the mood
comparable, yet musically they are quite different. The first is
bland and harks back to the earlier part of the century, the
second is quite up to date. Though of (almost) the same
length, in the former there are no unprepared discords on
strong beats (that is, on the first and third crotchets of the bar),
in the latter, seven. Jumps of imperfect intervals, sevenths and
ninths, taken in one or two steps number only one in the

Ex. 108a 'Amintas, to my grief I see'   Henry Purcell (*P1679*)

Ex. 108b 'I saw that you were grown so high'   Henry Purcell (senior? *B1678*)

former, nine in the latter, while false relations are one and five respectively (Ex. 108).

We get a foretaste of the expressive power of the mature Purcell, even if the style is still fairly primitive, in his elegy '*On the Death of his worthy Friend Mr.* MATTHEW LOCKE, . . . *who Dyed in* August, 1677' ('What hope for us remains now he is gone?'), in all probability written soon after the event though not published until 1679. It is thus one of the earliest samples we have of his vocal writing, though being recitative it can hardly be used as evidence in deciding the authenticity of the songs discussed above. Compared with the emotional luxuriance of later elegies on the death of John Playford in 1686, John Farmer about 1690 and especially the great epicideum '*Incassum Lesbia*' (*P1695c*) written in the last year of his life, this on the death of Locke seems quite austere. Yet within a relatively severe declamatory context the vocal line illustrates how important detailed expressivity was to Purcell even at this early stage. The antitheses in such a passage as:

> *His Layes to Anger, and to War could move,*
> *Then calm the Tempest they had rais'd with Love;*
> *And with soft Sounds to gentle thoughts incline,*
> *No Passion reign'd, where he did not combine . . .*

is pointed with a skill which, though modest by his own later standards, is masterly compared with William Gregory's in the elegy on the death of Pelham Humfrey ('Did you not hear the hideous groan?' in *P1681*). There the dramatic potential of the words

> *'Twas thou that mad'st dead words to live,*
> *Thou that dull Numbers didst inspire,*
> *With charming voice, and tuneful Lyre . . .*

fails to strike much response in the composer (Ex. 109).

Ex. 109a from 'What hope for us remains' *(On the Death of* . . . MATTHEW LOCKE)

Henry Purcell *(P1679)*

His lays to an - ger and to war could move, Then calm the tem-pest they had

rais'd with love, And with soft sounds to gent — — le thoughts in - cline,

No pas - sion reign'd where he did not com-bine. [etc.]

Ex. 109b from 'Did you not hear the hideous groan' (PASTORAL . . . *in memory of* . . .

Pelham Humphrys)

William Gregory *(P1681)*

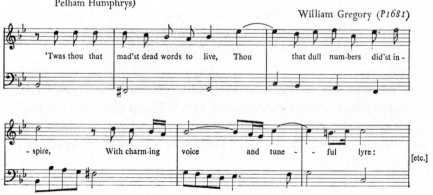

'Twas thou that mad'st dead words to live, Thou that dull num-bers did'st in -

- spire, With charm-ing voice and tune - - ful lyre : [etc.]

Purcell's example may have inspired Blow's 'PASTORAL ELEGY *on the Earl of* Rochester, *who died the* 26th *of* July, 1680.' ('As on his deathbed gasping Strephon lay' in *P1681*). For although Blow was the older composer and therefore, it

8 Matthew Locke, 'Aetat. 40 anno domini 1662' (Isaac Fuller (?). Faculty of Music, Oxford)

9 William Gregory, the younger (Faculty of Music, Oxford)

MVSICK.
Although the Cannon, and the Churlish Drum
Haue Brooke the Quire mate, and the Organs Dumb:
Yet Musicks Art with Ayre and String, and Voyce
Makes glad the Sad, and Sorrow to Reioyce.

10 Frontispiece of *Select Ayres and Dialogues* (1659)

11 Title page of Pietro Reggio's *Songs* (c. 1680)

12 John Blow (Sir Peter Lely.
St Michael's College, Tenbury)

13 John Weldon (?). (Faculty of
Music, Oxford)

14 Henry Purcell (John Closterman.
National Portrait Gallery, London)

might be thought, the maturer, at this stage in their development there was little to choose between them. Admittedly Blow lacked Purcell's happy gift for the tuneful triple-time song as represented by 'Hail to the myrtle shade' from Lee's *Theodosius* (1680). But when it came to airs in common time both were unable to achieve a natural line, and seemed intent on leaping about and crowding in false relations whether appropriate or not. There is no reason to suppose, for example, that 'Pastora's beauties' (*P1681*) were other than perfect, yet the melody is inexplicably contorted.

Ex. 110 'Pastora's beauties when unblown'   Henry Purcell (*P1681*)

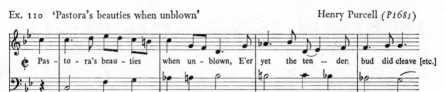

Pas- | to - ra's beau - ties | when un - blown, E'er | yet the ten — der: | bud did cleave [etc.]

That was Purcell. But Blow does the same sort of thing in his song 'In vain brisk god of love' (*P1683*)—and, indeed, never ceased to do it. Fortunately Purcell was able to control it, and use it in conjunction with an increasingly supple vocal line to superb effect.

This is the genesis of Purcell's mannered style of melody, and his growing control is evident in such a song as 'Retir'd from any mortal's sight' from Tate's *Richard II* (1681). It is a piece worth looking at closely in order to pin-point some of the salient features. Disjointed rhythms and vocal nuances combine to convey something of the dynamic quality of the verse. Thus the impression made by the line 'And curs'd the smiling day' is a disturbed one, due to the characteristic figures employed on 'curs'd' and 'smiling'—the one high-pitched yet downward in movement and highly emphatic, the other a gentler rippling figure.

Repeatedly we notice leaps up and, more often, down of a fourth or fifth within a slurred pair of notes, the first of which is accented but frequently the shorter: thus, '*retir'd*', '*of* his

Ex. 111a 'Retir'd from mortal's sight' (Tate: *Richard II*)   Henry Purcell *(P1683)*

pain', etc. There are jumps from unaccented discords (a kind of échappée effect) that we find at 'discont*ent*ed', 'ten*der*', and '*his* pain'. Accented discords from above or below a note are common, prepared or unprepared; thus, '*dis-con-tent*-ed', '*smil*ing', '*no long*er' etc. Less in evidence in this particular song is the two-note slide, as on '*curs'd*'.[8]

These are just some of the mannerisms that begin to characterize Purcell's vocal writing more strongly in the early 1680's; a pliable line which paid constant attention to details, matching rhythm and melody to the rhetorical and emotional quality of the words. Rhythm, ornament, dissonance, were all brought into play. But as yet all this was on rather a small scale. A larger framework was needed for a more complete realization of his expressive aims.

It was the application of this mannered style to recitative which was to release its full potential. This process can be traced in the increasingly extravagant recitatives which he wrote for the great bass singer John Gostling in the verse anthems up to about 1683, and in some of the Welcome Songs of this period. The same line of development is pursued in a number of Cowley settings. From *The Mistresse*, published as long before as 1674, he took 'The Thraldom' ('I came, I saw, and was undone'), 'The Rich Rival' ('They say you're angry') and 'The Concealment' ('No, to what purpose should I speak?'); the first displaying a hitherto unsurpassed intensity of affective declamation. The advance over the rather wooden recitative of earlier years is striking. Still more impassioned is the setting of Stanley's 'Draw near, you lovers' which also belongs to this stage in his development and survives uniquely in the autograph manuscript in the Royal Music Library where the Cowley settings are also to be found.[9] The evidence of this manuscript suggests that what might be called the 'recitative phase' of Purcell's career lasted for about five years (roughly from 1682 to 1687) during which time his declamatory style was becoming increasingly flamboyant. A number of sacred songs, later published in *Harmonia Sacra* (1688) belong to this period, including a setting of George Herbert's 'With sick and famished eyes'. and 'Job's Curse' ('Let the night perish'). Also contemporary are the 'Sighs for our late Sov'raign King Charles ye 2d' ('If pray'rs and tears') and 'Anacreon's defeat' again by Cowley.

Many of these and other recitatives form part of larger cantata-like structures. In one or two cases there are merely a few concluding bars of chorus for treble and bass; in others, the recitative leads into a tuneful section, usually in triple time and rather undeveloped melodically. Sometimes the sequence is extended so that recitative and airy passages form a succession of several movements as in the setting of Cowley's 'How pleasant is this flowery plain'—one of a number of cantatas for two or more voices written during this 'Cowley period'. It

begins with a 'Symphony For Flutes' in G minor and subsequently alternates tenor recitatives with short airs for soprano (twice) extolling the blessings of the pastoral life. The
final section is a concerted movement for the two flutes and the
two singers. Though the situation does not develop and the
tonal range is limited, variety is achieved through contrast of
tempo, metre and texture between the sections. There is
nothing in it to rival the wonderful ground in the cantata 'If
ever I more riches did desire' (Cowley again), but it is well
worth noticing in view of the fact that it is one of the items in
the Bodleian Library's set of *The Banquet of Musick* (*P1689*)

Ex. 111b 'How pleasant is this flowery plain' (Cowley)　　　Henry Purcell (*P1688*)

which contains manuscript indications of a worked-out continuo. The suggestion has already been made that quite elaborate realizations were an ideal to which those capable might aspire and this evidence is useful corroboration whether designed for theorbo or keyboard. Where chords were enough presumably, additional figuring supplements the meagre indications of Playford's original, but here and there passages have been added which impart a sense of movement and line to the accompaniment, as well as making it more expressive. The first recitative of Ex. 111b provides a good example.

Undoubtedly it is in their recitatives that the power of these cantatas lies. For not only are the tuneful sections often weak in themselves, they tend also to weaken the overall structure by being out of scale with the recitatives. The next stage in Purcell's development as a song writer seems to have concentrated upon remedying this defect—the disparity in size and expressive power between his recitatives and his airs. In practical terms the problem was the creation of a large-scale vocal form viable in itself, and though Purcell may not have realized this as a conscious aim, his admiration for Italian music made it inevitable that this was the direction in which he would move. Already in the preface of his *Sonnata's of III Parts* (1683) he confessed to having

> faithfully endeavour'd a just imitation of the most fam'd Italian Masters; principally, to bring the seriousness and gravity of that sort of Musick into vogue, and reputation among our Country-men, whose humor, 'tis time now, should begin to loath the levity, and balladry of our neighbours . . .

and we can see him attempting the same sort of thing in his vocal music. The models available to him included Carissimi, Cesti and Luigi Rossi, masters of the middle Baroque in whose work the *da capo* aria had yet to establish its dominance over binary form and ground bass. It was to the latter species of composition that he turned first, borrowing the bass of Reggio's setting of Cowley's 'She loves and she confesses too' in making his own version of the song (*P1683*).[10] His setting is notably more resourceful than Reggio's; for example, in the way phrase lengths are varied—overlapping and getting out of step with the bass. In his word-painting he shows considerable flair and though there is little attempt—indeed, little opportunity—to exploit the harmonic ambiguity of the ground, the staggered vocal line enables him to avoid making the expected cadences. In another ground published in the same book ('Let each gallant heart') he is able to make more of this device through the use of dominant or secondary dominant chords in treating the bass, though the song as a whole lacks the vitality of the other.

But it was in the Odes and Welcome Songs of this period that he practised the technique of the vocal ground bass assiduously. With a single exception, they contain at least one such movement from 1682 onwards, nearly always in common time and consisting of a regular quaver motion spread over three or four bars. The earliest is 'These had by their ill usage drove' in the Welcome Song for the King returning from Newmarket in 1682—a near relation of 'Oft she visits' in *Dido and Aeneas* (1689). (It also bears a resemblance to Blow's 'Of you, great Sir, our Druids spake' from the New Year's Ode of 1681, which seems to be Blow's first vocal ground and may have influenced Purcell.)

Ex. 112a Ground: 'Of you, great sir, our Druids spake' (*Great Sir, the joy of all our hearts*)

John Blow *(1681)*

Ex. 112b Ground: 'These had by their ill-usage drove' (*The Summer's absence unconcern'd we [bear)*

Henry Purcell *(1682)*

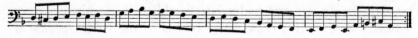

Of these early grounds the most famous is probably the chromatic 'Here the deities approve' from the Cecilia Ode of 1683, which was adapted for keyboard in the second part of *Musick's Hand-maid* (1689). It is amazing with what assurance these grounds are handled generally speaking; certainly they are the most accomplished solo movements in the Odes.

Yet there is a certain stiffness in this music, due as much to the empty heroics of the occasions as to the immaturity of the composer. In private he could experiment and win new freedom within the discipline of the ground bass. Transposition of the ground into keys other than the tonic was one device which offered an opportunity for much-needed tonal variety. 'Cease, anxious world' (*P1687*) provides an example. Here, after six statements of the bass in G minor, it moves into B flat and at each repetition rises a tone, through C minor and D minor, returning to the tonic for the last two repetitions before the metre changes to common time. The harmonic logic of this design is obvious and needs no comment beyond pointing out that it reproduces on a large scale the progression III – IV – V – I to the cadence. Then, having changed time, the bass appears in a new form, treated more freely in different keys but still retaining its basic shape. But interesting as it is from a technical point of view, and by no means lacking expressive moments, it does not bear comparison with the setting of Katherine Philips' 'O solitude' published in the same collection. This may fairly be described as his first truly great vocal ground. It has the broad sweep of the finest Italian *bel canto* of the mid-century, yet Purcell's own affective power. Chromaticism or abstruse harmony is absent, but a wide-leaping line and irregularity of phrase suggest the disturbance of the soul seeking solitude. He had used a five-bar version of the same bass a few years earlier (in the introductory symphony to the anthem 'In thee, O Lord, do I put my trust') but shortening it here he secures a more purposeful progression, telescoping the first and last bars into a single bar of tonic harmony. In all the bass repeats 28 times and remains in C minor throughout, yet

one is not conscious of a lack of variety in the harmonic treatment, because the phrase effect of the vocal line is so wonderfully free, both in itself and in relation to the ground.

To a great extent this freedom comes from the use of rests of
varying length between the lines, from rhetorical repetition,
and by expressively drawing out certain words to illustrate
their meaning. In the opening section it is noticeable that only
twice, at bars 13 and 29, do the two parts cadence together;
otherwise there is continual fluctuation of tension between the
two, so that when one is coming to rest the other is already on
the move, or poised for departure.

Ex. 113 'O solitude' (Philips)   Henry Purcell (*P1687*)

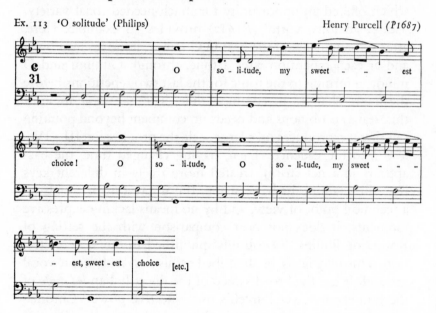

Purcell himself was poised on a point of departure for he
was about to embark on his career as an opera composer, and
it is within the context of the theatre that he achieves maturity
as a song writer. So far we have followed the development of
his recitative from something physically and emotionally
rather austere—austere, that is, by his own later standards—to
something extravagant, yet still controlled. The need to de-

velop the air as a larger and at the same time more powerful expressive vehicle had also been recognized, and the process begun in his ground basses.

When we turn to his other songs the accomplishment is less, although the direction he has taken is clear. For while the light, tuneful air patterned on the forms and rhythms of the dance was to retain its place to the end, at a deeper level it was necessary to break through the formal and emotional restrictiveness of its small-scale symmetries. The influence of verse and dance forms had therefore to recede, and techniques of abstract musical construction—motivic repetition, development, sequence, imitation, tonal prolongation—take their place. In other words, the application of the Italian instrumental style to vocal music becomes an accomplished fact; the transformation of air into aria.

An increasing use of repetition is a sign of Purcell's move towards a more Italianate idiom. To an extent the text becomes a vocalizing medium, and frequent, often inordinate, repetition of words and phrases an increasing phenomenon. On the whole, his early songs treat the text as it comes, only repeating a word or phrase here and there for dramatic effect, or to build up the end of a song. But more and more (and especially through various kinds of sequence) it becomes a necessity as a means of achieving a line that can be spun out beyond the four-bar phrase length, thus opening up new compositional possibilities as well as a wider expressive range.

The bass solos in two anthems of 1688—'The Lord is King' and 'My song shall be alway'—exhibit some of these features to a marked degree, and they may also be observed in the Mad Song 'I'll sail upon the dog-star' from D'Urfey's *A Fool's Preferment* staged the same year. A number of motives are employed in the course of the song, all more or less instrumental in character but at the same time representative of the verbal ideas they convey. In fact, the free canonic treatment throughout the song represents the idea of 'pursue' and 'chase' contained in the opening lines, while the pictorialism of successive motives is obvious (Ex. 114).

The modernity of the style is undeniable, especially the motivic treatment and the logic of the tonal structure. If it

Ex. 114a 'I'll sail upon the dog-star' (D'Urfey: *A Fool's Preferment*)   Henry Purcell (*1688*)

were longer it might well be taken for Handel—a fact which probably accounts for the song's continuing popularity in the eighteenth and nineteenth centuries.

There is very little as modern as this in *Dido and Aeneas* (1689). Through force of circumstances the scale of the songs in this opera is small, but this perhaps helped to ensure consistently high quality. Certainly it is hard to imagine the two grounds 'Ah Belinda' and Dido's Lament ('When I am laid in earth') being any better for being longer. The first especially consolidates all the techniques we have observed, and intensifies their effects—overlapping phrases between treble and bass, transposition of the ground, resourceful harmonic treatment, and, above all, a wonderfully flexible vocal line that reveals the full extent of Dido's anguish. In contrast, the mood of her final lament is one of heroic resignation, the voice soaring above a highly expressive four-part string accompaniment. The bass is of the chromatic chaconne type common enough in the middle Baroque and offers a great deal of scope for suspensions and affective dissonance, augmented chords and false relations which Purcell realizes in the richest way. In this company 'Oft she visits this lone mountain' seems rather four square and, here and there, not altogether happy from the harmonic point of view.

So far as the other songs are concerned some (e.g. 'Fear no danger') show trace of a French accent. On the other hand, Italian elements have little opportunity to flourish because of the diminutive scale of the opera, but it is worth looking at Belinda's song 'Pursue thy conquest love' to observe the same features already noted in 'I'll sail upon the dog-star' more tightly controlled and taken a stage further. The key is the same, and again the idea of 'pursue' prompts canonic treatment. Words and phrases are frequently repeated; there are only 12 words in 22 bars. The form is a miniature *da capo* although the reprise is written out, with a clearly defined middle section moving to the dominant and from there by sequential imitation of a brief motive ('Her eyes express the flame') to a cadence in A minor. The return begins straight away, and the final cadence is repeated as a coda. The concentration is remarkable, yet all the ingredients of a large scale aria are there. It required only a more suitable occasion.

The inhibitions of scale which affected *Dido and Aeneas* (by no means for the worse) were absent from *Dioclesian* (1690), for which Purcell wrote incidental music and a Masque. But it was the instrumental and choral movements which benefited most, although there are some charming songs. Foremost is the exquisite 'What shall I do to show how much I love her', the tune of which eventually found its way into the *Beggar's Opera*. Among others which attained popularity is the duet 'O the sweet delights of love'.

It is interesting to examine the role of instruments in this opera, particularly in their function as obbligato accompaniment but also as ritornellos to the songs. The use of instrumental ritornellos in English seventeenth-century vocal music goes back at least as far as Walter Porter's *Madrigales and Ayres* (1632). Henry Bowman's *Songs* (1677) were also printed 'With some Short Symphonies' as were many of the playsongs in Playford's *Theater of Music* (1685–87). Purcell's own use can be traced to his music for *Theodosius* (1680) where two flutes (i.e. recorders) accompany the song 'Hark, behold the heavenly choir'. The songs of *Circe* (1685?) are interesting, too, on account of the bass recitative 'Pluto arise' accompanied by strings. Increasingly this was to be the practice, not only in 'operas' but in plays also, especially in supernatural scenes. The song 'Great Diocles the boar has killed' in Act II of *Dioclesian* belongs to this category, and its solemn four-part string writing helps to create an atmosphere of awe and wonder. Following a chorus the celestial music continues with 'Charon the peaceful shade invites', a soprano air with accompaniment of two flutes. A few moments later a *'martial Song is sung; Trumpets and Hoboys joining with them'*. Then comes *'a Symphony of Flutes in the air'* and two flutes continue their accompaniment during the recitative and ground which follows.

The choice of instruments to accompany or introduce a play-song thus often depends on certain traditional associations or conventions appropriate to the dramatic context. The trumpet was used for martial effects naturally; the oboe too, though it seemed to serve equally well in pastoral or amatory situations. So did the flute, which was preferred in supernatural songs on account of its mysterious tone quality. The trumpet aria in Act IV of *Dioclesian* ('Sound fame') is an early example of a type of song which Purcell was to practise with increasing success in the remaining years of his life. It is after the manner of similar works by Italian opera composers, the trumpet answering the voice in echo. However, the limitations of the instrument as well as the one-bar bass ostinato sounding the notes of D major chord virtually kills the piece as anything more than a fanfare.

With *King Arthur* (1691) we again have an heroic subject, but for the most part Purcell's song forms are still not developed enough to function on that elevated level. Instead, they come into their own in the pastoral episodes, and there are some exquisite pieces among them: 'How blest are shepherds', 'Fairest isle' and the beguiling duet 'Shepherd, shepherd leave decoying'. But in two respects at least Purcell's solo writing for the voice takes a step forward in this opera. First, in recitatives such as 'What ho! thou genius of the isle', which so impressed North, especially as sung by Mrs. Butler—'beyond any thing I ever heard upon the English stage'.[11] Secondly, in the bass song 'Ye blust'ring brethren of the skies' which is an absolute *tour de force*. The stage directions at this point read:

Merlin *waves his Wand; the Scene changes, and discovers the British Ocean in a Storm.* Aeolus *in a Cloud above: Four Winds hanging, &c...*

and the first impression the music excites in our minds is of the turmoil of the winds, each of the four represented by the voices of a buffeting semiquaver fugue. Above this tumult the voice of Aeolus calls out:

> *Ye Blust'ring Brethern of the Skies*
> *Whose Breath has ruffl'd all the Wat'ry Plain,*
> *Retire . . .*

and immediately the movement begins to abate from semi-quavers to quavers, to crotchets, to minims, to semibreves, while Aeolus continues:

> *. . . and let* Britannia *Rise*
> *In Triumph o'er the Main.*

During this the voice soars majestically to top G and climbs down again through two octaves. Then C major changes to C minor, common time to triple time, and the soft tones of two flutes magically evoke a new mood:

> *Serene and Calm, and void of fear,*
> *The Queen of Islands must appear.*

after which a symphony sounds while 'An *Island* arises . . . *Britannia* seated in the *Island*, with Fishermen at her feet, *&c.*'

One is left breathless in more senses than one by such a piece. It proclaims Purcell's virtuosity unequivocally; beside it the storm music in *Dido and Aeneas* is pathetically naïve.

Even so, a great gulf separates the songs in *King Arthur* from those in the *Fairy Queen* (1692), Purcell's next opera. The technical advance in less than 12 months is phenomenal, although the composer had already pointed to the direction he was taking in the dedication of *Dioclesian*:

> Musick is yet in its Nonage, a forward Child . . . 'Tis now learning *Italian*, which is its best Master . . .

The lesson was indeed well learned for in *The Fairy Queen* we find not only thorough commitment to the Italian style, but thorough mastery. 'Ye gentle spirits of the air' (added in 1693) is a fully fledged *da capo* aria, complete with 'motto' opening, contrasting movement and metre in the middle section—in all 134 bars (29+76+29). Even longer is 'Thus the gloomy world' (164 bars: 56+52+56) in which the contrast of the middle section is heightened not only by change of key and time signature, but also of instrumental accompaniment; a pair of violins replacing the obbligato trumpet of the *da capo* section. Still more brilliant in effect is the famous 'Hark! the ech'ing air', a trumpet aria, while on a smaller scale 'A thousand ways' and 'Thus the ever grateful spring' are equally Italianate. Several features of 'Hark, how all things' may be cited in this connection; for example, the tonic iterations at the opening of the prelude and the broken-chord figuration that leads to the cadence hardly disguising the baldness of the progression. The voice enters with the opening phrase of the ritornello but soon branches off on its own, filling out the word 'sound' with coloratura, repeating, ornamenting and extending the treatment of the word 'rejoice' through sequences which eventually cadence on the dominant. Already eight words have extended over 19 bars and the whole section is repeated. The middle section sets the second line, with imitations between treble and bass and further sequences prolonging the word 'voice' over eight bars leading to a cadence in E minor. The return of G major is immediate and an expanded repeat of the first section is made with a modified close to end in the tonic.

Here then are the external features of the modern Italian style: an abstract instrumental idiom which utilizes various types of repetition at a higher and lower level to spin out the invention and at the same time make it coherent. Even so the personal accent is irrepressible, particular in such idioms as false relations, jerky rhythms and the exuberant discord treatment in a passage like the following.

Ex. 115 from 'Hark, how all things' (*Fairy Queen*)   Henry Purcell (*1692*)

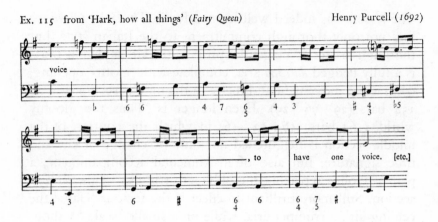

Of course, the authentic native voice speaks even more clearly in such songs as 'If love's a sweet passion', which became popular enough to remain in print for a century, passing through the *Beggar's Opera* on the way. The exquisite shaping of the final couplet is one of those things which every taste recognizes as being the work of genius.

Ex. 116 from 'If love's a sweet passion' (*Ibid*)   Henry Purcell

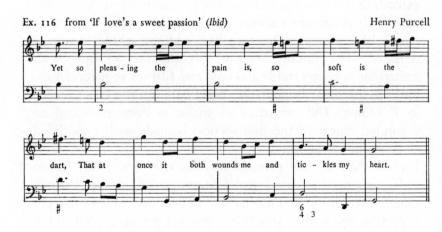

But for the first time Purcell's lyrical gifts are over-shadowed in this opera by the unprecedented number and importance of

the large-scale songs. Many possess subtle evocative powers of an impressionistic nature. The Song of Night ('See, even Night herself is here') with its mysterious accompaniment of muted violins unsupported by bass instruments is perhaps the most atmospheric, but hardly less so are the creeping chromatics of Winter's Song ('Next, Winter comes slowly'). Especially telling is the reversal of the last line where, instead of the mood of icy desolation evoked by the downward chromatic progression of the bass, the hopeful prospect of seasonal renewal is conveyed by the bass rising diatonically through an octave, leading into the return of the chorus 'Hail! great parent' and thus completing the seasonal cycle.

It is evident in *The Fairy Queen* that the days of Purcell's devotion to the strict treatment of the ground bass are at an end. In 'The Plaint' ('O let me ever weep'), for example, only the opening refrain is treated as a ground. The other verses function as episodes, free to move away from D minor and the discipline of the bass. The song itself is one of Purcell's finest, pathos overwhelming the senses as in Dido's Lament. But the sweep is broader still—155 bars of slow triple time for a mere seven lines of verse—the expression restrained rather than dramatic. In place of Dido's impassioned climax on top G, a hesitant, drooping, reiteration of the word 'never' echoed by the solo violin brings a feeling of utter sadness to the close. 'The Plaint' is strongly reminiscent of Euridice's aria *'Mio ben'* in Luigi Rossi's *L'Orfeo* (1647), but for all that both composers are employing conventions, clichés even, it does not seem to invalidate their power to move (Ex. 117).

With increasing length some relief from continual repetition of the ground at the same pitch became necessary. Transposition to related keys was one solution which he had already adopted, as we have seen. But the handling of such a bass becomes even freer in songs like 'Come all ye songsters of the sky', where, following five repetitions of the two-bar pattern in C major, and two in G, the motive is taken up as an ostinato and led by means of large and small scale sequences through A

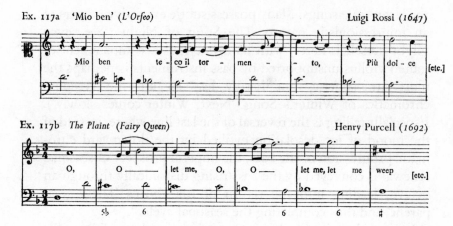

Ex. 117a 'Mio ben' (*L'Orfeo*)   Luigi Rossi (*1647*)

Mio | ben | te - co il tor - | men - | - to, | Più | dol - ce | [etc.]

Ex. 117b *The Plaint* (*Fairy Queen*)   Henry Purcell (*1692*)

O, | O ____ | let me, | O, | O ____ | let me, let | me | weep | [etc.]

minor, D minor and G major—in other words, the circle of
fifths—back to the tonic. In 'Yes Daphne' the motivic treatment of the bass takes over almost from the start, and there are
similar examples among the Queen's Birthday Odes of about
this time, notably 'I see the round years' in *Welcome, glorious
morn* (1691), and in the first section of the *da capo* song 'I see,
she flies me' from Dryden's *Aurengzebe* written in 1692 (or
1694). Another ground from a play of this period, Dryden
and Lee's *Oedipus* (1692), is the celebrated 'Music for a while'.
At first the bass is strictly treated, but later the cadential pattern
is modified in order to lead to statements in related keys (G
minor and B flat), then still more freely treated until a return
to the words and music of the opening couplet is made at the
end. This is one of a number of songs in which ground bass
and *da capo* forms came together in this way. It is a miracle of
intensity: one of the few playsongs of the time which manages
to convey the inner, psychological impulse of its dramatic
role; in this case, as part of a supernatural ritual in which the
ghost of Laius—the father of Oedipus—is raised in order to
discover the reason for the curse which hangs over the city of
Thebes. It is often thought of as a 'beautiful' song, and sung
as such. On the contrary, it is a song charged with menace,

as a look beyond the opening lines makes clear. Dryden's sinister imagery—

> *Till Alecto free the dead*
> *From their eternal bands,*
> *Till the snakes drop from her head*
> *And the whip from out her hands . . .*

finds a fitting response in Purcell's disturbed line.

Ex. 118   from 'Music for a while (Dryden and Lee: *Oedipus*)   Henry Purcell (*1692*)

The richness of this period in Purcell's creative life is amazing. Two songs from his incidental music to Shadwell's *The Libertine* (1692?) which must be mentioned are 'Nymphs and shepherds'—well enough known—and the bravura trumpet aria in the Italian style, 'To arms heroic prince', sung by 'the boy', Jemmy Bowen. It was for the same singer that Purcell wrote the second setting of 'Thy genius, lo!' in Lee's *The Massacre of Paris*, a florid recitative in his most mature style.

(Purcell said of young Jemmy Bowen when someone had tried to tell the boy how a certain passage should be ornamented, 'O let him alone . . . he will grace it more naturally than you, or I, can teach him.'[12]) Another singer who could do justice to this style was Mrs. Ayliff. Her singing of 'Ah me! to many deaths decreed' in Crowne's *Regulus* (1694) was described by Peter Motteaux in the following terms:

> had you heard it sung by Mrs. Ayliff, you would have owned that there is no pleasure like that which good notes, when so divinely sung can create.[13]

It is significant that Motteaux describes the song as 'set by *Mr. Purcell* the *Italian* way'. The same writer provides us with the well known account of ' 'Tis Nature's voice' from the Cecilia Ode of 1692 'sung with incredible Graces by *Mr. Purcell* himself', though in actual fact the song is marked 'Mr. Pate' in the score.[14] In it every idea for which a musical equivalent can be found is treated accordingly. Especially vivid is the pointing of the antitheses in the following passage:

> *From her it learn'd the mighty Art*
> *To court the Ear and strike the Heart:*
> *At once the Passions to express and move:*
> *We hear, and straight we grieve or hate, rejoice or love:*
> *In unseen Chains it does the Fancy bind;*
> *At once it charms the Sense and captivates the Mind . . .*

where, among other details, the voice dallies seductively over 'court', traces the trajectory of an arrow on 'strike', makes chromatic insinuations on 'express' and runs rapid divisions on 'move'. Still more remarkable are the chromatic wails on 'grieve', expected enough the coloratura on 'rejoice' and the slurs and ties on 'bind', but most amazing of all, an utterly fantastic conceit on 'charms'.

The large-scale works of Purcell's last years include the

Ex. 119   from 'Tis nature's voice' (Brady: *St. Cecilia's Ode*)   Henry Purcell (*1692*)

great Birthday Ode of 1694 for the Queen, *Come ye sons of Art* and *The Indian Queen* (1695). These contain much superb vocal music but technically little that is new, whereas the big Italianate *da capo* arias in *The Tempest* would represent an enormous stylistic advance if they could be shown to be by Purcell.[15] In some ways they do represent a logical culmination of traits which had become increasingly apparent—but culmination, not continuation. There is a stage missing in the development which not even Purcell could have omitted. The style of these arias is not the only disquieting feature in the Tempest music: there are others—the ground bass 'Dry those eyes', for example, is also far from what one would expect from Purcell at this time. Certainly fewer problems are raised by denying Purcell's authorship of most of the music (apart from the song 'Dear pretty one' about which there is no doubt) than asserting it. The main difficulty is to find a likely author, and though there is evidence that Purcell's pupil John Weldon wrote music for a production of *The Tempest* in 1712 which has not survived (unless this is it), other specimens of his work at all comparable give little indication of a technique that could have managed anything on the scale of 'Arise, ye subterranean winds' or with the assurance of 'See, see the heavens smile'— as close in letter and spirit to the early eighteenth-century Italian style as can be imagined. Perhaps in the years since writing his prize-opera *The Judgement of Paris* (1701) Weldon's style had developed sufficiently. It is not impossible and seems more credible than that Purcell could have written the music as early as 1695.

In any event we cannot use the vocal music in *The Tempest* as an illustration of the final stage of Purcell's development as a song writer, even if, superficially, it might seem a plausible sequel to *The Fairy Queen* in certain technical respects. One would be forced to conclude that romantic fertility of imagination and richness of invention had given way before the steely brilliance of Italian late Baroque. There is little sign of this in other works. The *air en rondeau* 'I attempt from love's sickness to fly' in *The Indian Queen* is as fine and delicate as anything in *The Fairy Queen*, and 'They tell us that you mighty powers' captures the same vein of lyrical ardour as 'If love's a sweet passion'. And whereas the recitative 'Your awful voice' in *The Tempest* is merely a perfunctory piece of eighteenth-century *recitativo secco* (though it would have offered Purcell plenty of scope for extravagant treatment), in other works he still employed his own highly personal style of affective declamation. The opening of Pandora's song 'Sweeter than roses' in Norton's *Pausanias* (1695), for example, is unmistakably erotic and as highly charged as anything in Wagner or Strauss. In a different way the noble lament of the death of Queen Mary (*'Incassum Lesbia'*) is profoundly moving, especially such passages as *'mens est immodulata'* in the first section and the impassioned opening of the third, *'Regina, heu! Arcadiae'*. He even refrains from writing a ground bass in the middle section, thereby leaving himself free to exploit opportunities for harmonic expression as at the wonderful passage *'ad modum fletur'*.

A further—and final—demonstration of Purcell's mastery of the flamboyant declamatory style are the Mad Songs in

Ex. 120a from 'Incassum Lesbia' (Herbert: *The Queen's Epicedium*)   Henry Purcell (*P1695c*)

D'Urfey's *The Comical History of Don Quixote* (1694–5). These occur in the first and third parts of the cycle, respectively Cardenio's 'Let the dreadful engines' and Altisidora's 'From rosy bow'rs'. (The Mad Song in part two of the play, 'I burn, I burn', was composed by John Eccles.) Both of Purcell's use the sectional form that he had employed earlier in such songs as 'Bess of Bedlam' ('From silent shades', *P1683*) and 'Beneath the poplar's shadow' in Lee's *Sophonisba*, but here with such intense and violent contrasts as to convey unmistakably the illogical train of thought of a deranged mind. Contrast of major and minor is one of the principal devices used in Cardenio's song: the vivid juxtaposition of 'manic' and 'depressive' states in the first two recitative sections is achieved largely by this means as well as by contrast in the manner of declamation. Later, following a dramatic outburst at 'Ye powers, I did but use her name' in emphatic *recitatio secco*, the key changes again and the movement slows to an expressive *arioso* with pathetic repetitions of the phrase 'where are now [those flow'ry groves]'. Then comes a return to fury and F major:

> *I glow, I glow, but 'tis with Hate*
> *Why must I burn for this Ingrate?*

followed by withdrawal and resignation into the minor:

> *Cool, cool it then, and rail,*
> *Since nothing will prevail.*

There follows a lively movement cynically analysing the motives of women's love, and at last Cardenio becomes calm. The fit has passed and with child-like simplicity he bids them (and the world) 'Good Night'.

The psychological truth of all this is profoundly affecting; yet much must have depended on the way it was performed. Undoubtedly John Bowman, who played Cardenio was immensely versatile. Indeed it must not be forgotten that one factor that enabled Purcell to make such technical progress during the last five or six years of his life, and which helped to liberate his style, was the excellent singers available to him. Among the women was Mrs. Ayliff, whom Motteaux praised, Charlotte Butler who so impressed Roger North, Arabella Hunt immortalized by Congreve in his ode *Upon a Lady's Singing*, and Anne Bracegirdle, whose singing of Eccles' 'I burn, I burn' inspired Purcell's 'Whilst I with grief' in Dryden's *The Spanish Friar* (1694). Mrs. Ayliff especially must have had formidable technical and interpretative powers judging by the recitative 'Let sullen discord' he wrote for her in the 1693 Birthday Song for Queen Mary (*Celebrate this Festival*). Then in the last year of his life Mrs. Cross came on the scene in time to sing 'I attempt from Love's sickness' and 'They tell us that you mighty powers' in *The Indian Queen*, 'O lead me to some peaceful gloom' in *Bonducca*, as well as 'From rosy bow'rs'—songs which testify to extraordinary gifts in one so young.

Laetitia Cross was known as 'The Girl', the female counterpart of 'The Boy'—Jemmy Bowen. Of his ability as a singer we have both Purcell's own reported testimony and the evidence of the songs that were composed for him, including 'Celia has a thousand charms' in Gould's *The Rival Sisters* (1695). He also took part in *The Indian Queen*, singing 'Seek not to know'.

It was in that opera that the great bass Richard Leveridge made his debut as Ismeron and thus became the first of a long line to sing 'Ye twice ten hundred deities'. Up to this time most of the important bass songs in Purcell's operas and incidental music had been written for Bowman. The countertenors Freeman and Pate must also have been skilful singers, for it was the former who sang 'Sound the Trumpet, beat the warlike drum' in the Birthday Song for the Duke of Gloucester in 1695, and the latter who, on one occasion at least, performed ''Tis Nature's voice'. Both were active on the stage, unlike the basses Gostling and Woodson—who were in holy orders—and the counter-tenors Boucher, Howell and Damascene, for all of whom he wrote difficult and elaborate music in his anthems and odes.

The women were probably lyric sopranos with pretty voices, though Mrs. Ayliff must have been more versatile. But it was the men, and particularly the basses, whose vocal resources provided Purcell with the means whereby the full splendour of his gifts as a song writer could be realized.

'From rosy bow'rs' was said in *Orpheus Britannicus* to be 'the last Song that Mr. *Purcell* Sett, it being in his Sickness'. The development thus concluded is truly amazing. He brought the melodic and harmonic refinement of the lighter type of song to a peak in such exquisite pieces as 'If love's a sweet passion', the second setting of 'If music be the food of love' and 'I attempt from love's sickness'. But in another direction his achievement was far greater, both as to the progress made as well as the intrinsic excellence of the final product, for it was actually to evolve forms capable of giving expression to the most powerful emotions.

Turning first to recitative, he developed its expressive capabilities from about 1683 onwards by the application of a technique which was basically ornamental but, true to the baroque aesthetic, dynamically conceived with the aim of stirring the affections. On the other hand, the air as Purcell inherited it was a puny thing, quite unequal to weighty subject matter. But in the ground bass the composer saw a means whereby he could achieve this ideal. Again the years around 1683 were critical. Over the next decade his handling of ground-bass technique became increasingly free, and this in itself enabled the form to expand. The practice of repeating the ground over and over in the same key brought with it dangers of monotony—a limiting factor. Transposition of the bass into related keys in the middle section of a song was a device which offered a remedy, and increasingly towards 1690 the repetitive element became less literal.

Indeed, the distinction between ground and free ostinato technique becomes blurred in Purcell's mature period, and it is evident that, strictly speaking, the ground had served its purpose in the evolutionary process by 1692. For by that time he had learned to apply the technique of abstract motivic composition within a large-scale tonal framework to vocal music. Italian instrumental music provided the model, yet in all he did he showed 'a peculiar Genius to express the Energy of *English Words*, whereby he mov'd the Passions as well as caus'd Admiration in all his Auditors.'[16] He died aged 36. As often, Roger North summarizes aptly and provides an epitaph:

Orpheus Brittanicus Mr. H. Purcell . . . began to shew his great skill before the reforme of musick *al'Italliana*, and while he was warm in the persuit of it, dyed; but a greater musicall genius England never had.[17]

2 The songs of Blow and some younger contemporaries

Orpheus Britannicus came out posthumously in two books dated 1698 and 1702 respectively, and subsequently in enlarged editions, the third (1721) containing a total of 185 songs. John Blow, in collecting together 50 of his own songs for *Amphion Anglicus* in 1700, did not perhaps trust immediate posterity to perform the same service for him, and with reason.[1] True, Blow was a formidable figure with an impressive and well deserved reputation as a choral composer second only to Purcell, but his standing as a songwriter was lower by a long way.

This much must be said of him (and it is why he is being considered alongside Purcell rather than his contemporaries Humfrey and Turner); he shared Purcell's view of song as something beyond the amorous trifles of court and theatre. For him, too, it had a high and serious purpose. But good intentions and high ideals are not enough. With Blow the spirit was willing, but the technique was weak.

The overall view makes it clear that the absolutely crucial weakness was his inability to absorb late seventeenth-century harmonic practice into his idiom. Thus the spacious proportions that derive from it eluded him—which is not to say that he did not write lengthy vocal pieces. But without the prop of polyphony his writing remained cramped and largely ineffectual to the end. False relations and other evidences of unstable scale forms were never eradicated, and expressive details unintegrated into the larger pattern added further confusion. It was rarely that he achieved such refinement as in his setting of Waller's 'It is not that I love you less', and then perhaps only because he had the form of the minuet before him.

Ex. 121 'The Self Banished; out of Waller. A Minuet.'   John Blow *(AA)*

We might expect, therefore, to find his most impressive achievements in serious vein, especially in recitative. Already in the elegy on the death of the Earl of Rochester ('As on his deathbed gasping Strephon lay' in *P1681*) there are signs that this is so, as also in parts of *Venus and Adonis* (*c*.1682). Many years later his deeply moving setting of Dryden's 'Ode on the Death of Mr. Henry Purcell' (1696) confirms the fact; the recitative 'So ceased the rival crew' surely ranking as Blow's finest piece of declamation—not in the objective sense, but as a subjective expression of inconsolable grief.

Ex. 122 from '*An Ode on the Death of Mr. Henry Purcell*'   John Blow (1696)

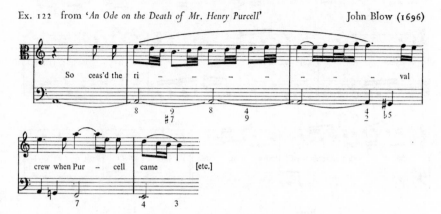

During the 1680's Blow, like Purcell, increasingly adopted a florid, more or less extravagant style in his recitatives, though he was less careful than Purcell to confine his flourishes to words that could logically bear them. Even so, he was able to explore a wide expressive range, as a song like 'Happy the man' illustrates. Beside the Purcell elegy it may seem pretty poor stuff, but though the occasion of the song may be trivial ('Sappho *to the Goddess of Beauty, Addres'd to the Dutchess of Grafton*') and the argument grotesque, the music does force us to take it seriously. (Sappho is struck dumb, blind and deaf by the wit and beauty of Paphiana—Her Grace!—and finally dies). The form is a short, sectional cantata alternating declamatory and tuneful passages. In the excerpt quoted below (Ex. 123) appoggiaturas suggest her faltering speech, the key changes to 'horrific' F minor and her agony ('Slow') continues with jagged leaps in the vocal line and in the bass squirming discords and false relations. Suddenly she becomes aware that her sight, too, is affected. At first she is agitated ('Brisk') and the excitement is reflected in a return to the major. But as her eyes cloud over, major fades to minor, 'Brisk' gives place to 'Slow', and discordant diminished fifths and sevenths mark the onset of

deafness. Thus afflicted she sings her final expressive lament:

> *Pale, cold and speechless, without Breath I lye,*
> *In the sweet transports of my Soul, I die.*

Like Purcell, Blow was drawn to the ground bass though he was never able to accept its discipline completely. Perhaps he misunderstood the nature of the freedoms that Purcell enjoyed; certainly his handling of the form is often diffuse compared with the younger composer. The basses themselves rarely show the same tight construction as Purcell's. Compare, for example, Purcell's 'The sparrow and the gentle dove' from the 1683 Marriage Ode for Princess Anne, with Blow's 'See, see the pausing lustres stand' from the New Year Ode of 1686. Not only does the strict sequential patterning of the former give a thrust to the bass that is lacking in the latter, but its harmonic progression is more purposeful.

Ex. 124a 'The sparrow and the gentle dove' (*From Hardy climes*)   Henry Purcell (*1683*)

Ex. 124b 'See, see the pausing lustres stand' (*Hail Monarch sprung of Race Divine*)
John Blow (*1686*)

Blow's basses being less strongly motivated by tonality tend to modulate haphazardly, and sometimes lose their way altogether. At such times he is prone to abandon the strict form of the bass and not infrequently upset the phrase structure by introducing (or losing) an odd half bar. Even when the bass is a strong one, there is often an almost perverse irregularity in its handling. In the English version of the Queen's Epicideum, which Blow set and published together with Purcell's Latin setting, Blow uses the ground bass form in all but the third of four verses. In the first ('No, Lesbia, no, you ask in vain') and the last, the bass is in three time and well managed on the whole but in the second verse the same bass is transformed into common time and indiscriminately cut about and

Ex. 125 Bass of verse 3 'No, Lesbia, no' (The Queen's *Epicedium*)

John Blow (*P1695c*)

transposed. Already in the third statement half a bar is omitted, while in the fifth, following a modulation to the dominant, only the first half of the bass is given before another repetition in the tonic intervenes. The example below (Ex. 125) indicates how structurally disorganized this section is in general, and how lacking in clear purpose are the excursions from key to key. None of this is made any more convincing by the loose phraseology of the vocal line.

Though not without its moments, the whole effect is confused. Yet by standards other than Purcell's, Blow was not particularly inept at this type of composition. Among the ground basses in *Amphion Anglicus* which illustrate his characteristic waywardness, yet manage to triumph over self-made difficulties 'The sacred nine, observe the mode' and 'The sullen years are past' may be mentioned. The former is actually part of a larger piece ('Welcome, welcome, ev'ry guest') probably a Cecilia Ode. It serves as Prologue to the whole collection, beginning with a flamboyant recitative in D major followed by the ground in question. The Muses are invited to 'observe the mode' (which promptly changes at that point) and to inspect such 'dainties from abroad' as 'the delicious Thracian lute', 'Dodona's mellow flute' and 'Cremona's racy fruit'—the violin. Already the bass, which began in A minor, has moved via C major and D minor back to A minor again, when a ritornello of flutes answered by violins interposes by way of illustrating the last two items respectively. But the voice sings—

> *At home you have the freshest Air;*
> *Vocal, Instrumental Fare.*

and after a repeat of the ritornello to drive home the point, moves (appropriately enough in view of the words) to D major for the conclusion:

> *Our English Trumpet nothing has surpast.*

Ex. 126 from 'Welcome, welcome, ev'ry guest'   John Blow (*AA*)

The whole thing has enormous panache and is, despite some untidy details, as effective a song as any Blow wrote.

For reasons that will be obvious enough by now, the ground bass was for Blow a less satisfactory means of achieving dimensional expansion than for Purcell. Yet his undeniably weighty musical personality was ill-suited to light airs, and though his songs continued to be included in the miscellanies, very few (and virtually none of any length) are completely satisfactory. Such melodic gift as he had could rarely sustain itself throughout the course of a song, yet his undeveloped harmonic sense could not support it either. 'Born with the vices of my kind' (*P1689*)—an apt title—provides a typical example (Ex. 127). The first two bars seem to promise good things (the flattened seventh being an attractive idiosyncrasy of Blow's melodic style) and the next two bars are elegant enough. However, the balancing phrase destroys the effect so far created; it is flat in more ways than one. So irrational is the harmonic sense here that at first one doubts that the accidentals are correctly placed until trial and error in an attempt to rectify a likely printer's mistake fails to produce much of an improvement, even assuming that the flat on the second note of the fifth bar belongs to the preceding note. In fact, the whole approach to the dominant cadence in bar 9 is confused, and there is little to compensate by way of melody to carry the phrase through. Just possibly all this is supposed to convey the idea of 'rambling' which occurs in the text. If so, it shows an over-zealous approach to the expressive function of music—which, first and foremost, has to be music before it can express anything.

Following the double bar, the next line reproduces in a condensed form the virtues and vices of the first two. A perfectly respectable continuation is followed by another plunge into flat regions and an utter break-down in the melody, which limps apologetically to a cadence in F major at 'grown low'. Blow recovers in the last line and another flattened seventh suggests the possibility that some at least of the peculiarities we have noted may be intended as characteristics of a 'Scotch Song'. (But on reflection it is difficult to believe that there can

Ex. 127 'Born with the vices of my kind'   John Blow (*P1689*)

Born with the vi - ces of my kind, I should in - con - stant be; Dear

Ce - lia could I ramb - ling find, More beau - ty, more beau - ty, than in

thee: The rol - ling sur - ges of my blood, By vir-tue now, now grown low,

Should a new show'r in - crease the flood, Too soon would o - - ver - flow.

be anything in this: if there were it would only mean that the song had failed as a parody too.)

This song has been examined in some detail because it is an average specimen which allows us to pinpoint some characteristic weaknesses within a few bars. The melancholy fact, so far as Blow's songs are concerned, is that he remained at the mercy of his weaknesses until the end. As we have seen, they stem, in the main, from his failure to absorb the new tonal idiom fully into his system. Among other consquences it meant that he was unable to expand his solo songs as successfully as Purcell had done.

For though he might adopt ostinato techniques, employ instrumental motives and extend his phrases through repetition and coloratura writing, the tonal organization too often remains haphazard to the detriment of the song as a whole. The opening section of 'At looser hours in the shade' will illustrate most of these points without too much adverse reflection on the composer (Ex. 128). It begins as if it were to be a ground bass, but after a single repetition the bass moves to the dominant where it cadences. The rhythmic character and firm C major harmonic basis of this opening is distinctly Italian in style, and offers promise of easy, if mechanical, development through a circle of related keys. In fact, having arrived at the dominant in bar 8 a restatement of the opening material in the new key might have been expected, and this is what Blow seems inclined to do at first. But instead, he retreats to the tonic immediately. The effect is disappointing, though he gives signs of being able to retrieve the situation with a sequence in the bass beginning at bar 9 which might have spun out the line to a close in G some bars ahead. However, this expectation is again frustrated. The sequence does not take shape, nor does another which offers itself at bar 11. And though the tonal direction at this point is towards sharp keys, the bass finds itself unaccountably in F major at bar 12, and has to retrace its harmonic steps before cadencing in the dominant at bar 16. Yet in other respects the structure is fairly tight. Significantly the

cadences have occurred at bars 8 and 16, and the initial motive
has stamped its rhythmic character, somewhat untidily to be
sure, on most of the material.

The conclusion seems inescapable then, that Blow, as a song
writer, fails at all levels. He either cannot or will not please
with trifles, and though he aspires to something higher he just
has not got what it takes. Naturally there are a few songs to

Ex. 128 'At looser hours in the shade'   John Blow (*AA*)

contradict both these statements, but not enough to prove them wrong.

Many of the younger generation of composers acknowledged Purcell and Blow as their teachers and none could escape the influence of Purcell, at least. It remains to follow them to the turn of the century leaving them stranded on the shore without compunction to await the tidal wave of Italian music which was to submerge them and sweep in Handel on its crest. Inevitably they suffer in comparison with Purcell on the one hand and Handel on the other, yet they could all write pleasant and tuneful songs even if large-scale vocal composition was beyond most of them. In many ways they deserve respect, especially Daniel Purcell, the younger brother of Henry, John Eccles and John Weldon who are by no means negligible composers.

Daniel Purcell and Eccles had made their mark even before Henry Purcell's death. We know that Henry Purcell had been stirred by Mrs. Butler's singing of Eccles' Mad Song 'I burn, I burn' in *Don Quixote*, Part II (1694), though it seems mechanical and harmonically bald compared with Purcell's own mad songs in *Don Quixote*. Daniel Purcell had been represented in the song collections since 1687, and in 1696 'Additional Musick to the *Indian Queen*, by Mr. *Daniel Purcell*' was published in *Deliciae Musicae*, thus completing what his brother had been unable to do before his death. From then on he wrote music for the 'operas' regularly—for Powell's *Brutus of Alba* (1697), for Settle's *The World in the Moon* (1697) with Jeremiah Clarke, and for Gildon's *Phaeton* (1698) not to mention dozens of play-songs. 'Underneath a gloomy shade', one of his songs in Oldmixon's *The Grove* (1700) gives a good idea of his ability. The opening recitative strikes a nice balance between expressive ornament and straightforward musical declamation, while the air is a well-turned dance song (Ex. 129).

Daniel Purcell seems to have been regularly employed by

Rich's newly formed Patent Company, while Eccles served Betterton's. He was the major contributor to Motteaux's *Loves of Mars and Venus* (1696) which contains the simple yet touching duet 'How sweet, how lovely' between the protagonists. In the same year he provided a score for a revival of *Macbeth*.

While these two composers were writing for the opposing theatrical companies and trying between them to fill the gap

Ex. 129a   'Underneath a gloomy shade' (Oldmixon: *The Grove*)   Daniel Purcell (*1700*)

Ex. 129b

left by Henry Purcell, John Weldon was organist of New College, Oxford. Probably most of his energies were devoted to church music at this stage, yet when the three of them came together to contend for the 'Musick Prize', setting Congreve's *Judgement of Paris* (1701), it was Weldon who won the first prize of a hundred guineas, followed by Eccles (fifty guineas) and Daniel Purcell (thirty guineas). Gottfried Finger, an emigré musician 'reputed a very good composer' had to be content with the fourth prize of twenty guineas, but left the country in a huff saying that 'he thought he was to be judged by men and not by boys.'[2] Up to that time Weldon seems to have had no dramatic experience at all.

Having left Oxford for London he published *A Collection of New Songs* in 1702, containing his well known setting of 'Take, O take those lips away'. If one accepts Wilson's version as being close to an ideal, then this is absurdly pretentious in style. The opening recitative surely represents the misapplica-

Ex. 130 'Take, O take those lips away' (Shakespeare: *Measure for measure*)

John Weldon (*1702*)

tion of undoubted musical gifts; the air, for all its sequences, is too loosely constructed and cannot bring together diverse materials (Ex. 30).

On the other hand, 'Peace babbling brook' is a good ground bass with obbligato parts for two flutes, and Weldon shows again in his second (or third) *Book of Songs* (1703) that he had inherited Purcell's predilection for this type of composition and some of his skill. The second section of 'My cruel fair one has the art' enables us to compare his handling of a similar ground bass to that of Dido's lament. True, it is changed then abandoned later in the song, but it is not this which dissipates the feeling of the opening so much as lapsing into easy sequences and irrelevant coloratura (Ex. 131).

Gottfried Finger, the fourth prize winner, had published numerous songs since coming to England about 1685, especially in *Thesaurus Musicus* (1694–96). He shows Italianate leanings in his setting of Congreve's 'I tell thee Charmion' (*Love*

Ex. 131 from 'My cruel fair one has the art'   John Weldon *(1703)*

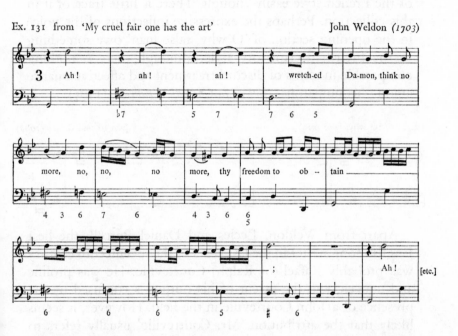

for Love, 1695) though he is equally able to satisfy less sophisticated tastes. Another German musician, the opera composer Johann Wolfgang Franck who had arrived in London from Hamburg about the same time as Finger, quickly made himself at home in the popular idiom, as the contents of *Remedium Melancholiae* (1690) show. His style was smooth and graceful and is seen to best advantage in songs published in the *Gentleman's Journal* (1692–94).[3] Nicola Matteis we have already encountered. He is more important as an instrumental composer, but he published two books of songs entitled *A Collection of New Songs* in 1696 and 1699. There is nothing very remarkable in either although the songs in the second book are quite ambitious.

In 1698 yet another foreign musician in London, Jean Claude Gillier, published *A Collection of New Songs*. Despite many songs and dances written for the *comédie française* between visits to London, he seems to have been able to divest himself of the French style easily enough. There is little trace of it in this collection. Perhaps the expressive inflections of the voice in the opening section of 'O why, false man' owe something to the French declamatory style, although there is nothing comparable in terms of discord treatment and affective nuance among his numerous *Airs de la Comédie Françoise* (1705).

Ex. 132 'O why, false man'   Jean Claude Gillier *(1698)*

Apart from Weldon, Eccles and Daniel Purcell, the best English song writer in the last years of the seventeenth century was probably Rafael (or Ralph) Courteville. He was prolific and uneven, and the extent of his output is confused by the presence of a John Courteville in the field. However, it seems likely that the attribution 'Mr. Courteville' usually refers to Rafael. Many of his songs demonstrate quite a well developed technique. 'Cease, Hymen, cease' from *Don Quixote*, III (1695) gives evidence of expressive power in recitative and suggests

Ex. 133 from 'Cease Hymen, cease' (Durfey: *Don Quixote*, III)   Rafael Courteville *(1696)*

that he is able to spread himself without becoming diffuse (Ex. 133).

Richard Leveridge, on the other hand, inclines to a more robust vein—as one might expect of the composer of 'The Roast Beef of old England'. His career as a singer and composer extended well into the eighteenth century (indeed, he belongs properly to that century), but already in 1697 a collection of his songs had been issued, and *A Second Book of Songs* followed in 1699. There were to be others later, as well as many songs published in single sheets. His score for *Macbeth* (1702) certainly indicates an inferior technique, but as Dent remarks 'it is effective stage music' and shows at least that operatic composition was not beyond him.[4]

In this he proved himself superior to others such as John Lenton, Jeremiah Clarke and John Barrett—the last two pupils of Blow. The best of Clarke's popular songs are to be found in *Mercurius Musicus* (1699–1700), but on the whole his gift of melody is slender. This is not to say that he lacked ability as a composer of vocal music, for on a more elevated plane his Elegy of the Death of Henry Purcell proves otherwise—especially the moving recitative 'Hold shepherd, hold' and the Italianate aria with obbligato flutes 'The glory of th' Arcadian groves'.[5] Barrett's contributions to *Mercurius Musicus* are neatly turned. This is more than can be said of *A Collection of New Songs . . . by Mr. Morgan* issued in 1697; his recitative 'What would Europa' in Motteaux's *Europe's Revels* (1697) is pretentious but hardly competent. No doubt a combination of spectacle and splendid singing helped to bring it off, as we may guess from the rubric '*Jupiter descends on his Eagle Sung by Mr. Leveridge*'.

Other individual collections were devoted to the songs of John Abell and Vaughan Richardson. Overcome with gratitude at being allowed to return to his native country from a picaresque exile as a Papist, Abell published in 1701 *A Collection of Songs in Several Languages*, distinguished more for patriotic fervour than musical excellence. He also published *A*

Collection of Songs in English the same year, and *A Choice Collection of Italian Ayres* in 1703. Italian inflence is evident in the former too, not only by reason of the *da capo* form of some of the songs, but in the rhythmic and motivic character of the vocal line. The opening of 'I'll press, I'll bless thee' and the start of the middle section in the relative minor give an idea of the extent of this influence.

Ex. 134a   'I'll press, I'll bless thee, charming fair'   John Abell *(1701)*

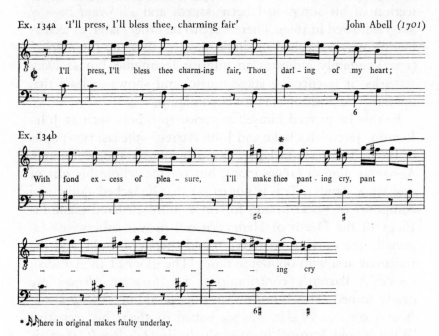

Ex. 134b

* ♪♪ here in original makes faulty underlay.

Vaughan Richardson's *Collection of New Songs* (1701) contains few tuneful settings of negligible worth. He is slightly more impressive in chamber duets that give scope for imitative treatment of the voices.

And so on . . . There seems little point in continuing this catalogue of mediocrity. Luminaries such as these shine only to the extent that they reflect Purcell's brightness. For Henry Purcell brings the development of English song in the seventeenth century to a peak and to an end. What follows is anticlimax. The Enlightenment had dawned and the lyric Muse was already numb in the cool light of Reason. Materialism and rationalism led Englishmen to discover their genius for commerce and politics. They saw themselves as patrons of the arts, not practitioners. More and more foreigners flooded in; not that all singing stopped, for the well-springs of a nation's song can never dry up. Indeed, what is arguably the true tradition of English Song from the lute ayre onwards continued unchecked into the eighteenth and nineteenth centuries in the songs of Arne, Linley and Bishop. But on another plane English Song in the seventeenth century presents a development complete and remarkable in itself—one giving primacy to the expression of feeling through words and music acting more powerfully together than either could separately. In the course of the century the means changed though the aim remained the same. The subjective intensity of Dowland's musical language was still based on contrapuntal principles, but Henry Lawes's ardent rhetoric was monodic and required only the harmonic support of a thorough bass. Purcell exploited the dramatic possibilities of recitative to the utmost and created large scale vocal forms to carry the force of what he had to say.

In fact, the scale was too great. Being larger than life it was more suited to the stage. The tendency of the century as a whole had been towards increasing dramatization, and it is hardly surprising that opera and symphony should hold such sway throughout Europe in the century to follow. It was not until the rebirth of lyricism in the Romantic period, and then in Germany, that poetry and music came together again with such mutual sympathy as they had done in seventeenth-century England.

Bibliography of seventeenth century song-books

This list is primarily a key to song-book abbreviations used in the text. It includes publications of lutesong writers (but not madrigalists) and most of the larger and more important collections of songs published between 1651 and 1703 (but not collections of songs from operas). The titles themselves have been shortened in most cases, and no attempt has been made to indicate the whereabouts of surviving copies. Some modern editions and reprints have been referred to. For more complete bibliographical details see Fellowes *EMV* and Day *ESB*.

B1596   William Barley: *A new Booke of Tabliture . . . 1596* (ed. Wilburn W. Newcombe, *Lute Music of Shakespeare's Time* [1966])

D1597   John Dowland: *The First Booke of Songes or Ayres of fowre partes with Tableture for the Lute . . . 1597* (²/1600, ³/1603, ⁴/1606, ⁵/1613, ELS-1 vol. 1/2, ELS-R vol. 4)

M1597   Thomas Morley: *Canzonets Or Little Short Aers To Five And Sixe Voices . . . 1597* (*EM* vol. 3)

C1598   Michael Cavendish: *14. Ayres in Tabletorie to the Lute . . . 1598* (ELS-2 vol. 7, ELS-R vol. 5)

D1600   John Dowland: *The Second Booke of Songs or Ayres . . . 1600* (ELS-2 vol. 5/6, ELS-R vol. 4)

J1600   Robert Jones: *The First Booke Of Songes & Ayres Of foure partes with Tableture for the Lute . . . 1600* (ELS-2 vol. 4, ELS-R vol. 7)

M1600   Thomas Morley: *The First Booke Of Ayres, Or Little Short Songs, To Sing And Play To The Lute, With The Base Viole . . . 1600* (ELS-1, vol. 16, ELS-R vol. 8)

J*1601*   Robert Jones: *The Second Booke of Songes and Ayres, Set out to the Lute, the base Violl the playne way, or the Base by tableture after the leero fashion* . . . *1601* (ELS-2 vol. 5, ELS-R vol. 7)

R*1601*   Philip Rosseter [and Thomas Campion]: *A Booke of Ayres, Set foorth to be song to the Lute, Orpherian, and Base Violl* . . . *1601* (21 songs by Campion in Part I; 21 songs by Rosseter in Part II: ELS-1 vols. 4/13 and 8/9 respectively, ELS-R vol. 9)

D*1603*   John Dowland: *The Third And Last Booke Of Songs Or Aires. Newly composed to sing to the Lute, Orpharion, or viols* . . . *1603* (ELS-1 vol. 10/11, ELS-R vol. 4)

G*1604*   Thomas Greaves: *Songes of Sundrie kindes: First, Aires To Be Sung To the Lute, and Base Violl. Next, Songes of sadnesse, for the Viols and Voyce. Lastly, Madrigalles, for five voyces* . . . *1604* (ELS-2 vol. 18, ELS-R vol. 5)

H*1605*   Tobias Hume: [*Musicall Humors*] *The First Part of Ayres, French, Pollish, and others together, some in Tabliture, and some in Prickle-Song* . . . *1605* (ELS-2 vol. 21, ELS-R vol. 6)

J*1605*   Robert Jones: *Ultimum Vale* . . . *Whereof The first part is for the Lute, the Voyce, and the Viole Degambo, The 2, part is for the Lute, the Viole, and foure partes to sing, The third part is for two Trebles, to sing either to the Lute, or the Viole or to both* . . . *1605* (ELS-2 vol. 16, ELS-R vol. 7)

P*1605*   Francis Pilkington: *The First Booke of Songs or Ayres of 4. parts: with Tableture for the Lute or Orpherian, with the Violl de Gamba* . . . *1605* (ELS-2 vols. 7/15, ELS-R vol. 8)

B*1606*   John Bartlet: *A Booke Of Ayres* . . . *the third part is for the Lute and one Voyce, and the Viole de Gamba* . . . *1606* (ELS-2 vol. 3, ELS-R vol. 1)

C*1606*   Giovanni Coprario [John Cooper]: *Funeral Teares. For the death of the* . . . *Earle of Devonshire. Figured In seaven songes, whereof sixe* . . . *may be exprest by a treble voice alone to the Lute and Base Viole, or else that the meane part may bee added* . . . *1606* (ELS-1 vol. 17, ELS-R vol. 3)

D*1606*   John Danyel: *Songs For The Lute Viol and Voice* . . . *1606* (ELS-2 vol. 8, ELS-R vol. 3)

C*1607*   Thomas Campion: *The Description Of A Maske* . . . *in honour of the Lord Hayes* . . . *1607* (ELS-2 vol. 2)

F*1607*   Thomas Ford: *Musicke Of Sundrie Kindes* . . . *The First Whereof Are, Aries for 4. Voices to the Lute, Orphorion, or Basse-Biol* . . . *1607* (ELS-1 vol. 3, ELS-R vol. 5)

H1607   Tobias Hume: *Captaine Humes Poeticall Musicke . . . 1607* (*ELS*-R vol. 6)

F1609   Alfonso Ferrabosco: *Ayres . . . 1609* (*ELS*-*2* vol. 16, *ELS*-R vol. 5)

J1609   Robert Jones: *A Musicall Dreame, Or The Fourth Booke of Ayres . . . the Third part is for one Voyce alone, or to the Lute, the Basse Viole, or to both if you please, Whereof, two are Italian Ayres . . . 1609* (*ELS*-*2* vol. 14, *ELS*-R vol. 7)

R1609a   [Thomas Ravenscroft]: *Pammelia, Musicke Miscellanie. Or, Mixed Varietie of Pleasant Roundelayes, and delightfull Catches . . . 1609* (²/1618)

R1609b   [Thomas Ravenscroft]: *Deuteromelia: Or The Second part of Musicks melodie . . . Of Pleasant Roundelaies; K. H. mirth, or Freemens Songs. And such delightfull Catches . . . Catch that catch can . . . 1609*

C1610   William Corkine: *Ayres, To sing And Play To The Lute And Basse Violl . . . 1610* (*ELS*-*2* vol. 12, *ELS*-R vol. 3)

D1610   [Robert Dowland]: *A Musicall Banquet. Furnished with varietie of delicious Ayres. Collected out of the best Authors in English, French, Spanish, and Italian . . . 1610* (*ELS*-*2* vol. 20, *ELS*-R vol. 4)

J1610   Robert Jones: *The Muses Gardin for Delights . . . 1610* (*ELS*-*2* vol. 14, *ELS*-R vol. 7)

M1611   John Maynard: *The XII. Wonders Of The World . . . 1611* (*ELS*-R vol. 8)

R1611   [Thomas Ravenscroft]: *Melismata. Musicall Phansies . . . 1611*

C1612   William Corkine: *The Second Booke Of Ayres, Some, to Sing and Play to the Base-Violl alone: Others, to be sung to the Lute and Base Violl . . . 1612* (*ELS*-*2* vol. 13, *ELS*-R vol. 3)

D1612   John Dowland: *A Pilgrimes Solace . . . 1612* (*ELS*-*1* vol. 12/14, *ELS*-R vol. 4)

C1613   Giovanni Coprario [John Cooper]: *Songs of Mourning: Bewailing the untimely death of Prince Henry . . . set forth to bee sung with one voyce to the Lute, or Violl . . . 1613* (*ELS*-*1* vol. 17, *ELS*-R vol. 3)

C1613 a & b   Thomas Campion: *Two Bookes Of Ayres . . . To be sung to the Lute and Viols, in two, three, and foure Parts: or by one Voyce to an Instrument . . .* (c. 1613, *ELS*-*2* vol. 1/2, *ELS*-R vol. 2)

N1613   Angelo Notari: *Prime Musiche Nuove . . .* (1613, engraved)

C1614   Thomas Campion: *The Description of a Maske . . . At the Marriage of the . . . Earle of Somerset . . . 1614* (*ELS*-R vol. 2)

—— [I.G., W.D. and T.B.]: *The Maske of Flowers . . . Being the last of the Solemnities . . . performed at the marriage of the . . . Earle of Somerset . . . 1614*

M*1618* George Mason [and John Earsden:] *The Ayres That Were Sung And Played, at Brougham Castle in Westmerland, in the Kings Entertainment . . . 1618* (ELS-2 vol. 18, ELS-R vol. 8)

C*1618* a & b Thomas Campion: *The Third And Fourth Booke Of Ayres) Composed . . . So as they may be expressed by one Voyce, with a Violl, Lute, or Orpharion . . .* (c. 1618, ELS-2 vol. 10/11, ELS-R vol. 2)

P*1620* Martin Peerson: *Private Musicke. Or The First Booke of Ayres and Dialogues: Contayning Songs of 4. 5. and 6. parts, of severall sorts, and being Verse and Chorus, is fit for Voyces and Viols. And for want of Viols, they may be performed to either the Virginall or Lute, where the Proficient can play upon the Ground, or for a shift to the Base Viol alone . . . 1620*

A*1622* John Attey: *The First Booke Of Ayres Of Foure Parts, With Tableture for the Lute: So made, that all the parts may be plaide together with the Lute, or one voyce with the Lute and Base-Vyoll . . . . 1622* (ELS-2 vol. 9, ELS-R vol. 1)

—— [Edward Filmer]: *French court-aires, With their ditties Englished, of foure and five parts. Together with that of the Lute . . . 1629*

—— Walter Porter: *Madrigales and Ayres . . . with the continued Base . . . After the manner of Consort Musique. To be performed with the Harpesechord, Lutes, Theorbos, Base Violl, two Violins, or two Viols . . . 1632* (ELS-R vol. 8)

—— [John Benson and John Playford]: *A Musicall Banquet . . . The third Part contains New and Choyce Catches or Rounds for three or foure Voyces . . . 1651*

H*1652* [John Hilton]: *Catch that Catch can . . . 1652*

P*1652* [John Playford]: *Select Musicall Ayres, And Dialogues, for one and two Voyces, to sing to the Theorbo, Lute, or Basse Violl . . . 1652* (ESB-R vol. 1)

L*1653* Henry Lawes: *Ayres and Dialogues, For One, Two, and Three Voyces . . . 1653*

P*1653* [John Playford]: *Select Musicall Ayres and Dialogues . . . 1653* (ESB-R vol. 1)

L*1655* Henry Lawes: *The Second Book Of Ayres, And Dialogues . . . 1655*

G1656 John Gamble: *Ayres And Dialogues (To be Sung to the Theorbo-Lute or Base-Violl))* . . . *1656* (²/1657)

H1658 [John Hilton]: *Catch that Catch can* . . . *The Second Edition Corrected and Enlarged by J. Playford* . . . *1658*

L1658 Henry Lawes: *Ayres, And Dialogues* . . . *M.DC.LVIII* (Reprinted as Book III of *The Treasury of Musick* . . . *1669*)

G1659 John Gamble: *Ayres And Dialogues* . . . *1659*

P1659 [John Playford]: *Select Ayres And Dialogues* . . . *1659* (Reprinted as Book I of *The Treasury of Musick* . . . *1669*, *ESB-R* vol. 1)

W1660 John Wilson: *Cheerful Ayres Or Ballads First composed for one single Voice and since set for three Voices* . . . *M DC LX*

——— [John Forbes]: *Songs and Fancies. To Thre, Foure, or Five Partes, both apt for Voices and Viols* . . . *M, DC, LXII* (²/1666; *Cantus* part only was published)

P1663 [John Playford and Zachariah Watkins]: *Catch that Catch can* . . . *1663* (The 1658 edition with additions.)

P1667 [John Playford: *Catch that Catch can: Or*] *The Musical Companion* . . . *To which is now added a Second Book Containing Dialogues, Glees, Ayres, & Ballads* . . . *1667*

K1668 William King: *Songs and Ayres with a Thorough Basse to the Theorbo, Harpsecon, or Base-Violl* . . . *1668*

P1669 [John Playford]: *Select Ayres And Dialogues* . . . *1669* (Book II of *The Treasury of Musick* . . . *1669*, and possibly a reissue of a lost edition advertised in 1663. The first and third books of the 'Treasury' are respectively *P1659* and *L1658*. The complete collection has been reprinted in facsimile by The Gregg Press [1966]; see also *ESB-R* vol. 1)

P1673a [John Playford]: *Choice Songs and Ayres For One Voyce To Sing to a TheorboL-ute, or Bass-Viol. Being Most of the Newest Songs sung at Court, and at the Publick Theatres* . . . *1673* (Enlarged editions in 1675 and 1676)

P1673b [John Playford]: *The Musical Companion* . . . *1673* (An enlarged edition of *P1667*.)

P1675 [John Playford]: *Choice Ayres, Songs, & Dialogues* . . . *1675* (An enlarged edition of *P1673a*)

P1676 [John Playford]: *Choice Ayres, Songs & Dialogues* . . . *1676* (An enlarged edition of *P1675*; *ESB-R* vol. 2)

B1677 Henry Bowman: *Songs for i 2 & 3 Voyces* . . . (1677, engraved; further editions are dated 1678 and 1679)

B1678 [John Banister and Thomas Low]: *New Ayres and Dialogues
. . . MDCLXXVIII [Girolamo Pignani]: Scelta di Canzonette
Italiane di diversi Autori . . . J. Playford . . . 1679*

P1679 [John Playford]: *Choice Ayres & Songs . . . The Second Book . . .
1679 (ESB-R vol. 2)*

R1680 Pietro Reggio: *Songs* (1680: engraved; reprinted in 1692)

P1681 [John Playford]: *Choice Ayres and Songs . . . The Third Book
. . . 1681 (ESB-R vol. 2)*

—— [John Forbes]: *Songs and Fancies . . . The Third Edition . . .
With severall of the choisest Italian Songs, and New English Ayres,
all in three parts . . . 1682 (Cantus part only of the songs in the
original edition, F1662.* A facsimile edition was published by
Alex. Gardner of Paisley in 'The New Club Series' [1879])

—— [Joseph Hindmarsh]: *A New Collection Of Songs And Poems.
By Thomas D'urfey . . . 1683*

P1683 [John Playford]: *Choice Ayres and Songs . . . The Fourth Book
1683* (Reprinted in *P1695; ESB-R vol. 2)*

—— [Joseph Hindmarsh]: *Choice New Songs . . . 1684*

P1684 [John Playford]: *Choice Ayres and Songs . . . The Fifth Book . . .
1684* (Reprinted in *P1695; ESB-R vol. 2)*

—— [Joseph Hindmarsh]: *A Third Collection Of New Songs . . .
1685*

P1685a [Henry Playford and Richard Carr]: *The Theatre of Music: Or,
A Choice Collection of the newest and best Songs Sung at the Court,
and Public Theaters . . . With A Theorbo-Bass to each Song for the
Theorbo, or Bass-Viol. Also Symphonies and Retornels in 3 Parts
to several of them for the Violins and Flutes. The First Book . . .
1685* (Reprinted in *P1695; ESB-R vol. 3)*

P1685b [Henry Playford and Richard Carr]: *The Theatre of Music . . .
The Second Book . . . 1685* (Reprinted in *P1695; ESB-R vol. 3)*

—— [John Playford]: *Catch that Catch can; Or, The Second Part Of
The Musical Companion: Being A Collection Of New Catches,
Songs, and Glees . . . 1685*

—— *A Choice Collection Of 180 Loyal Songs, All of them written
since the Two late Plots (Viz.) The Horrid Salamanca Plot in
1678. And The Fanatical Conspiracy in 1683 . . . To which is
added, The Musical Notes to each Song. The Third Edition . . .
1685* (Reprinted in 1694)

P1686 [Henry Playford and Richard Carr]: *The Theater of Music . . .
The Third Book . . . 1686 (ESB-R vol. 3)*

—— [John Playford]: *The Second Book of the Pleasant Musical Companion: Being a New Collection of Select Catches, Songs, and Glees . . . The Second Edition . . . 1686* (Further editions were issued in 1694, 1701, 1707 and 1720, and supplementary sheets at other times.)

—— [John Carr and Samuel Scott]: *Comes Amoris: Or The Companion of Love. Being a Choice Collection Of the Newest Songs now in Use. With A Thorow Bass to each Song for the Harpsichord, Theorbo, or Bass-Viol. The First Book . . . 1687 (ESB-R* vol. 5)

—— [John Carr and Richard Carr]: *Vinculum Societatis . . . Being a Choice Collection Of the Newest Songs now in Use. With Thorow Bass to each Song for the Harpsichord, Theorbo, or Bass-Viol. The First Book . . . 1687 (ESB-R* vol. 4)

—— [John Crouch]: *A Collection of the Choyest and newest Songs. Sett by severall Masters with a Thorow Bass to each Song for ye Harpsichord Theorbo or Bass-Violl The Second Book . . . 1687* (Engraved)

P1687 [Henry Playford): *The Theater of Music . . . The Fourth and Last Book . . . 1687* (Reprinted in *P1695; ESB-R* vol. 3)

—— [John Carr and Samuel Scott]: *Comes Amoris . . . The Second Book . . . 1688 (ESB-R* vol. 5)

—— [John Carr and Samuel Scott]: *Vinculum Societatis . . . The Second Book . . . MDCLXXXVIII (ESB-R* vol. 4)

P1688a [Henry Playford]: *The Banquet of Musick: Or, A Collection of the newest and best Songs sung at Court, and at Publick Theatres. With A Thorow-Bass for the Theorbo-Lute, Bass-Violl, Harpsichord, or Organ . . . The First Book . . . 1688 (ESB-R* vol. 6)

—— [Henry Playford]: *The Banquet of Musick . . . The Second Book . . . 1688 (ESB-R* vol. 6)

HS-1 [Henry Playford]: *Harmonia Sacra: Or, Divine Hymns And Dialogues: With A thorow-bass for the theorbo-lute, bass-viol, harpsichord, or organ . . . 1688* (^{2}/1696; enlarged editions were published in 1702, 1714, and 1726. A facsimile of the 1726 edition is published by The Gregg Press [1966]).

—— [John Carr and Samuel Scott]: *Comes Amoris . . . The Third Book . . . 1689 (ESB-R* vol. 5)

P1689 [Henry Playford]: *The Banquet of Musick . . . The Third Book . . . 1689 (ESB-R* vol. 6)

—— Johann Wolfgang Franck: *Remedium Melancholiae, Or The Remedy of Melancholy. Being A Choice Collection Of New Songs:*

*With A Thorow-Bass for the Harpsichord, Theorbo, or Bass-viol
. . . 1690*

——— [Henry Playford]: *The Banquet of Musick . . . The Fourth and
Last Book . . . 1690 (ESB-R* vol. 6)

——— [John Carr]: *Vinculum Societatis . . . The Third Book . . .
MDCXCI (ESB-R* vol. 4)

——— [Henry Playford]: *The Banquet of Musick . . . The Fifth Book
. . . 1691 (ESB-R* vol. 6)

——— [Henry Playford]: *The Banquet of Musick . . . The Sixth and
Last Book . . . 1692 (ESB-R* vol. 6)

——— Robert King: *Songs for One Two and Three Voices Composed to
a Through Basse For ye Organ or Harpsichord* (c. 1692, engraved)

——— [John Carr and Samuel Scott]: *Comes Amoris . . . The Fourth
Book . . . 1693 (ESB-R* vol. 5)

——— [John Hudgebut]: *Thesaurus Musicus: Being A Collection of the
Newest Songs Performed At Their Majesties Theatres; and at the
Consorts in Viller-street in York-Buildings, and in Charles-street
Covent-Garden. With a Thorow-Bass to each Song for the Harpsi-
chord, Theorbo, or Bass-Viol . . . The First Book . . . 1693
(ESB-R* vol. 7)

HS-2 [Henry Playford]: *Harmonia Sacra . . . The Second Book . . .
1693* (Further editions were published in 1714 and 1720: a
facsimile of the 1726 edition is published by The Gregg
Press [1966]).

——— [John Carr]: *Comes Amoris . . . The Fifth Book . . . 1694
(ESB-R* vol. 5)

——— [John Hudgebutt]: *Thesaurus Musicus . . . The Second Book . . .
1694 (ESB-R* vol. 7)

——— [John Hudgebutt]: *Thesaurus Musicus . . . The Third Book . . .
1695 (ESB-R* vol. 7)

——— [John Hudgebutt]: *Thesaurus Musicus . . . The Fourth Book . . .
1695 (ESB-R* vol. 7)

——— [Henry Playford]: *Deliciae Musicae: Being, A Collection of the
newest and best Songs Sung at Court and at the Publick Theatres
. . . With A Thorow-Bass, for the Theorbo-Lute, Bass-Viol,
Harpsichord, or Organ . . . The First Book . . . 1695 (ESB-R*
vol. 8)

——— [Henry Playford]: *Deliciae Musicae . . . The Second Book . . .
1695 (ESB-R* vol. 8)

P*1695*   [Henry Playford]: *The New Treasury of Musick . . . 1695*
(Made up of P*1683*, P*1684*, P*1685a*, P*1685b*, P*1687*)

——   [Henry Playford]: *Three Elegies Upon The Much Lamented Loss
Of . . . Queen Mary . . . 1695*

——   Robert King: *A Second Booke of Songs* . . . (c. 1695, engraved).

——   [John Hudgebutt]: *Thesaurus Musicus . . . The Fifth Book . . .
1696* (ESB-R vol. 7)

——   Nicola Matteis: *A Collection of New Songs . . . made purposely
for the use of his Scholars, with a thorough Bass to each Song, for the
Harpsichord Theorboe or Bass Viol . . . 1696* (Engraved)

——   [Henry Playford]: *Deliciae Musicae . . . The Third Book . . .
MDCXVI* (ESB-R vol. 8)

——   [Henry Playford]: *Deliciae Musicae . . . The Fourth Book . . .
1696* (ESB-R vol. 8)

——   [Henry Playford]: *Deliciae Musicae . . . The First Book of the
Second Volume . . . 1696* (ESB-R vol. 8)

——   [Henry Playford]: *Deliciae Musicae . . . The Second Book of the
Second Volume . . . 1696* (ESB-R vol. 8)

——   Richard Leveridge: [*A New Book of Songs...*] (1697; engraved)

——   [Thomas] Morgan: *A Collection of new Songs . . . Compos'd by
Mr. Morgan . . . 1697* (Engraved)

——   Jean Claude Gillier: *A Collection Of New Songs . . . 1698*

——   Henry Purcell: *Orpheus Britannicus. A Collection Of All The
Choicest Songs For One, Two, and Three Voices . . . Figur'd for the
Organ, Harpsichord, or Theorbo-Lute . . . MDCXCVIII* (A
Second book was published in 1702, and second editions of
both books in 1706 and 1711 respectively. A facsimile of the
third edition (1721) has been published by The Gregg Press
[1965]).

——   Richard Leveridge: *A Second Book of Songs...* (1699; engraved)

——   Nicola Matteis: *A Collection of new Songs . . . The Second Book*
(1699)

——   [William Pearson]: *Twelve New Songs, With A Thorow-Bass to
each Song, Figur'd for the Organ, Harpsichord, or Theorboe . . . 1699*

——   [Henry Playford]: *Mercurius Musicus: Or, The Monthly Collection Of New Teaching Songs, Compos'd for the Theatres, and other
Occasions(With a Thorow Bass for the Harpsichord, or Spinett . . .*
(Monthly numbers running from January 1699 to October
1702)

—— [Henry Playford]: *Wit and Mirth: Or, Pills to Purge Melancholy; Being A Collection of the best Merry Ballads and Songs, Old and New . . . 1699* (A further five parts were to follow in 1700, 1702, 1706, 1714 and 1720, each, except the last, reaching several editions.)

AA John Blow: *Amphion Anglicus: A Work Of Many Compositions, For One, Two, Three and Four Voices: With Several Accompagnements of Instrumental Musick; And A Thorow-Bass to each Song: Figur'd for an Organ, Harpsichord, or Theorboe-Lute . . . MDCC* (A facsimile edition has been published by The Gregg Press [1965]).

—— John Abell: *A Collection Of Songs, In English . . . 1701*

—— John Abell: *A Collection Of Songs, In Several Languages . . . 1701*

—— Vaughan Richardson: *A Collection of New Songs, For One, Two, and Three Voices . . . 1701*

—— John Weldon: *A Collection of new Songs . . .* (1702, engraved)

——– John Abell: *A Choice Collection of Italian Ayres . . . 1703*

List of principal manuscript song-books, 1600-1660

Abbreviations used in the text are the same as those in the author's 'English Songs, 1625–60', *Musica Britannica*, XXXIII (1971) pp. 189–90. The arrangement is roughly chronological. References are to works listed in the Select Bibliography.

I *Manuscripts representing a single composer*

—   Cambridge, Trinity College, MS R. 16. 29. Songs by George Handford, 1609; see Edward Doughtie, 'George Handford's "Ayres": Unpublished Jacobean Song Verse' *Anglia*, LXXXII (1964) pp. 474–84

A   London, British Museum, Add. MS 53723. Henry Lawes' autograph songbook, compiled *c*.1634–1650; see WillettsHL

B   Oxford, Bodleian Library, MS Mus. b.l. Songs by John Wilson, *c*.1656, probably in the hand of Edward Lowe (at least in part); see CuttsSCL and CrumM

C   London, British Museum, Add. MS 31432. William Lawes' autograph songbook, *c*.1639–41; see CuttsBM and CrumN

D   London, British Museum, Add. MS 10338. George Jeffreys' autograph containing a few solo songs as well as motets, madrigals, etc: *c*.1669

—   London, British Museum, Add. MS 32339. Seventy-nine songs by John Gamble, *c*.1680, probably a fair copy of a third book of ayres which Gamble proposed to publish, but for some reason never did

II *Manuscript collections of songs by various composers* (1600–1630)

—   Cambridge, King's College, Rowe Library, MS 2. Turpyn's songbook; see OboussierT

—   London, British Museum, Add. MS 15117, see JoinerBM

— London, British Museum, Egerton MS 2971, see Cyr*S*

— London, British Museum, Add. MS 24665, Giles Earle's song-book

— Oxford, Christ Church Library, MS 439

Tenb Tenbury, St. Michael's College Library, MS 1018/9, see Cutts *ESCL*

E Dublin, Trinity College Library, MS F.5.13. The quintus of Thomas Wode's Psalter, with treble part of songs etc: *c.*1615

F Edinburgh, University Library, MS La. III.483. The tenor and bass of Wode's Psalter, with bass part to some of the songs in *E*

G Cambridge, Fitzwilliam Museum, MS 52.D.25. The so-called 'John Bull MS' containing mostly virginal pieces and viol fantasies. Songs added *c.*1620 or later.

H Oxford, Christ Church Library, MS 87. Songs in the oldest part of the book which belonged to 'Mrs. Elizabeth Davenant' in 1624; see Cutts*ED*

I Oxford, Bodleian Library, Music School, MS f.575. Mostly lyra-viol music, but including some songs *c.*1630

J New York, Public Library, Drexel MS 4175. 'Ann Twice, Her Booke': songs, some with tablature accompaniments, probably before 1630; see Cutts*SV*

K London, British Museum, Add. MS 29481. Songs, some ornamented, probably before 1630

— Edinburgh, National Library of Scotland, Advocate's Library, MS.5.2.14 (Leyden MS), songs by Campion and others, 1639; see Nelly Diem, *Beiträge zur Geschichte der Schottischen Musik im XVII Jahrhundert* (1919) pp. 21–4

(1630–1660)

L Oxford, Bodleian Library, MS Don.c.57. Songs probably entered over the period 1631–1660; see Cutts*BS* and Thewlis*N*

M New York, Public Library, Drexel MS 4041. Songs, mostly entered before 1650; see Cutts*D*

N London, British Museum, Egerton MS 2013. Songs probably dating from before 1650. Many version carelessly notated and a considerable number provided with tablature

O London, Lambeth Palace, MS 1041. Songbook belonging to 'The Lady Ann Blount', the first part probably before 1655, the latter part post-Restoration

P   London, British Museum, Add. MS 11608. Songs *c*.1652–1660: among the most interesting and important collections of the period, not least on account of its added vocal embellishments. Of the two hands, the first (*c*.1652) is more authoritative than the second (?) 'T.C.' (*c*.1659)

Q   London, British Museum, Add. MS 10337. 'Elizabeth Rogers hir Virginal Booke: Februarye ye 27, 1656' contains a few texted keyboard versions of songs. If the book is reversed more songs in two-stave score are revealed in another hand, hardly later than that in which the virginal music was written

R   New York, Public Library, Drexel MS 4257. 'John Gamble his booke amen 1659'. Probably compiled over a period of years prior to 1659; see Duckles*GM*, Duckles*JG* and Hughes*JG*

(after 1660, though contents belong to the earlier period)
S   Edinburgh, University Library, MS Dc.1.69. Songs in the hand of Edward Lowe after 1660; see Cutts*SCSE*. Bodleian MS Mus d.238, acquired in 1972, is a companion volume containing *cantus secundus* parts.

T   London, British Museum, Add. MS 29396; songs in the hand of Edward Lowe, *c*.1661–1680

U   Glasgow, University Library, Anderson MS R.d.58–61. Four part-books in the hand of John Playford; a source of glees for P*1667* and P*1673*

V   Paris, Bibliothèque Nationale, MS Rés. 2489. Part of a songbook in the hand of John Playford; a source for P*1669; c.1665;* see Cutts*SCSP*

—   London, British Museum, Add. MS 14399. Songs in the hand of Matthew Locke (?), *c*.1680

—   Edinburgh, National Library of Scotland, Advocate's Library, MS 5.2.17; the contents seem related to the 'Leyden MS' (see above) and F*1662*

Select Bibliography

Works cited in footnotes in abbreviated form are listed in this bibliography along with other relevant writings. For the most part general works have been excluded as have a number of books and articles dealing with various peripheral matters. Nothing exhaustive has been attempted by way of a bibliography of modern editions of the music. Those which were thought to be the most comprehensive and representative have been included. See the *Bibliography of Song Books* for further details about modern editions.

	Arundell, D.	'Purcell and Natural Speech' *Musical Times*, (1959) p. 323
Ault*SCL*	Ault, N.	*Seventeenth-Century Lyrics* (²/1950)
Bentley*JCS*	Bentley, G.E.	*The Jacobean and Caroline Stage*, 7 vols. (1941–68)
	Boorman, S.	'Notari, Porter and the Lute', *Lute Society Journal*, XIII (1971) pp. 28–35.
	Bowden, W.R.	*The English Dramatic Lyric* (1951).
Brett*ECS*	Brett, P.	'The English Consort Song, 1570–1625' *Proceedings of the Royal Musical Association*, LXXXVIII, (1962) pp. 73–88.
Brett*EP*	——————	'Edward Paston (1550–1630): a Norfolk Gentleman and his Musical Collection' *Transactions of the Cambridge Bibliographical Society*, IV (1964) pp. 51–69.
Burney*H*	Burney, C.	*A General History of Music*, 4 vols. (1776–1789).
Colles*VV*	Colles, H.C.	*Voice and Verse* (1928).
Covell*T*	Covell, R.	'Seventeenth Century Music for "The Tempest"' *Studies in Music*, II (1968) pp. 43–65.

Crum*M*	Crum, M.C.	'A Manuscript of John Wilson's Songs' *The Library* (1955) pp. 55–57.
Crum*N*	————————	'Notes on the Texts of William Lawes's Songs in B.M. MS Add. 31432' *The Library*, (1954) pp. 122–127
Cutts*BM*	————————	'British Museum Add MS 31432: William Lawes' writing for the Theatre and the Court' *The Library*, (1952) pp. 225–34.
Cutts*BS*	Cutts, J.P.	'A Bodleian Song-Book: Don.c.57' *Music & Letters*, XXXIV (1953) pp. 192–211.
Cutts*D*	————————	'Drexel MS 4041' *Musica Disciplina*, XVIII (1964) pp. 151–201.
Cutts*ED*	————————	' "M^{ris} Elizabeth Davenant 1624" Christ Church MS. Mus. 87' *Review of English Studies*, X (1959) pp. 26–37.
Cutts*ESCL*	————————	'Early Seventeenth-Century Lyrics at St. Michael's College' *Music & Letters*, XXXVII (1956) pp. 221–33.
Cutts*JPC*	————————	'A John Payne Collier unfabricated "fabrication"' *Notes & Queries*, (1959) pp. 104–6.
Cutts*M*	————————	*La Musique de la Troupe de Shakespeare* (1959 rev. 1971).
	————————	'Original Music to Browne's Inner Temple Masque and other JacobeanMasqueMusic' *Notes & Queries*, (1954) pp. 194–195.
	————————	'Robert Johnson: King's Musician in His Majesty's Public Entertainment' *Music & Letters*, XXXVI (1955) pp. 110–25.

CuttsR ——————— 'Le Rôle de la Musique dans les Masques de Ben Jonson' in *Les Fêtes de la Renaissance,* ed. J. Jacquot (1956) pp. 285–303

Cutts*SCL* ——————— 'Seventeenth-Century Lyrics: Oxford Bodleian MS. Mus. b.l.' *Musica Disciplina,* X (1956) pp. 142–209.

Cutts*SCS* ——————— *Seventeenth Century Songs and Lyrics* (1959).

Cutts*SCSE* ——————— 'Seventeenth Century Songs and Lyrics in Edinburgh University Library Music MS Dc.1.69' *Musica Disciplina,* XIII (1959) pp. 169–94.

Cutts*SCSP* ——————— 'Seventeenth-Century Songs and Lyrics in Paris Conservatoire MS. Rés. 2489' *Musica Disciplina,* XXIII (1969) pp. 117–39.

Cutts*SV* ——————— 'Songs unto the Violl and Lute: Drexel MS 4175' *Musica Disciplina,* XVI (1962) pp. 73–92.

Cutts*TH* ——————— 'Thomas Heywood's "The Gentry to the King's Head" in "The Rape of Lucrece" and John Wilson's Setting' *Notes & Queries,* (1961) pp. 384–87.
'Two Jacobean Theatre Songs' *Music & Letters* XXXIII (1952) pp. 333–34.

Cyr*S*   Cyr, M.   'A Seventeenth-Century Source of Ornamentation for Voice and Viol: British Museum MS Egerton 2971' *Royal Musical Association Research Chronicle,* IX (1971) pp. 53–72

Davis*C*   Davis, W. (ed.)   *The Works of Thomas Campion* (1967).

	Dart, R.T. and N. Fortune (eds)	'John Dowland: Ayres for four voices' *Musica Britannica*, VI (1953).
Dart*HL*	Dart, R.T. (ed.)	*Ten Ayres by Henry Lawes* (1956).
Dart*R*	————————	'Rôle de la danse dans l' "ayre" anglais' in *Musique et Poésie au XVIᵉ Siècle*, (1954) pp. 203–9.
Day*ESB*	Day, C.L. and E.B. Murrie	*English Song-Books, 1651–1702* (1940).
Day*S*	Day, C.L.	*The Songs of John Dryden* (1932)
Dent*F*	Dent, E.J.	*The Foundations of English Opera* (1928).
	Dolmetsch, A. (ed.)	*Select English Songs and Dialogues of the 16th and 17th centuries*, 2 vols (1898–1912).
	Duckles, V.	'The "Curious Art" of John Wilson (1595–1674)' *Journal of the American Musicological Society*, VII, (1954) pp. 93–112.
Duckles*ES*	————————	'English Song and the Challenge of Italian Monody' in *Words to Music, Papers on English Seventeenth - Century Song* (1967).
Duckles*FE*	————————	'Florid Embellishment in English Song of the late 16th and early 17th Century' *Annales Musicologues*, V (1957) pp. 329–45.
Duckles*GM*	————————	'The Gamble Manuscript as a Source of Continuo Song in England' *Journal of the American Musicological Society* I/2 (1948) pp. 23–40.
	————————	'Jacobean Theatre Songs' *Music & Letters* XXXIV, (1953) pp. 88–9.

Duckles*JG* ——————— *John Gamble's Commonplace Book: A Critical Edition of New York Public Library MS Drexel 4257* (Ph.D. dissertation, 1953, University of California).

Duckles*JJ* ——————— 'John Jenkins's Setting of Lyrics by George Herbert' *Musical Quarterly*, XLVIII (1962) pp. 461–75.

Duckles*ML* ——————— 'The Music for the Lyrics in Early Seventeenth-Century English Drama: A Bibliography of Primary Sources' in *Music in English Renaissance Drama*, ed. John H. Long, (1968) pp. 117–60.

Elliott, K. (ed.)   *Musa Jocosa Mihi* (1966).

ELS-1   *English Lute-Songs,* First series, originally 16 vols in *English School of Lutenist Song Writers,* First series (1920–1932), with original tablature, transcribed and edited by E.H. Fellowes, revised R.T. Dart; see also Hendrie, G.

ELS-2   *English Lute-Songs,* Second series, originally 16 vols. in *English School of Lutenist Song Writers,* Second series (1925–1927), without tablature, transcribed and edited by E.H. Fellowes, revised R.T. Dart; see also Spink, I.

ELS-R   *English Lute Songs, 1597–1632: A Collection of facsimile reprints* (1968–71), photographic reprints of lutesong books in 9 vols. by Scolar Press under general editorship of F.W. Sternfeld.

Emslie*M*	Emslie, McD.	'Milton on Lawes: the Trinity MS Revisions' in *Music in English Renaissance Drama*, ed. John H. Long (1968) pp. 96–102.
Emslie*NL*	————————	'Nicholas Lanier's Innovations in English Song' *Music & Letters*, XLI (1960) pp. 13–27.
	————————	'Pepys's Songs and Songbooks in the Diary Period' *The Library*, (1957) pp. 240–
Emslie*T*	————————	'Three early settings of Jonson' *Notes & Queries* (1953) pp. 466–468.
ES		'English Songs, 1625–1660' ed. I. Spink, *Musica Britannica*, XXXIII (1971).
Evans*C*	Evans, W.McC.	'Cartwright's debt to Lawes' in *Music in English Renaissance Drama*, ed. John H. Long (1968) pp. 103–16.
	————————	'Henry Lawes and Charles Cotton' *Publications of the Modern Language Association*, LIII (1938) pp. 724–29.
Evans*HL*	————————	*Henry Lawes, Musician and Friend of Poets* (1941).
Fellows*EMC*	Fellowes, E.H.	*The English Madrigal Composers* (²/1948).
Fellowes*EMV*	——— (ed.)	*English Madrigal Verse* (1920, ²/1929, ³/1967 rev. F.W. Sternfeld and D. Greer).
Fellowes*S*	————————	*Songs and Lyrics from the Plays of Beaumont and Fletcher* (1929).
	————————	'The Text of the Song-Books of Robert Jones' *Music & Letters*, VIII (1927) pp. 25–37
Fiske*M*	Fiske, R.	'The "Macbeth Music"' *Music & Letters*, XLV (1964) pp. 114–25.

Fortune*PA*	Fortune, N. and F. Zimmerman	'Purcell's Autographs' in *Henry Purcell, 1659–1695* ed. Imogen Holst (1959) pp. 106–21.
Fortune*PR*	————————	'Philip Rosseter and his Songs' *Lute Society Journal* VII (1965) pp. 7–14.
Gérold*AC*	Gérold, T.	*L'art du chant en France au XVIIᵉ siècle* (1921).
	Gladding, B.	'Music as a Social Force during the English Commonwealth and Restoration' *Musical Quarterly*, XV (1929) pp. 506–521.
	Gombosi, O.	'Some Musical Aspects of the English Court Masque' *Journal of the American Musicological Society* I/3 (1948) pp. 3–19.
Greer*C*	Greer, D.	'Campion the Musician' *Lute Society Journal*, IX (1967) pp. 7–16.
Greer*M*	————————	'The Lute Songs of Thomas Morley' *Lute Society Journal*, VIII (1966) pp. 25–35.
Greer*P*	————————	'The Part-Songs of the English Lutenists' *Proceedings of the Royal Musical Association*, XCIV (1968) pp. 97–110.
	Harbage, A.	*Annals of English Drama, 975–1700* (1940, rev. 1964).
Hart*CL*	Hart, E.F.	'Caroline lyrics and contemporary song-books' *The Library* (1953) pp. 89–110.
Hart*HL*	————————	'Introduction to Henry Lawes' *Music & Letters*, XXXII, (1951) pp. 217–25 and pp. 328–44.

Henderson*JW*	Henderson, H.P.	*The Vocal Music of John Wilson* (Ph.D. dissertation, 1962, University of North Carolina).
	Hendrie, G. and R.T. Dart (eds.)	'John Coprario, Funeral Teares (1606), Songs of Mourning (1613), The Masque of Squires (1614), *The English Lute-Songs*, First series, vol. 17 (1959).
Hughes*JG*	Hughes, C.W.	'John Gamble's Commonplace Book' *Music & Letters* XXVI (1945) pp. 215–29.
	Ingram, R.W.	*Dramatic use of music in English drama, 1603–42* (Ph.D. dissertation, 1955, University of London)
Joiner*BM*	Joiner, M.	'British Museum Add MS 15117: An Index, Commentary and Bibliography' *Royal Musical Association Research Chronicle*, VII (1969) pp. 51–109.
Joiner*C*	————————	'Caccini's "Amarilli mia bella"—Its influence on "Miserere my Maker" ' *Lute Society Journal*, X (1968) pp. 6–14.
Judd*D*	Judd, P.	'The Songs of John Danyel' *Music & Letters*, XVII, (1936) pp. 118–23.
Kastendieck*C*	Kastendieck, M.M.	*England's Musical Poet, Thomas Campion* (1938).
	Kerman, J.	*The Elizabethan Madrigal* (1962).
Kerr*MH*	Kerr, J.M.	'Mary Harvey—the Lady Dering' *Music & Letters*, XXV (1944) pp. 23–33.
	Lafontaine, H.C. de.	*The King's Musick* (1909).

	Laurie, M.	*Purcell's Stage Works* (Ph.D. dissertation, 1962, University of Cambridge).
Laurie*T*	————	'Did Purcell set "The Tempest"?' *Proceedings of the Royal Musical Association*, XC (1964) pp. 43–57.
	Lawrence, W.J.	'Notes on a collection of masque music' *Music & Letters* III (1922) pp. 49–58.
Lefkowitz*TP*	Lefkowitz, M.	'The Longleat papers of Bulstrode Whitelocke; New light on Shirley's "Triumph of Peace"' *Journal of the American Musicological Society*, XVIII (1965) pp. 42–60.
Lefkowitz*TM*	————	*Trois Masques à la Cour de Charles Ier d'Angleterre* (1970).
Lefkowitz*WL*	————	*William Lawes* (1960).
Lennep*LS*	Lennep, W. van.	*The London Stage, 1660–1700* (1965).
Lewis*L*	Lewis, A.	*The language of Purcell* (1968).
	————	'The Tempest of The Enchanted Island' *Musical Times*, C (1959) pp. 321–22.
Lowbury*C*	Lowbury, E., T. Salter and A. Young	*Thomas Campion: poet, composer, physician* (1970).
Luhring*JB*	Luhring, A.A.	*The Music of John Banister* (Ph.D. dissertation, 1966, Stanford University).
Mace*MM*	Mace, T.	*Musick's Monument* (1676, reprinted 1958, ²/1966).
McGrady*ESS*	McGrady, R.	*The English Solo Song from William Byrd to Henry Lawes* (Ph.D. dissertation, 1963, University of Manchester).
McGrady*HL*	————	'Henry Lawes and the concept of "Just Note and Accent"' *Music & Letters*, L (1969) pp. 86–102.

	McGuinness, R.	'The Ground Bass in the English Court Ode' *Music & Letters,* LI (1970) pp. 118–40 and pp. 265–79.
McManaway*T*	McManaway, J.G.	'Songs and Masques in "The Tempest"' *Theatre Miscellany* (1953) pp. 71–96
	Manifold, J.S.	*The Music in English Drama* (1956).
	———————	'Theatre Music in the 16th and 17th Centuries' *Music & Letters,* XXIX (1948) pp. 366–97.
Maze*T*	Maze, N.	'Tenbury MS 1018: a key to Cassini's Art of Embellishment' *Journal of the American Musicological Society* IX (1956) pp. 61–63.
Meltzer*S*	Meltzer, E.C.	*Henry Purcell's Secular Solo Songs: a stylistic analysis* (Ph.D. dissertation, 1957, University of California, Los Angeles).
Miller*GB*	Miller, H.M.	'Henry Purcell and the Ground Bass' *Music & Letters,* XXIX (1948) pp. 340–47.
Nicoll*RD*	Nicoll, A.	*A History of Restoration Drama, 1660–1700* (1955).
	———————	*Stuart Masques and the Renaissance Stage* (1938).
Noble*PCR*	Noble, J.	'Purcell and the Chapel Royal', in *Henry Purcell, 1659–1695,* ed. Imogen Holst (1959) pp. 52–66.
Noyes*C*	Noyes, R.C.	'Conventions of Song in Restoration Tragedy' *Publications of the Modern Language Association,* LIII (1938) pp. 162–88.

Oboussier*T*	Oboussier, P.	'Turpyn's Book of Lute-songs' *Music & Letters*, XXXIV (1953) pp. 145–49.
Olshausen*L*	Olshausen, U.	*Das Lautenbegleitete Sololied in England um 1600* (1963).
Pattison*MP*	Pattison, B.	*Music and Poetry of the English Renaissance* (1948, ²/1970).
Pereya*M*	Pereya, M-L.	'La musique écrite sur "La Tempête" d'après Shakespeare par Pelham Humfrey' *Revue de Musicologie*, II (1921) pp. 75–85.
Pereya*T*	————	'"La Tempête" d'après Shakespeare et la Musique de Pelham Humfrey' *Revue Musicale*, II/3 (1921) pp. 32–42.
Platt*RD*	Platt, P. (ed.)	'Richard Dering, Secular Vocal Music' *Musica Britannica*, XXV (1969).
Porter*O*	Porter, W.V.	*The origins of Baroque solo song: a study of Italian manuscripts and prints from 1590–1610* (Ph.D. dissertation, 1962, Yale University).
Poulton*D*	Poulton, D.	*John Dowland* (1972).
	Reyher, P.	*Les masques anglais* (1909).
Riley*G*	Riley J.	'The Identity of William Gregory', *Music & Letters*, XLVIII (1967), pp. 236–46.
Rose*PR*	Rose, G.	'Pietro Reggio—A Wandering Musician' *Music & Letters*, XLVI (1965) pp. 207–16.
Sabol*N*	Sabol, A.	'New Documents on Shirley's Masque "The Triumph of Peace"' *Music & Letters*, XLVII (1966) pp. 10–26.
Sabol*S*	————	*Songs and Dances for the Stuart Masque* (1959).

SchofieldT	Schofield, B. and R.T. Dart	'Tregian's Anthology' *Music & Letters,* XXXII (1951) pp. 205–16.
ScottD	Scholes, P. Scott, D.	*The Puritans and Music* (1934). 'John Danyel: His Life and Songs' *Lute Society Journal,* XIII (1971) pp. 7–17.
	Shaw, H.W.	'The Secular music of John Blow', *Proceedings of the [Royal] Musical Association',* LXIII (1937) pp. 1–19.
SimpsonB	Simpson, C.M.	*The British Broadside Ballad and its Music* (1967).
SmallmanER	Smallman, B.	'Endor Revisited: English Biblical Dialogues of the Seventeenth Century' *Music & Letters,* XLVI (1965) pp. 137–45.
	Spink, I (ed.)	'Alfonso Ferrabosco II, Manuscript Songs' *The English Lute-Songs,* Second Series, vol. 19 (1966).
SpinkAN	——————	'AngeloNotariandhis"Prime Musiche Nuove"' *Monthly Musical Record,* LXXXVII (1957) pp. 168–77.
	——————	'Anne Twice, Her Booke' *Musical Times,* CIII (1962) p. 316.
SpinkC	——————	'Campion's Entertainment at Brougham Castle, 1617' in *Music in English Renaissance Drama* ed. J.H. Long (1968) pp. 57–74.
	——————	'An Early English Strophic Cantata *Acta Musicologica,* XXVII (1955) pp. 138–140.
SpinkECS	——————	'English Cavalier Songs, 1620–1660' *Proceedings of the Royal Musical Association,* LIIIVI (1960) pp. 61–78.

Spink*ED* ———————— 'English Seventeenth-Century Dialogues' *Music & Letters*, XXXVIII (1957) pp. 155–63.

——— (ed.) 'English Songs, 1625–1660' *Musica Britannica*, XXXIII (1971).

——— (ed.) 'Greaves, Mason, Earsden; Songs (1604) and Ayres (1618)' *The English Lute-Songs*, Second Series, vol. 18 (1963).

Spink*L* ———————— 'Lanier in Italy' *Music & Letters*, XL (1959) pp. 242–52.

Spink*OJ* ———————— 'The Old Jewry "Musick-Society": A 17th-Century Catch Club' *Musicology*, II (1967) pp. 35–41.

Spink*P* ———————— 'Playford's "Directions for Singing after the Italian Manner"' *Monthly Musical Record*, LXXXIX (1959) pp. 130–35.

——— (ed.) 'Robert Johnson, Ayres, Songs and Dialogues' *The English Lute-Songs*, Second series, vol. 17 (1961).

——————— 'Sources of English Song 1620–1660: A Survey' *Miscellanea Musicologie*, I (1966) pp. 117–36.

Spink*WP* ———————— 'Walter Porter and the last book of English Madrigals' *Acta Musicologica*, XXVI (1954) pp. 18–36.

Squire*F* Squire, W.B. 'J.W. Franck in England' *Musical Antiquarian*, III (1912), pp. 181–90.

Squire*T* ———————— 'The Music of Shadwell's "Tempest"' *Musical Quarterly*, VII (1921) pp. 565–78.

	Steele, M.S.	*Plays and Masques at Court during the reigns of Elizabeth James and Charles* (1926).
	Sternfeld, F.W.	*Music in Shakespearean Tragedy* (1963).
Stevens*MP*	Stevens, J.	*Music and Poetry in the Early Tudor Court* (1961).
	Terry, C.S.	'John Forbes's "Songs and Fancies"' *Musical Quarterly*, XXII (1936) pp. 402–419.
Thewlis*N*	Thewlis, G.A.	'Some notes on a Bodleian Manuscript' *Music & Letters*, XXII (1941) pp. 32–5.
Tilmouth*LC*	Tilmouth, M.	'Some early London concerts and music clubs' *Proceedings of the Royal Musical Association*, LXXXIV (1958) pp. 13–26.
	Verchaly, A.	*Airs de cour pour voix et luth, 1603–1643* (1961).
	Walker, D.P.	'Musical Humanism in the 16th and early 17th Centuries' *Music Review*, II (1941) pp. 1–13, 111–21, 220–27. 288–308, and III (1942) pp. 55–71.
Ward*B*	Ward, J.M.	'Barley's Songs without Words' *Lute Society Journal*, XII (1970) pp. 5–22.
Warlock*EA*	Warlock, P.	*The English Ayre* (1926)
	————	and P. Wilson. *English Ayres*, 6 vols (1927–31).
	Westrup, J.A.	'Domestic Music under the Stuarts' *Proceedings of the [Royal] Musical Association*, LXVIII (1942) pp. 19–53.
Westrup*FM*	————	'Foreign Musicians in Stuart England' *Musical Quarterly*, XXVII (1941) pp. 70–89.
Westrup*P*	————	*Purcell* (1937, rev. 1965).

Willetts*A*	Willetts, P.J.	'Autographs of Angelo Notari' *Music & Letters,* L (1969) pp. 124–26.
Willetts*HL*	————————	*The Henry Lawes Manuscript* (1969).
Willetts*M*	————————	'Music from the circle of Anthony Wood at Oxford'. *British Museum Quarterly,* XXIV (1961) pp. 71–5.
Willetts*N*	————————	'A neglected source of Monody and Madrigal' *Music & Letters,* XLIII (1962) pp. 329–39.
Wilson*RN*	Wilson, J.	*Roger North on Music* (1959).
Wood*AO*	Wood, A.	*Athenae Oxonienses,* 4 vols. ed. P. Bliss (1813–1820).
Woodfill*M*	Woodfill, W.L.	*Musicians in English Society from Elizabeth to Charles I* (1953).
Zimmerman*C*	Zimmerman, F.B.	*Henry Purcell, 1659–1695: An Analytical Catalogue of his Music* (1963).
	————————	*Henry Purcell, 1659–95: His Life and Times* (1967).
Zimmerman*S*	————————	'Sound and Sense in Purcell's "Single Songs" ' in *Words to Music; Papers on English Seventeenth-Century Song* (1967).

Notes

Part I Chapter I (*pp. 15–37*)

1. Sixteenth-century sources of English lute-songs are of three kinds. The earliest MSS (such as MS 448.16 in the Folger Library, Washington, and MS Royal Appendix 58 in the British Museum) contain songs arranged for lute which may have been used to accompany a singer. Later sources (such as the Brogyntyn MS 27 in the National Library of Wales, Aberystwyth, and the somewhat later BM. Add. MS 31992) provide tablatures which omit the vocal line (presumably supplied in a separate part-book), while later still there are lutesong MSS which give melody and tablature together. Surprisingly perhaps, none of this third category is earlier than 1600, though the most important (BM Add. MSS 4900 and 15117, and the Turpyn MS in the Rowe Library, King's College, Cambridge) contain songs dating from the middle of the sixteenth century. See Stevens*MP* p. 279, Brett*EP*, Oboussier*T*, Joiner*BM* and Poulton *JD*, pp. 185–7.

2. Most of the English lutesong publications are available in facsimile published by the Scolar Press under the general editorship of F. W. Sternfeld (*ELS-R*), and in modern edition published by Stainer & Bell under the editorship of E. H. Fellowes, with revisions by R. T. Dart (*ELS-1, ELS-2*) A useful selection is *English Ayres* transcribed and edited by P. Warlock and P. Wilson, published by O.U.P. in six volumes (1927–31) and now reprinted. Warlock*EA* is still the best book on the subject. The section on lutesong writers in Fellowes *EMC* is rather perfunctory. Olshausen*L* is highly analytical. McGrady*ESS* pays particular attention to Morley, Jones, Campion, Danyel and Dowland—they are, indeed, the composers most worthy of attention. He traces the growth of the declamatory element through the songs of Ferrabosco, Coperario, Johnson and Lanier to Henry Lawes, though the latter's contemporaries are hardly touched upon. David Greer's book on the English Ayres was still in preparation at the time of writing.

3. Ward*B*, pp. 9–12.

4. Brett*ECS* covers the development of the Consort Song.

5. Greer*M*, pp. 29–30.

6. Dart*R*, pp. 205–8.

7. William Webbe, *A Discourse of English Poetrie, 1586* (ed. E. Arber, 1895), p. 61.

8. The matter is dealt with in Greer*P*.

9. Treated sympathetically in Warlock*EA*, pp. 106–10, and Fortune *PR*.

10. Apart from Warlock*EA* and Fellowes*EMC* the bibliography on Campion as a musician includes Kastendick*C*, Lowbury*C* and Greer *C*. Davis*C* considers the music briefly in his introduction and prints some of the best songs.

11. In 1629 Edward Filmer published his *French Court-Aires, with their Ditties Englished* dedicated to Charles I's Queen, Henrietta-Maria.

But not even under the protection of a French Queen could the arbitary rhythms of the *air de cour* influence the English ayre significantly.

12. See Warlock*EA*, pp. 63–81.

13. See Greer*M*.

14. See Warlock*EA*, pp. 82–90.

15. *Ibid.*, pp. 52–63, Judd*D*; Scott *D*.

16. Warlock*EA*, p. 125.

Part I Chapter 2 (pp. 38–71)

1. The last line of Orlando Gibbons' 'Silver Swan' in his *Madrigals and Mottets* (1612).

2. Details of appointments etc. in Woodfill*M*, Appendix E. The bibliography on Dowland is copious and includes more or less extensive treatments in Warlock*EA*, pp. 21–51, and Fellowes*EMC* pp. 307–313. At the time of writing Poulton*D* had not been published.

3. According to Miss Poulton's note to the Scolar Press facsimile of *D1610*. I had earlier thought it might refer to a visit King James made in September 1603.

4. Editions in Sabol*S* nos. 7–16, also in Cutts*R* pp. 298–300 as well as *ELS-2* vols. 16 and 19.

5. Egerton MS 3665; see Schofield*T*.

6. A. Bertolotti, *Musici alla Corte dei Gonzaga in Mantova* (1890), pp. 80–81.

7. Spink*AN*; see also Willetts*A* following on from Willetts*N*.

8. Joiner*C*, pp. 8–10.

9. See Maze*T*, also Porter*O*, p. 72–73, 295–300. The English songs are discussed in Cutts *ESCL*. Another English MS containing Italian monodies is Egerton 2971 (ff.24–28v), including Caccini's '*Amarilli*' and '*Dolcissimo sospiro*', see Cyr*S*.

10. *ELS-2* vol. 19, nos 11–14.

11. G. Pulver, *A Biographical Dictionary of Old English Music* (1927), p. 114, via Sir Frederick Bridge who got it from the Rev. Spooner Lillington! Even so, it is not impossible.

12. Sabol*S*, no. 18. A version of this song with the words 'Weep no more my wearied eyes' occurs in several MSS (*E*,*G*,*R*); see *ES* no. 1. A Comparison with Pierre Guédron's '*Quel espoir de guerir*' in Bataille's third book of *Airs de Différent Autheurs* . . . 1611, reveals a number of similar details. The French song is in P. Warlock's *French Ayres* (1926) p. 26; also in Gérold*AC* p. 43. It seems unlikely

that Lanier would have known
Guédron's *air*, but the resemblance
underlines the fact that both composers were moving in similar
directions.

13. The vocal music for this masque
is the most complete surviving
from the period; see Spink*C*. The
songs are in *ELS-2* vol. 18.

14. Wilson*RN*, p. 294.

15. C. H. Herford and P. & E.
Simpson (eds.), *Ben Jonson* (1925–52)
vol. VII, pp. 454, 463.

16. Emslie*T*, p. 466. The first
mention of 'recitative' in English
seems to occur in the description of
Aurelian Townsend's *Albion's
Triumph* (1631): "*MERCURY* . . .
In voce Recitativa, he declares the
substance of his Commission" (p.5).

17. Sabol*S*, no. 28.

18. Spink*ED*.

19. *ES* no. 11.

20. *Ibid.*, nos. 19, 60, 74, 77, 95.

21. Smallman*ER*; also E. Thomp-
son's follow-up letter in *Music &
Letters* (1965), pp. 289–90.

22. *On the University Carrier* . . .
'Here lies old *Hobson*, Death hath
broke his girt'; see W. McC. Evans,
'Hobson appears in Comic Song'
Philological Quarterly, *XXVI* (1947),
pp. 321–27.

23. F. W. Moorman, *Robert Herrick,
A Bibliographical and Critical Study*
(1910), p. 54.

24. *ES*, nos. 15, 67.

25. *Ibid.*, nos. 14, 61.

26. The 'Lanier' versions are in BM
Add. MSS 22100 and 31460;
Purcell's setting in *HS-2*.

27. It would be interesting to trace
the musical settings of various
'Charon-dialogues' back into the
sixteenth century. C. H. Wilkinson
in *The Poems of Richard Lovelace*
(1930), pp. 312–14 follows the clue
to Olivier de Magny's '*Hola, Charon,
nautonnier infernal*' (no. 124 in the
Oxford Book of French Verse, ed. P.
Mansell Jones [1957], pp. 123–24),
itself written in imitation of an
Italian *strambotto* according to
Gérold*AC* p. 54. This dialogue was
set by Boësset in Bataille's fifth
book of *Airs de Différents Autheurs*
(1615), p. 53. English 'Charon-
dialogues' include: 'Charon, O
Charon, come away' by Robert
Johnson (*Tenb. G*); 'Charon, O
Charon, row thy boat'—anon.
(*Tenb*)—which occurs with an Italian
text as 'Caron', Caronte, voltam'il
tuo legno' in the Bibliothèque du
Conservatoire Royal de Musique,
Brussels, MS 704, pp. 221–3;
'Charon, O Charon, thou wafter of
the souls' by Mr. [Alfonso ?] Balls
(*Q,V*) from Beaumont and Flet-
cher's *The Mad Lover* (*c*.1617);
'Charon, O Charon, hear a wretch
oppressed' by Robert Ramsey (*L*);
'Charon, come hither Charon' by
John Hilton (*L,P*, also *M* where
attributed to John Wilson);
'Charon, O Charon, hear a wretch
oppressed' by William Lawes
(*P1669*); 'Charon, O Charon, let
me woo thee' by William Lawes
(*C, L, U, P1652*); 'Charon, O
Charon, draw thy boat' by Henry
Lawes (*P1652*). The last two are by
Herrick.

28. Theatrical details from A. Har-
bage, *Annals of English Drama, 975–
1700* (1964), pp. 303–06.

29. The dramatic function of the playsong has been studied in W. R. Bowden, *The English Dramatic Lyric, 1603–1643* (1951), but without taking into account the actual music. In fact it would seem as if the effect of the music often blunts some of the fine distinctions Bowden makes.

30. Those with music surviving from the pre-Commonwealth period have been listed with sources in Duckles*ML*. Music for many of these songs is in Cutts*M*. Fellowes*S* transcribes some playsongs from *L*. Johnson's playsongs are edited in *ELS-2* vol. 17; 3 of Wilson's in *ES*.

31. Cutts*M* is eager to attribute songs to Johnson which more likely belong to Wilson; but see the checklist of Wilson's playsongs in Cutts*TH*. Songs apparently by both survive from Beaumont and Fletcher's *Valentinian* (not later than 1614) and *The Mad Lover* (*c*.1617), and from Middleton's *The Witch* (*c*.1616), though it is possible that Wilson's settings were written for revivals.

32. The theory put forward by J. P. Collier in 'John Wilson, the Singer' *Shakespeare Society's Papers* (1845), II, pp. 33–36, and taken up by E. F. Rimbault in 'Who was Jack Wilson, the Singer of Shakespeare's Stage', *Musical Tracts*, III/I (1846), is out of fashion at present, and neither Henderson*JW* nor

Cutts*JPC* supports it. But, in fact, there is no evidence to contradict the hypothesis that he was the Wilson referred to in the folio, and in the circumstances it seems extremely probable.

33. *ES*, no. 22.

34. *Ibid.*, no. 21.

35. *Ibid.*, no. 24.

36. Duckles*JG*, p. 317.

37. *ES*, no. 120.

38. *Ibid.*, no. 7.

39. *Ibid.*, no. 1; the music is the same as 'Bring away this sacred tree' (*C1614*).

40. *Ibid.*, no. 87.

41. *Ibid.*, no. 20.

42. *Ibid.*, no. 120.

43. *Ibid.*, no. 121.

44. *Ibid.*, no. 16.

45. See Duckles*FE*, p. 343.

46. *ES*, no. 12.

47. Printed in Cutts*SCS*, pp. 15, 139, 188, 220.

48. *ES*, no. 61; Ramsey's setting is no. 14.

49. *Ibid.*, no. 63.

50. *Ibid.*, no. 62.

51. *The Lives of John Donne . . . By Izaak Walton . . . The Fourth Edition . . . 1675* ed. G. Saintsbury (1927) p. 62.

52. *ES*, no. 64.

53. *Ibid.*, no. 65.

Part II   Chapter 1   (pp. 75–99)

1. Evans*HL* is still the only full-scale treatment of Lawes' life and works, though by now it is rather out of date. Hart*HL* and McGrady

Notes

HL provide some useful insights into the development of his musical techniques, as does WillettsHL.

2. The significance of Milton's revisions of this sonnet are considered in EmslieM; also McGradyHL, pp. 361–62.

3. An inventory of the contents is given in WillettsHL, pp. 34–83; also McGradyESS, pp. 432–66.

4. ES, nos. 33, 34 and 36.

5. Respectively in D1612 and D1600.

6. A rule of the octave is given (with minor variations between them) by Campion, Simpson, Locke and Mace—the last referring specifically to a theorbo continuo (*Musick's Monument*, [1676] pp. 217–30, especially 225–27). Locke is clearest: "On the *half-Note* below the *Tone* you play in, on the Third and Sixt *Major* above the *Tone* . . . and on all *sharp Notes* out of the *Tone*, Play a *Sixth Minor* . . . " (Quoted in F. T. Arnold, *The Art of Accompaniment from a Thorough-Bass* [1931] p. 155).

7. HartCL, pp. 91–2 says: "Of the 318 songs with English words, 38 are settings of poems by Carew, and 35 are to words by a minor poet called Dr. Henry Hughes . . . Herrick and Waller have twelve settings each, Cartwright seven, Aurelian Townshend six, Milton five (the *Comus* lyrics), and Suckling, Lovelace, Davenant, Strode, and other lesser men, two or three each" WillettsHL's figures do not quite tally since not all ascriptions are agreed. It is worth noting that most of Carew's settings are concentrated

between f.95v and f.121, and the Hughes settings between f.128 and f.176v. The Herrick settings are more dispersed, but there are nine between f.70 and f.80v: the same goes for Waller's with five between f.86 and f.90v. These facts suggest that the songs in question were set in batches as they came to hand. Whether the poets themselves sent their MSS to Lawes, more or less requesting him to set their songs, or whether the composer exercised his own choice in the matter is hard to say—probably it was a bit of both.

8. ES, no. 55.

9. *Ibid.*, no. 49.

10. *Ibid.*, no. 37.

11. BurneyH, vol. III, pp. 382–5.

12. CollesVV, p. 63.

13. PattisonMP, p. 147.

14. BurneyH, vol. III, p. 398. The same tune is used by Lawes to set Townsend's 'Thou shepherd, whose inventive eye' (A,R,L1653).

15. ES, nos. 35 and 36.

16. *Ibid.*, no. 42.

17. *Ibid.*, no. 33.

18. *Ibid.*, no. 50.

19. The terms 'single' and 'through-set' were actually used by John Gamble to distinguish what we now call 'strophic' from 'through-composed'.

20. SpinkECS, pp. 76–77.

21. Modern edition in SabolS pp. 91–99 from an eighteenth-century copy of A (Add. MS 11518); also by Hubert Foss in E. H. Visiak, *The Mask of Comus* (1937) pp. 35–44.

22. *ES*, nos. 43–46. Songs for *The Floating Island* are in *A*: see Evans *HL*, pp. 122–37, also Evans *C*, pp. 103–16.

23. The introduction in *A* is more to the point: "Ariadne deserted by Theseus Sittinge uppon a Rock in ye Island Naxos thus Complaines."

24. See Kerr*MH*.

25. Comendatory poems in *L1655*; Katherine Philips ('Matchless Orinda') also contributed.

26. *The Life of William Cavendish, Duke of Newcastle . . . by Margaret, Duchess of Newcastle . . .* ed. C. H. Firth (1906) p. 169.

27. Commendatory poem in *L1653*.

28. *ES*, no. 114.

29. See 'Dialogues for two voices and continuo by William and Henry Lawes' (ed. Roy Jesson for *The Penn State Music Series*, No. 3), also *ES*, no. 60.

Part II Chapter 2 (*pp.* 100–127)

1. *ES*, no. 7.

2. Sabol*S*, no. 18, Davis*C*, pp. 278–79, *ES*, no. 1.

3. It is ironical that Lanier's setting should approach Ferrabosco's normal style in this case, while Ferrabosco's setting is rather uncharacteristic and more like Dowland.

4. *ES*, no. 5.

5. *Ibid.*, no. 9.

6. Duckles*ES*, pp. 3–25, especially pp. 16–22, deals at some length with this recitative and to a lesser extent with Lawes' 'Ariadne'. See also Emslie*NL*, pp. 17–20; Spink*ECS*, pp. 70–2, and *ES*, no. 10.

7. Spink*L*.

8. Wilson*RN*, p. 265.

9. References are to *ES*, no. 10.

10. *Ibid.*, no. 4.

11. The Preface to *Poems, written by . . . Earl of Pembroke* (1660).

12. In the poem "To M. Henry Lawes, *the excellent Composer of his*

Lyrics" in *Hesperides* (1648).

13. *ES* nos. 31–32.

14. *Ibid.*, nos. 26–27.

15. Concerning the contents of *B* see Cutts*SCL*. Crum*M* challenged the long-held view that this MS was autograph, but supposed that it was corrected by Wilson. The hand seems to be that of Edward Lowe.

16. *ES*, no. 20a/b.

17. *Ibid.*, no. 23.

18. *Ibid.*, no. 30.

19. *Ibid.*, nos. 20–21.

20. See Lefkowitz*WL* pp. 149–186 and Appendix C for a list of songs.

21. *ES*, no. 84a/b.

22. *Ibid.*, no. 85.

23. *Ibid.*, no. 83.

24. *Ibid.*, nos. 79–80.

25. Leftkowitz*WL* pp. 187–204.

26. For Lawes' masque music, especially the *Triumph of Peace* see Dent*F*, pp. 29–39; Sabol*S*, nos. 30–31; Sabol*N*, Lefkowitz*TP* and Lefkowitz*WL*, pp. 205–34. The

principal musical source is Bodleian MS Mus. Sch.B.2, but isolated numbers are in *C*, *M* and *S* (see Lefkowitz*TM*).

27. *ES*, no. 74.

28. *Ibid*., no. 73.

29. *Ibid*., no. 68.

30. As shown by the table of contents. It occurs also in *L*, and as a glee in *P1652*.

31. *ES*, no. 87 a/b.

32. *Ibid*., no. 88.

33. Sabol*S*, no. 29; Bentley*JCS* IV, pp. 643–44, 660–63.

34. *ES*, nos. 75 and 94.

35. *Ibid*., no. 76.

36. *Ibid*., no. 104.

37. Spink*P*, pp. 132–33

38. See Duckles*FE*, pp. 337f and Duckles*GM*, pp. 31–33.

39. *Synopsis of Vocal Musick . . . By A.B. Philo-Mus . . .1680*, p. 44

40. *A Brief Introduction To the Skill of Musick* (1666) p. 58.

41. Respectively nos. 102 and 99 in *ES*.

42. *Ibid*., no. 100.

43. *Ibid*., no. 107.

44. *Ibid*., no. 106.

45. Wilson, whether or not he is referring to Gamble in his commendatory poem to *L1655* makes valid comment: "Not like those . . . /Take words that creep half way to sense;/ . . . /And sing them too with Notes as meet;/Songs as all th'way to *Gam ut* tend,/But in *F Fa ut* make an end;/ . . ./These with their brave *Chromaticks* bring/Noise to the Ear; but mean No-thing: . . . "

46. Wood*AO*, I, p. xxxii.

47. BM Add. MS 32339, with many treble parts copied out in BM Harleian MS 6947 ff.368–408.

48. See Duckles*GM* and an edition of the MS in Duckles*JG*. An earlier study is Hughes*JG*.

49. *ES*, no. 113.

50. *Ibid*., no. 110.

51. *Ibid*., no. 111.

52. Commendatory poem in *Choice Psalmes* (1648).

Part III   Chapter 1   (pp. 131–47)

1. Wood*AO*, pp. xxv-vi, xxxii, xxxiv-vi. See also Willetts*M*.

2. Further details of this club in Spink*OJ*, and of later meetings in Tilmouth*LC* and Wilson*RN* pp. 302–05, 351–53.

3. See Day*ESB* for bibliographical details of songbooks published in the second half of the century.

4. 'Advertisement' in *P1673*.

5. *Compendium of Practical Musick* (1667), p. 174.

6. Wilson*RN*, p. 4.

7. See Duckles*JJ* for examples.

8. Spink*WP*, pp. 27–33.

9. Spink*OJ*, pp. 36–7.

10. Platt*RD*, nos. 1, 11, 16, 18 and 21.

Part IV Chapter 1 (pp. 151–83)

1. Theatrical details and background in this chapter rely mainly on LennepL*S* unless otherwise stated.

2. Details of these and other series are in Day*ESB*.

3. The following figures derive from Day*ESB*, pp. 409–15.

4. Also in Day*S*, p. 33.

5. Setting by Playford in *P1673:* regarding the identity of Black Bess see Ault*SCL* p. 510.

6. Wilson*RN*, p. 350.

7. Mace*MM*, p. 207.

8. *Ibid.*, p. 221; see pp. 217–30.

9. Humfrey was of an age with Turner and Blow but developed much quicker.

10. Day*S*, p. 25.

11. *Ibid.*, pp. 39, 45 and 47.

12. Luhring*JB* deals with the biography (pp. 1–49) and the songs (pp. 103–32, transcribed pp. 207–39).

13. Day*S*, pp. 31 and 14.

14. See Riley*G*.

15. Dent*F*, pp. 165–70.

Part IV Chapter 2 (pp. 184–200)

1. Much of the literary content of what follows is based on Noyes*C*.

2. Noyes*C*, p. 188.

3. Day*S*, pp. 7–8.

4. *Ibid.*, p. 55.

5. Simpson*B*, pp. 498–501.

6. The Davenant/Dryden version was first performed on 7 November 1667. The exact date of Shadwell's 'operatic' version is uncertain, though W. J. Lawrence (*The Elizabethan Playhouse and Other Studies* [1912] I, p. 203) has argued in favour of *c.* 30 April 1674. McManaway*T* pp. 80–3 proposes a date earlier than 26 March 1674.

7. Covell*T*, pp. 52–61.

8. Diary; 11 May 1668 (also 7 November 1667).

9. See Squire*T*, Pereya*M* and Pereya*T*, the latter containing a transcription of 'Arise ye subterranean winds'.

10. A notable dialogue on quite an extended scale is that between Orpheus, Pluto and Proserpine ('The groans of ghosts and sighs of souls' in *Ch. Ch. MS 692*) which Locke provided for Settle's *Empress of Morocco* (1673), but was 'scandalously performed' according to North (Wilson*RN* p. 306).

Part V Chapter 1 (pp. 203–240)

1. I am grateful to Dr Rosamond McGuinness for putting at my disposal her transcriptions of many of these works which will be referred

to at times during this chapter.

2. See Westrup*FM*, pp. 77–80 and 85.

3. See Rose*PR*, 208–11.

4. All the works of Purcell referred to are in the Purcell Society's Complete Edition, from which most of the music examples are taken. The Secular Songs and Cantatas (vol. 25) were edited by Arthur Somervell and published in 1928. Other relevant volumes are vols 16, 20 and 21 edited by Alan Gray (1906–1917).

5. Zimmerman*C*, pp. 178–214, Meltzer*P*, pp. 162–79; Westrup*P*, pp. 308–12.

6. It should be pointed out that dates affixed to plays in the following pages are those of performances for which Purcell provided music. In most cases they are not first performances, but revivals.

7. In addition to those mentioned, the authenticity of the following songs is thus very much in question: 'Cease O my sad soul', 'I saw that

you were grown so high', 'More love or more disdain I crave', 'Sweet be no longer sad' and 'When I a lover pale do see'—all in *B1678*.

8. See Lewis*L*, pp. 17–22 and Zimmerman*S*, pp. 55–78.

9. Fortune*PA*, pp. 114–5.

10. Miller*GB*, pp. 341–2 notes that there are 65 vocal grounds (57 for solo voice) roughly divided equally between those in triple time and those in four.

11. Wilson*RN*, p. 217.

12. Westrup*P*, p. 76.

13. Zimmerman*C*, p. 263.

14. Noble*PCR*, pp. 60–1 notes this discrepancy. Purcell and Pate probably sang this song on separate occasions.

15. Dr Margaret Laurie has come down strongly against Purcell in Laurie*T*, while other scholars have had their doubts.

16. Playford's 'Publisher to the Reader' in *Orpheus Britannicus* (1721).

17. Wilson*RN*, p. 307.

Part V   Chapter 2   (pp. 241–59)

1. When no specific reference is made to the source of a song in what follows, it is to be found in *Amphion Anglicus* (1700, reprinted by Gregg Press Inc., 1965).

2. Wilson*RN*, p. 312.

3. Squire*F* prints the recitative

'Still must I grieve' and the air 'By warring winds'.

4. Dent*F*, p. 136, Fiske *Mp*. 118.

5. BM Add. MS; modern edition by Walter Bergmann (Schott, 1961).

Index

Abell, John (1653–1724), 270
  'Choice Collection of Italian Ayres, A', 258
  'Collection of Songs in English, A', 257
  'Collection of Songs in Several Languages, A', 257
  I'll press thee, I'll bless thee (Ex. 134), 258
académie de musique; see Baïf, J. A. de
Ackroyde, Samuel (*fl.* 1684–1706), 182, 184
Albrici, Bartolomeo (*fl.* 1663–88), 204–5
Albrici, Vincenzo (1631–96), 204–5
Allen, John (*fl. c.* 1609), 41
almain, 155–6
Anne of Denmark, Queen (1574–1619), 38, 40, 43
Anonymous
  Down afflicted soul (Ex. 26), 64–5
  Eyes gaze no more (Ex. 25), 64–5
  Eyes look off (Ex. 24), 62–4
  Have you seen the bright lily grow, 55
  How short a time of breath, 49, 67
  If when I die, 63
  Like as the lark, 61
  Miserere my maker, 43
  Must your fair inflaming eye, 60, 62
  My lodging is in the cold ground, 193
  Venus went wand'ring (Ex. 22), 61–2
  Wrong not dear Empress of my heart, (Ex. 23), 62–3
anthem, 144, 215, 219, 221
Arne, T. A. (1710–78), 259
Atkins, John (*d.* 1671), 123
  I can love for an hour, 123
  Wert thou yet fairer, 123
  This lady ripe, 123
Attey, John (*fl. c.* 1622), 36–7, 264

'First Booke of Ayres, The', 36–7
  On a time, 37
  Vain hope, adieu, 37
  Sweet was the song the Virgin sang, 37
Ayliff, Mrs (*fl. c.* 1694), 185, 232, 238–9

Baïf, J. A. de (1532–89), 25, 86
ballad, 17, 55, 107, 110, 114, 193
Balls, Mr. (Bales, Alfonso or Richard?) (*fl.* 1613–35), 65–6
  Chloris sigh'd (Ex. 27), 65–6
Banister, John (*d.* 1679), 160–2, 164, 171, 179, 184, 186, 195, 266
  Beneath a myrtle shade, 164
  Come unto these yellow sands, 195–6
  Dry those eyes (Ex. 78), 164, 196
  Full fathom five, 195–6
  Go thy way (Ex. 103), 196–7
  Lo behind a scene of seas, 186
Barley, William (*fl.* 1592–1614)
  'New Booke of Tabliture, A', 15, 261
Barrett, John (*fl.* 1693–1735), 257
Bartlett, John (*fl.* 1606–10), 33, 37, 262
  'Booke of Ayres, A', 33
  Go wailing verse, 33
  Of all the birds, 33
  Whither runneth my sweet-heart, 33
Batchelar, Daniel (*fl. c.* 1610)
  To plead my faith, 36
Beaumont, Francis; see Fletcher, John
Beggar's Opera, The, 178, 224, 228
Behn, Mrs Aphra (1640–89), 174–5
  The Rover, II, 174
Benson, John (*fl.* 1635–58), 132, 264
Betterton, Thomas (*d.* 1710), 184, 253
  Dioclesian, 224–5

298

Index

3 6289 000525490

Index

Riley, Thomas (*fl. c.* 1630), 49

Rinuccini, Ottavio (1562–1621), 43

Rochester, John Wilmot, Earl of (1647–80), 153, 190, 212, 242
    Valentinian, 191

Roffey, John (*fl. c.* 1685), 182

rogero; see *ruggiero*

Rogers, Benjamin (1614–98), 144

Rontani, Raffaello (*d.* 1622)
    'Varie Musiche', 43

Rosseter, Philip (1568–1623), 15, 20, 23, 25, 33, 37, 41, 62
    'Booke of Ayres, A' (with Campion), 23, 262
    If I hope, I pine, 24
    What then is love, 25

Rossi, Luigi (1598–1653), 204, 217
    Mio ben (Ex. 117), 229–30

round; see catch

ruggiero (rogero), 17

Salisbury, Robert Cecil, Earl of (1563–1612), 40

Sambrooke, Francis (*fl.* 1633–62), 127

saraband, 113–14, 155–6

Savile, Jeremy (*fl.* 1651–65), 132, 144, 146–7
    Here's a health (Ex. 71), 146–7

'Scotch' songs, 166

Scott, Samuel (*fl.* 1687–99), 151, 267–8

Sebenico, Girolamo (*fl.* 1668–92), 204

Sedley, Sir Charles (1639–1701), 153

Settle, Elkanah (1648–1724)
    The Fairy Queen (?), 226–30
    The World in the Moon, 252

Shadwell, Thomas (*d.* 1692), 153, 191
    The Libertine, 191, 231
    The Tempest, 195–9, 234–5

Shakespeare, William (1564–1616)
    As you like it, 31
    Hamlet, 193
    Macbeth, 55, 253
    Measure for Measure, 58, 254
    Much ado about nothing, 57
    The Tempest, 54, 164, 195–8, 234–5

Short, Peter (*fl.* 1589–1603), 15

Shirley, James (1596–1666)
    Ajax and Ullyses, 125
    Triumph of Peace, 115

Sidney, Sir Philip (1554–86), 16, 78

Simpson, Christopher (*d.* 1669), 121, 135

Smith, Robert (i) (*d.* 1647), 132

Smith, Robert (ii) (*d.* 1675), 161–2, 172, 184
    Farewell, fair Armida (Ex. 77), 163–4
    Hark, the storm grows loud, 171
    Long betwixt hope and fear, 163
    The day you wished arrived at last, 163

Snow, Moses (*d.* 1702)
    When you have broke (Ex. 75), 160, 182

Somerset, Robert Carr, Earl of (1589–1645), 44

Staggins, Nicholas (*d.* 1700), 159, 178, 184, 189
    As Amoret with Phyllis sat (Ex. 74), 159–60
    How severe is fate (Ex. 98), 189
    How unhappy a lover am I, 178

Stanley, Thomas (1625–78), 111, 124, 215

Stradella, Alessandro (1642–82), 177, 204

Strode, William (*d.* 1645)
    The Floating Island, 95

Suckling, Sir John (1609–42), 89–91, 93–4, 114, 124
    Aglaura, 114

Synopsis of Vocal Musick, 122

Tate, Nahum (1652–1715), 153
    Brutus of Alba, 190
    Dido and Aeneas, 218, 223–4, 226
    Richard II, 213

Tatham, John (*fl.* 1632–64), 113, 120–1, 123

Taylor, Charles (*fl. c.* 1685), 182

Taylor, John (*fl.* 1637–45), 132
    Lay that sullen garland by thee, 123
    Tell me not that I die, 123
    Then let us be friends, 123

311

3 6289 000525490